Praise for the Bad L̲u̲c̲k̲ C̲a̲t̲

"*Black Cat Crossing* has everything a cozy mystery reader could want—intrigue, memorable characters, a small-town setting, and even a few mouthwatering recipes . . . A purr-fectly cozy read."
— Ellery Adams, *New York Times* bestselling author

"*Black Cat Crossing* is an entertaining introduction to Sabrina's world, and I look forward to Hitchcock's future exploits."
— *Open Book Society*

"Murderous bad luck may follow the characters in the Bad Luck Cat Mysteries, but there's only good luck for anyone reading *The Black Cat Sees His Shadow!*"
— *Lisa K's Book Review*

"Finch has, yet again, offered a great tale of female and feline that cozy readers will love."
— *Suspense Magazine*

"I believe Hitchcock and Sabrina make a wonderful detective team and can't wait to read about their next big case."
— TheBookReview.com

"Don't miss out on this humorous well-written cozy! You'll be turning pages as fast as you can to find out whodunit!"
— MyShelf

Books by Kay Finch

The Bad Luck Cat Mysteries

Black Cat Crossing
The Black Cat Knocks on Wood
The Black Cat Sees His Shadow
The Black Cat Steps on a Crack
The Black Cat Breaks a Mirror

The Corie McKenna PI Mysteries

Final Decree
Final Cut

Klutter Killer Mysteries

Relative Chaos

THE BLACK CAT BREAKS A MIRROR

KAY FINCH

BEYOND THE PAGE
PUBLISHING

The Black Cat Breaks a Mirror
Kay Finch
Beyond the Page Books
are published by
Beyond the Page Publishing
www.beyondthepagepub.com

For Hudson, the whirling dervish of our family

Acknowledgments

I am blessed with an abundance of team members who are always available to me when I need them. First, many thanks to my social media pals at Cozy Mystery Share-A-Palooza — Victoria Abbott, Ellery Adams, Leslie Budewitz, Peg Cochran, Miranda James, Mary Kennedy, Molly MacRae, Leann Sweeney, and Heather Blake Webber — for your unflagging support and encouragement.

Thanks also to Bill Harris, my editor, and Jessica Faust, my agent, along with all the staff members behind the scenes at Beyond the Page and BookEnds Literary Agency. I couldn't do this without you.

I continue to count on my fabulous critique partners, Laura Elvebak, Julie Herman, Kay Kendall, Bob Miller, and Amy Sharp, as well as Susie, Charlie, and Bindi, whose home we invade for our meetings.

Special mention to my nephews Matthew and Adam — as I tried to decide on the right names for Sabrina's nephews, I finally realized that my own already had the perfect names that I could use for these characters.

I can always rely on my family for moral support and understanding. Thanks to my husband, Benton, for enduring my many hours spent locked away in my office.

Last but not least, thanks to my mom, Betty Bittner, for teaching me the love of books and reading that will endure for all my years.

Chapter 1

Back when my little friends played house with their dolls, I sat off in a corner and played book club with mine. In my imagination, I always played the guest author. My older brother Nick made fun of my games, though I never understood his reasoning. After all, he pretended to be a lawyer on a regular basis while his friends played baseball. Dad encouraged both of us, whatever our endeavors. Mom simply said "that's nice, dear" in a tone that implied she hadn't even noticed what the heck we were doing.

I felt pride in my accomplishments during those childhood games, and today was no different. I'd arrived at the book club meeting — my first as a published author — ecstatic about the invitation and well prepared, or so I thought. I'd rehearsed answers to the common questions asked by readers. Where do you get your ideas? How long did it take you to write the book? Who should play your heroine in the movie?

I wanted to impress the club members so they would rush out to buy my second book, and the third. A few minutes into our discussion, though, I felt a distinct chill in the air. A coldness in attitudes, mood, definitely not temperature. We'd gathered in the screened porch of Tower of Pizza on an August afternoon in the Texas Hill Country.

Hot was an understatement, in spite of the lazily spinning ceiling fans and the big oak that shaded the roof. We met here because Noah, the four-year-old grandson of the shop owner, had made a special request for my cat, Hitchcock, to come along for a playdate. I was happy to oblige even if that meant forgoing the air-conditioned restaurant.

The little boy was ecstatic, chasing Hitchcock around the patio like a whirling dervish. He dropped to all fours every so often to growl like a tiger. Hitchcock wasn't fazed.

The food was another plus for this meeting site. Bruno Krause, the shop owner and book club president, brought out trays filled with pizza finger-foods and poured a glass of full-bodied red wine for each of us. The air was fragrant with pungent scents of garlic and oregano.

But there was definitely something up with the people. After my brief introductory talk, the group members said they were so happy I'd agreed to come. They told me my book deserved great reviews. I wanted to say "show, don't tell," an admonition well known by writers, because these people didn't appear happy in the least. Rather than sound critical, I kept my mouth shut.

Maybe they'd had some kind of big blowup before I arrived. They seemed edgy, especially the middle-aged blonde in the body-hugging hot pink tank top. Tracey, according to her name tag. She had a ticked-off look in her eye, and the wine wasn't helping.

She drank quickly, then twirled her empty glass on the red-and-white-checked tablecloth. She seemed oblivious to the cute antics of the boy and cat. She ran a hand over her copy of my book, *Scarlet's Run*, then fixed her sober gaze on me.

"I'll betcha you do a lot of research about perfect ways to commit murder," she said.

That wasn't a question, and I couldn't decide how to respond. Tracey was a big-boned and muscular woman who I wouldn't want to cross. I wondered if her husband—if she had one—was home quaking in his boots as he awaited her return. Or maybe he was out carousing, the very reason she had thoughts of doing him in. Could be she wanted to write a book about a murder.

Stop it, Sabrina. Try to focus.

"I do *some* research," I said carefully. "Not as much as I would if I were writing from the point of view of, say, a medical examiner. I prefer to leave out the gory details."

Tracey leaned in so far her bosom rested on the tabletop. "Tell me this, hon."

Elise, sitting to Tracey's left, put a hand on the other woman's forearm. "Let it go," she said.

Tracey shook her off like a gnat. "What I wanna know is how can a person one hundred percent, teetotally get away with murder?"

I blinked. I hadn't exactly prepared for this.

Bruno straightened in his chair. "First off, you don't spout off in front of a dozen witnesses that you're thinking about knocking somebody off."

Jeff, a middle-aged man who'd told me about his novel-in-progress, nodded in agreement. "You dispose of the body," he said.

"Can't prove murder when there's no body. Less chance of conviction."

"Good point, Jeff," I said, "but don't forget, the more trouble you throw at a character, the more conflict you have on the page, the better the book. Finding a body can get your character in a boatload of trouble."

"I'm not talkin' about no danged book." Tracey pounded the cover of my book with her fist like a judge hitting the bench with a gavel. "We got plenty of freakin' conflict around here already."

Bruno pushed his chair back and stood. "I sure as heck hope you're not talking about committing a crime, 'cause that would be dumber than—"

"Stop it, both of you." Elise turned to check on Noah and Hitchcock. She lowered her voice. "The boy doesn't need to hear this kind of talk."

Noah had apparently worn himself down and lay sprawled on the cement floor in the corner, trailing an apron sash for my cat to chase.

Conversation buzzed at the other tables. Comments about Tracey's behavior, no doubt.

I met her angry glare and smiled as if she'd asked nothing more alarming than "What's your favorite place for Italian food here in Lavender?" Which of course would be easy to answer. Tower of Pizza. But that's not what she'd asked.

"Sorry if I said something to upset you," I said. "The truth is there's no way anyone could be sure they would get away with a crime. Law enforcement professionals have so many tools at their disposal these days. I would never try to get away with anything."

I paused and snagged my fifth pepperoni puff from the snack tray. Bruno stood to fetch another bottle of wine and refilled glasses.

When he finished, he sat and turned to me. "Tell us, Sabrina. What's next up for you? A worldwide book tour?"

He knew better, and we both chuckled. New authors like me only went on tour if they footed the bill themselves.

"I'm celebrating having typed *The End* on my second manuscript," I said. "It's a draft, but I feel good about the story."

"Here's to you." Jeff raised his arm in a toast, and everyone joined in to clink glasses.

"I'm taking a little time off from writing this week," I told the group, "to focus on family. My brother and his boys are coming to visit. The nephews want to go tubing on the river, but the real draw is Saturday night's Colt Jamison concert."

"Of course it is," Tracey said in a disgruntled tone.

Bruno ignored her. "Heard something about a show, but I don't know Colt Jamison's music."

"He's a new country singer from Austin, so the boys tell me," I said. "I'm sure we'll have a crowd here in Lavender for the event. Lots of pizza eaters."

Bruno grinned and lifted his glass. "That's what I like to — "

He stopped midsentence, his gaze drawn to Tracey. She glared in the direction of the street. Bruno appeared to pinpoint what had captured her attention, and his expression darkened.

I turned in my chair to see what was going on. A lanky blond man with a pointy goatee and wearing skinny jeans climbed out of a cherry red Corvette parked near the shop. He straightened to his full height of six feet or more, placed a black cowboy hat on his head, and turned toward the pizza shop entrance.

Tracey pounded my book with her fist again. "I knew it. Y'all tried to tell me different, but I knew in my bones we hadn't seen the last of that s.o.b." She shoved her chair so hard it flew over backward. Elise and Jeff tried to block her path, but Tracey barreled past them and out the door.

Elise went after Tracey. Bruno popped up from his chair and went straight to Noah. He bent to take his grandson's hand and pulled the boy to his feet. "C'mon with me, bud. Let's go out back."

"Why, Papa?" Noah said.

"Your mom needs you." Bruno and Noah went out through the back screen door with the little boy whining about wanting to take the cat with him. I looked toward the kitchen, where a young woman visible through a glass window — Noah's mother, I thought — twirled pizza dough in the air.

Hitchcock came over and jumped up on the chair next to me. "Mrreow."

I put a reassuring hand on the cat's head and looked at Jeff, who was still seated and doing his best to finish off the treats.

He looked up when he noticed me watching him. "What?"

I pointed toward the kitchen. "Isn't that Charlotte, Noah's mother?"

He raised his hands at his sides. "Hey, I know nothing."

"I don't buy that. You're a writer. We notice details."

Outside, Elise and Tracey stood on the side lawn. Elise had hold of the larger woman's arm, but Tracey was trying to wriggle free. Corvette guy proceeded up the walk toward the door.

"What's going on, Jeff?" I said. "Who's the guy in the hat?"

"Don't know his name," Jeff said, "but if I had to guess, I'd say he's the guy Tracey's fixin' to snuff out if we don't do something to stop her."

Chapter 2

I would have liked to bring the book club meeting to a nice peaceful close and thank everyone for inviting me, but that wasn't going to happen. Jeff and I were the only ones left in the room, aside from Hitchcock. Time to wrap things up. If I left now, I'd be home to greet Nick and the boys when they arrived in an hour or so.

I unlooped Hitchcock's leash from the back of my chair and hooked it to his harness, then faced Jeff. "Guess the meeting's over."

"Looks that way." He picked up his wineglass and motioned toward the window. "Might wanna stick around for the show, though. Things are gettin' dicey out there."

I turned to the window to see Elise guarding Tracey like a basketball player trying to prevent the star shooter from making a basket. Corvette guy seemed oblivious to the women. He was busy watching the street, and I heard the unmistakable beat of Alan Jackson's "Chattahoochee" playing at ear-splitting volume. The music seemed to grow louder, and then the source of the noise appeared. Two pickups loaded with teenagers — most of them riding illegally in the beds — rounded the corner.

The trucks pulled to the curb and parked behind the red sports car. The music died when the trucks shut off, quickly replaced by the teenage chatter of bikini-clad girls and shirtless boys. Judging by the sunburns, I figured they'd spent the afternoon on the river.

Tracey took advantage of the distraction to slip around her friend. She raced to the man and grabbed a fistful of his black T-shirt adorned with silver script that read *Colt Jamison*. She was in the guy's face and spouting off something I couldn't hear. He swatted her away and focused on the kids, waving them toward the building.

"C'mon in," he said. "Free pizzas for all, courtesy of Colt Jamison."

The kids cheered and piled out of the trucks to head into Tower of Pizza.

"Sounds like we're about to be invaded by a swarm of freakin' locusts." Jeff picked up his copy of my book, pushed his chair back, and stood. "Don't know about you, but I'm clearing out."

"Good idea." I grabbed my tote and picked up Hitchcock, then followed Jeff through the screen door Bruno had used a few minutes ago. The exit led to a small, well-manicured backyard. When I rounded the building to head for my car, there was no sign of Bruno or his grandson.

Whatever problem Tracey had with the man giving away the pizza, she wasn't about to let it slide. She grabbed him again. This time her fingernails dug into the flesh of his arm and held. He tried to yank his arm free, but she had a tight grip.

Elise's forehead creased with worry. "Tracey, for pity's sake, leave him alone. Remember what happened last time."

Her words appeared to fall on deaf ears, but they piqued my curiosity about the history between Tracey and the man. Sweat trickled down my back with the late afternoon humidity. I should get Hitchcock into the air-conditioned car, but the action playing out in front of us had captured my attention.

"You have some nerve showing your face around here, Dixon," Tracey hollered. "This town doesn't need your kind ruining the lives of honest, hardworkin' people. You should turn right around and get out while the gettin' is good."

"Or what?" he said with a smirk. "I have as much right here as you do, sweetheart."

Tracey's complexion turned a purplish hue. "I am *not* your sweetheart."

"Havin' a little trouble accepting my success, are ya?" he said.

Without hesitation, she hauled off and kicked him in the shin. Her tennis shoe connected with a thwack. He hollered and hopped on his good leg.

"I don't give a rat's patootie about you or your so-called success." Tracey delivered a new kick with each of her next words. "I. Want. You. Gone."

"Whoa, whoa," Dixon yelled as he wobbled.

I wondered why Tracey thought she could tell this guy what to do and if she honestly thought he would obey orders from her. Why would he?

Hitchcock had a nervous purr going in my ear.

"I know, buddy, we should leave." I stroked the cat's head, but I couldn't make myself walk away. I hated to leave Elise standing by helplessly and literally wringing her hands, but I wasn't jumping into the fray when I had Hitchcock to protect.

One of the boys who'd gone inside opened the door to stick his head out and yelled, "Hey, Dix. You need a hand?"

The man waved for him to stay back. "Nah, I got this."

"That's what you think." This time Tracey aimed a karate-like kick at his head.

Dixon dodged her foot and his hat flew off. He came around behind Tracey to encircle her waist. Chuckling, he lifted her off the ground. "Don't go startin' something you can't finish."

Tracey's legs bicycled. "Oh, I'll finish you all right."

Elise danced closer to them, raising her hands. "Put her down, Dixon."

Tracey dipped her head and sank her teeth into Dixon's arm. He yelped and dropped her. They both went down in a tangle of arms and legs and rolled on the lawn, grappling like wrestlers. Someone needed to intervene. I turned to see if Jeff was still here.

"We need to help—" I stopped and stared. Jeff held his phone high, obviously videotaping the action.

"For crying out loud," I said. "What are you thinking?"

"This sucker could bring some money." He held his phone higher as I approached him.

"Are you kidding me? I thought Tracey was your friend." I shifted Hitchcock into my other arm and made a grab at his phone.

"Uh, uh, uh." Jeff backed away. "Let me finish. The fun's about to come to an end anyway."

"What do you mean?" I said. "This isn't fun."

"Mrreow," Hitchcock said, in what I'm sure was complete agreement.

I put the cat down and looped the end of his leash around my wrist, then pulled out my phone to dial nine-one-one. Before I could punch in the numbers, I saw a sheriff's department car coast to a stop at the curb. The blurp of its siren caught the attention of Tracey and Dixon. They froze as if a director had yelled "Cut" to end the scene.

Deputy Patricia Rosales got out of the car, and I sighed softly. Why did it always have to be this woman who found me in awkward situations? A question I wouldn't voice aloud lest someone blame the legendary bad luck cat—the infuriatingly awful nickname sometimes used for Hitchcock.

Rosales usually rode alone, but this time a male officer I didn't recognize climbed out of the car's passenger side. I hoped having a partner had a good effect on her personality.

Over my shoulder, I saw Jeff lower his phone and slide it into his shorts pocket.

Rosales strode across the lawn. Her gaze slid over Tracey and Dixon before her focus narrowed and zoomed in, one hundred percent, on me.

Why would I expect any less?

"Well, well, well," Rosales said. "Sabrina Tate. Imagine my surprise to find you and your cat here in the middle of a brawl."

"We are not *in* the brawl," I said.

The officer with Rosales reached us. He glanced at Tracey and Dixon before looking to Rosales, as if for instruction. Elise went to Tracey's side and took her arm to help the other woman up. Dixon stood and brushed his jeans off.

Rosales pointed at Hitchcock. "See this cat?" she said to the other officer. "You ever hear about the bad luck cat? Well, this is him, right here in the thick of things. As usual."

Oh, for the love of Pete.

"Mrreow," Hitchcock said.

"He doesn't look like bad luck," the new guy said. "He's kind of cute."

I nodded to him. "Thank you, Officer—" I paused for a moment, then offered my hand. "I'm sorry, I didn't catch your name."

"Denny Salazar, ma'am." He shook my hand. "Sheriff Crawford hired me on as a deputy, special security detail. Crowd's expected this weekend for the concert."

"So nice to meet you, Deputy Salazar," I said. "By the way, my cat is absolutely not bad luck. His name is Hitchcock, and he wasn't even around when that ridiculous bad luck story began, none of us were. Plus, we're not involved in the altercation. Hitchcock and I were here at the pizza shop this afternoon for a very innocent book club meeting."

"Book club?" he said.

"That's right. I just had a book pub—"

"Enough already," Rosales interrupted. "Salazar, we have business to tend to. Separate these folks and start interviews. I'll handle *him*."

She turned away from me and Hitchcock, thank goodness, but what was with the intent to interview people? She could simply say, "Break it up, folks. Move along now." Was she insinuating we all had to stay here for some sort of investigation?

The man named Dixon bent to retrieve his hat and faced Rosales as he stood. "Hey there, Pat. Look at you, mighty fine in that fancy uniform."

Rosales stared daggers at him.

"*Mr.* Dixon," she said. "I hoped I had dealt with you for the last time."

"Talk to her." He pointed at Tracey. "She ran out here and attacked me for no reason at all. I didn't even know she was around."

Rosales continued as if he hadn't spoken. "We brought in security reinforcements for this weekend, but now we're wasting those resources on you. I don't like that. Seems you don't take warnings very seriously. I don't like that either."

"I hear you," Dixon said, "but I got a job to do, and Colt Jamison depends on me. I'm here for the duration, so you'll have to deal with me a while longer, Pat, like it or not."

There he went again with the nickname. The guy had some nerve talking to Rosales in that tone of voice.

The deputy set her mouth in a grim line and raised one eyebrow. "I don't believe a word that comes out of your mouth. Salazar, lock this man up in the cruiser for now, until we get everybody's story straight."

Dixon's shoulders slumped. "Aw, Pat, that's not—"

"I am *Deputy* Rosales." She pointed at him. "Don't you forget that."

I wondered what kind of warning this man had been given and why. And why did we need security reinforcements?

Sure, things sometimes turned rowdy when crowds of teens were involved, but I hated that my brother and the boys were coming to visit during a week that called for heightened security.

Maybe this brawl between Tracey and Dixon would be the worst that would happen, and it was all over with now. Dixon had done something to tick Tracey off, she had a short fuse, and she went off on the guy.

But Rosales had a major problem with Dixon as well. Odd that the deputy hadn't said one word to Tracey.

Not your business, Sabrina.

Time for me to look forward. My brother was bringing the boys here for a fun-filled getaway, and I wanted them to experience the peaceful and laid-back atmosphere of Lavender that I loved. I only hoped that the troublemaker named Dixon would keep his distance from my family.

Chapter 3

After the scene outside the pizza shop, I was happy to return to the tranquility of Around-the-World Cottages. Rather than drive straight to the Monte Carlo cottage where Hitchcock and I live, I pulled into the driveway at Aunt Rowe's house. A charcoal gray Explorer sat in the driveway next to Aunt Rowe's car.

"Wait 'til you meet Nick and my nephews," I told Hitchcock. "You'll love them, except you'll need to watch out for the boys' practical jokes." In the year and a half since Hitchcock came into my life, I had visited my brother's family in Houston. They had not been to Lavender to meet my cat.

I grabbed the end of Hitchcock's leash and hurried to the back door. At ages fifteen and twelve, Matthew and Adam were voracious eaters, and I expected to find them in the kitchen. Aunt Rowe's housekeeper had stocked up on extra soft drinks and snacks in anticipation of their arrival, not to mention the brownies and lemon meringue pie she'd baked. If the boys had already spotted the brownies, it might be too late for me to have a taste.

I smelled enchilada sauce the second I opened the door. After eating pizza snacks at the book club meeting I wasn't hungry, but I'd never pass up Glenda's cheese enchiladas.

"Hello," I called as I entered the empty kitchen. "Anybody home?"

Glenda poked her head out from the laundry room doorway. "I'm here."

"Nick and the kids?" I said. "Where are they?" I unhooked Hitchcock's leash, and he went straight to his water bowl.

"Boys are down on the river," Glenda said. "Nick went into town. Said he had to run an errand."

"Oh." I felt a pang of disappointment. "What kind of errand?"

"I asked, but I didn't get an answer."

That seemed odd. "I thought that was his car in the driveway."

"Nope." Glenda shook her head and ducked back into the laundry room. "Belongs to Rowe's new friend."

The words *new friend* came out with a sarcastic slant.

"Oh? Who's the friend?"

"Violet Howe," she said.

I took a soft drink from the refrigerator and walked to the laundry room so I could see her expression. "And you don't like the woman."

"I never said that." Glenda moved laundry from the washer to the dryer. "You'll see for yourself. They're out on the deck. How'd your book club meeting go?"

She was changing the subject, but I decided to go with the flow.

"Good, at least until this dude showed up and a fight broke out."

Glenda straightened and turned to me. "Are you serious?"

"Completely," I said. "Sheriff's deputies came, questioned witnesses and all." I told her how Tracey took off like a firecracker the second she saw Dixon, and about the ensuing fight. "This guy Dixon says he works for Colt Jamison."

"The singer everyone's talking about?" Glenda said.

"Yes, but I thought the most interesting part is Deputy Rosales knows the guy. He called her Pat, and she was none too happy to see him. Seemed like she overdid the interrogation to jack with him."

"Huh." Glenda turned back to her laundry. "Wonder what that's about."

"If I knew, I'd tell you." I popped the top of my drink. "How about you tell me why you don't like Aunt Rowe's friend?"

Glenda finished loading and started the dryer, then leaned against the washer and sighed. "Lord knows why Rowe is falling for this woman's shtick."

"What's up with her?"

"Claims she's a 'life coach.'" Glenda made air quotes.

I digested that for a few seconds. "Aunt Rowe might be the last person I can imagine needing help with her life."

"Exactly." Glenda nodded, happy that I'd validated her opinion.

"On the other hand, Aunt Rowe is a grown woman and entitled to do whatever she wants."

"Chime in on this again," Glenda said, "after you meet Violet."

"Will do." I took a swig of my drink and headed for the deck. When I pushed the door open, Hitchcock darted out ahead of me.

"Oh, how precious," a woman said.

On hearing the words *life coach* I had conjured up a female Tony Robbins, a woman dressed for success in a business-office style. Violet Howe didn't fit the image. The woman with Aunt Rowe was fiftyish and wore a flowing maxi-dress of vibrant colors and high platform sandals. Her shoulder-length blonde hair had a purple streak with a pink feather tied to one section.

"This is my niece's cat, Hitchcock," Aunt Rowe said.

"Mrreow." Hitchcock sidled up to Aunt Rowe and rubbed against the leg of her chair.

She bent to pat his head, then noticed me. "Sabrina, I knew you wouldn't be far behind." She introduced me to the other woman and added, "Violet is a life strategist. She checked into the Melbourne cottage this morning."

Violet stood and we shook hands. Her fingernails were long and painted deep purple. Hitchcock had jumped up on the patio table to eye her from a distance. He sat near a sheaf of papers fanned out from a teal folder.

"I adore your cat." Violet took a step toward Hitchcock with a hand outstretched. "Will he be okay with me petting him?"

"Sure." One point in Violet's favor—she wasn't one of the bad luck crazies. I glanced at the papers on the table and caught the phrase "Renew Your Life—With Violet" and a card that said "Save Now—$500 Value" in bold print.

The woman stroked Hitchcock's head. He stood still for the attention, but I didn't hear any purring. The cat and I were reserving judgment until we had more information on this woman.

Violet looked at me. "Do you have much trouble with people saying your cat will cause bad luck?"

"Does she ever," Aunt Rowe said.

I frowned at her.

She shrugged. "I didn't say one word about Hitchcock before you came out here."

Violet's gaze focused on me. "I can feel this topic causes you angst. We could work on transformational therapy."

"We what?"

"There are ways to adjust the way people perceive things," she said.

Hitchcock had backed away from her, and I found myself doing the same.

I said, "The last person who discussed changing people's attitudes about my cat ended up—"

"Sabrina's not interested, Violet," Aunt Rowe interrupted. "Why don't we get back to what we were working on?"

She didn't want me telling her friend about the murder of Jane Alcott, a librarian who'd suggested trying a social media campaign to turn around the bad luck cat legend—shortly before she was murdered.

"What is it you're working on?" I said.

"My discovery packet," Aunt Rowe said. "Violet is pulling information out of me that I never knew existed."

My brows drew together. "What does that mean?"

Violet turned a beatific smile on me. "I'm helping Rowe determine what she wants to do with her one wild and precious life."

I didn't have a comeback for that, so I excused myself and went back inside with Hitchcock on my heels. I selfishly wished Violet would leave so I could get the real scoop about the life strategy session from Aunt Rowe, ask her what errand my brother had gone off on when he could have been here visiting with us, and go down to the river to catch up with the boys—in that order. Glenda stood at the kitchen island scooping melon balls from half of a large watermelon. She looked up as I walked into the room.

"Well?" she said.

"My scam alarm is going off," I said in a low voice. "I saw what looked like a coupon for five hundred dollars off, so Lord knows what she charges people. She wanted me to try transformational therapy."

"What's that?"

"I have no idea and no urge to find out. Where did Aunt Rowe meet this woman?"

"As far as I can tell, they met for the first time today."

"Maybe there's more to it," I said. "Aunt Rowe isn't gullible. What if she's drawing Violet in for some reason and not the other way around?"

"Why would Rowe do such a thing?"

"I don't know." I walked over to the counter where Glenda kept the baked goods and lifted plastic wrap from the brownie pan. The boys hadn't discovered them yet, and I took the first one. "If Aunt Rowe thought she needed help with her life or wanted to make some changes, she could have come to us." I took a bite of the treat and chewed thoughtfully.

"Would you come to me and your aunt if you needed help?" Glenda said.

The doorbell rang before I had a chance to respond. Hitchcock, curious as always, sprinted toward the front door. Glenda followed close behind. I heard the door open and muffled voices came from that direction. I enjoyed my brownie and didn't pay much attention until a man's irritated tone reached me.

"I need to see Gary Weber *now*," he said. "Which one of these little huts is he stayin' in?"

I took a few steps in their direction so I could hear better. The guy's nasal twang sounded familiar. I looked out a window and saw a red Corvette parked in the drive.

"They are called cottages, sir, not huts," Glenda said, "but I can't help you. As I said, there's no one here by that name."

"You refusing to help me?"

"No, I don't have any information for you."

"Gary is stayin' here," he said. "Right here. This is Around-the-World, ain't it? I saw the sign."

"You have the right place, but that doesn't change anything."

"I need to see Weber about a mutual problem. No excuses." He paused for two beats. "Hold on. Is this the same freakin' cat I saw in town earlier? When that wild woman attacked me?"

I nearly choked on my last swallow of brownie and marched in their direction. He'd better not bring up the ridiculous bad luck cat legend. I came up behind Glenda. Hitchcock sat on the windowsill by the door, like a spectator waiting for a sporting event to begin. Dixon still wore his Colt Jamison T-shirt, now dirt-streaked from his wrestling match on the pizza shop lawn.

"I don't believe you came here to talk about a cat," I said.

"No, I—" He swung his attention to me, lifted an index finger, and pointed at me. "Wait. You were there, too. You and the cat."

"Enough about the cat." I sliced my hand through the air to cut off his train of thought. "You mentioned a problem."

"Right." He shuffled his feet. Maybe he was afraid Glenda and I would gang up on him to finish what Tracey had started. "It's between me and Gary Weber. You don't need the details."

I looked at Glenda. "This is the man from the pizza shop. Deputy Rosales's friend."

Glenda folded her arms over her chest. "I gathered."

"Let's not start trouble," Dixon said. "I came to see Gary, that's all."

"We'd be happy to take a message," I said. "If we happen to come across your friend, we'll let him know you stopped by. Is Dixon your first or last name?"

"Last," he said. "Marty Dixon. Look, is Weber here or not?"

I didn't want to help this weasely little guy even if I knew the name of every person registered at the cottages this week, which I didn't. "Maybe you could try calling Mr. Weber to find out his whereabouts. Sorry we can't help." I put a hand on the door to swing it closed.

His hand shot out to catch the door. With his other hand he pulled out a wallet. "I want to rent a room," he said. "How much?"

"We're filled up, aren't we, Glenda?" I looked at her, and she nodded.

"Booked solid the next two months, I believe," she said. "You really have to call by March if you want an August reservation."

He blew out a breath. "I can make this worth your while." He pulled out cash that appeared to be all hundred-dollar bills.

"Mr. Dixon," I said, "please. We can't pull an empty room out of thin air."

He leaned in and whispered in a conspiratorial way, "You happen to know where Colt Jamison is hangin' his hat while he's here in Lavender?"

I wondered why this man who'd been buying pizza for a gang of fans on behalf of the singer didn't already have this information.

"I never even heard of Jamison until last week," I said, "so he doesn't share news with me. Now, if you'll excuse us."

This time I succeeded in shutting the door.

"Can you believe that guy?" I said to Glenda.

Aunt Rowe came down the hall from the direction of the kitchen. "Violet and I wrapped things up. That was *such* an interesting session."

"Has she gone?" I said.

"Only as far as the Melbourne cottage," Aunt Rowe said, "where she's staying."

"Oh." I had a new topic that momentarily trumped my desire to discuss Violet. "Have we ever heard of a man named Gary Weber?"

"He's supposed to be here undercover," Aunt Rowe said.

Glenda and I exchanged a glance.

"Undercover?" I said. "What do you mean?"

"He's Colt Jamison's general manager," she said.

"What does that have to do with us?" Glenda said.

"You both have to swear you never heard a word of this." Aunt Rowe looked from me to Glenda.

I traced an X over my heart and Glenda followed suit.

"Weber is on our books as renting the Athens cottage," Aunt Rowe said.

I turned my palms up. "Okay. So what?"

"Weber's not here at all, and he doesn't plan to stay here."

"So we *do* have an empty cottage," Glenda said.

"No, we don't." Aunt Rowe dropped her voice to a whisper. "The singer is staying in the Athens cottage. Colt Jamison. He's writing some new songs and needs total privacy. We can't leak his whereabouts to a soul."

Aunt Rowe hadn't seen the truckloads of screaming Colt Jamison fans that I saw at the pizza shop. Those kids might not expect the singer to be in Lavender this soon, but they'd be on the lookout for him before long.

"What about Matt and Adam?" I said. "They're two of his biggest fans, and they're staying right here with you."

"I know that, Sabrina," Aunt Rowe said. "It's a sticky situation."

She could say that again.

"You're going to lie to your great-nephews?" I said.

"No, no." She shook her head. "They won't expect to see the singer here. He plans to hole up in the cottage and work on his songwriting."

The cottage wasn't soundproof, and I couldn't imagine his plan working.

"He had that one big hit—'Broken Mirror,'" Aunt Rowe went on, "and he's hoping to pull himself out of a dry spell. You know what that feels like, right, Sabrina?"

I didn't respond.

"What's he going to do for food?" Glenda said.

"That's Gary Weber's problem," Aunt Rowe said. "All I promised was a quiet and uninterrupted place to stay."

Off the top of my head, I could think of a dozen reasons this plan could go wrong. Aunt Rowe wouldn't want to hear them. I looked at Hitchcock. "What do you think, buddy?"

"Mrreow," he said.

"He's right, ladies." Aunt Rowe clapped her hands together. "Our plan is set, and we'll make it work. I gave Gary Weber my word."

Chapter 4

I started to ask Aunt Rowe why Colt Jamison had chosen to stay here—of all the places he might go to write songs—but I could guess the answer. Our setting on the bank of the Glidden River was as perfect for a songwriter as the Monte Carlo cottage was for me to write novels. A good place to unplug and let the words—or music—flow.

Thoughts of Aunt Rowe's secret guest had overshadowed my curiosity about the life coach for a few minutes. I was considering exactly how to approach my aunt with my questions when my phone rang.

Luke Griffin calling. Summer was a busy and stressful season for a Texas game warden, and I was surprised to hear from him.

I snatched a second brownie and went out to the deck to take the call.

"Hey," he said when I answered. "Are you in town?"

"No. I'm at Aunt Rowe's house. Why?" I plopped into a chaise and nibbled the brownie.

He paused for a moment. "I'm taking an early dinner break and wondered if you'd join me."

The answer would normally be a resounding yes. "Sorry, I thought I mentioned my family dinner tonight."

Luke and I had dated for nearly a year, and he was usually an attentive listener.

"Right," he said. "You did."

Something seemed off with him. "Are you all right?"

"Me? Yeah. Your family make it in okay?"

"I'm told they did. Haven't seen them yet."

He went quiet again. "Today was your book club meeting."

"Sure was, and it was a doozy."

He groaned. "I hoped you were gone by the time the fight broke out."

"How'd you hear about that?" I said.

Deputy Rosales seemed to stalk Luke at times. I wouldn't be surprised if she'd told him Hitchcock and I had caused the problem at the pizza shop.

"Not from Rosales," he said, as though reading my mind, "but I heard she was there. Some kids on the river were bragging about free pizza. Telling stories about the fight."

I laughed. "The pizza benefactor showed up here a little bit ago."

"For what?" he said. "Is he staying at the cottages?"

"No. He was looking for someone." If I continued this line of conversation, I might say something I shouldn't reveal. "I'm about to join my nephews down at the river."

"I'll let you go," he said.

"Lunch tomorrow?"

"Sure thing."

We ended the call. I sat there for a moment, looking at my phone. He'd seemed distracted, and I tried not to take it personally. No telling what was going on around him with all the tourists in town.

Back inside, I found Hitchcock alone in the kitchen. "Where'd everyone go?"

"Mrreow," he said.

I glanced out a side window and saw Glenda driving the golf cart, complete with baskets of fresh folded towels, toward the cottages. Aunt Rowe and Thomas, her handyman at the cottages, headed into the storage building. I wondered if she was letting him in on her secret.

I didn't want to have my life coach discussion in front of Thomas, so I'd save my questions for later. With Hitchcock trotting beside me, I took a slightly longer route to the river so I could peek at what I now thought of as the singer's hideout.

Laughter and music drifted up from the river. At the Athens cottage, all was quiet. A nondescript white pickup sat in the parking space. If I were to write a song, I'd begin with the words. I wondered how songwriters typically worked.

Not the time to explore songwriting, Sabrina.

As I walked and mulled this over, a black SUV came down the drive and pulled to a stop near the Athens cottage's front door. For a moment, I feared Marty Dixon had returned, but he'd been driving a red Corvette earlier. The man who climbed out of the SUV was fortyish, shorter and wider than Dixon. He wore Wranglers, expensive-looking boots, and a Western shirt cut a little too tight for his midsection. His dark hair reminded me of Elvis.

The man stood and stretched. He scanned the area and spotted me, then jumped as if another person was the last thing on earth he expected to see. Or maybe Hitchcock had startled him. I couldn't be sure.

I was a little far from the man for conversation, but I waved and greeted him. "Hello. Welcome to Around-the-World Cottages."

He nodded. "Howdy."

He had to be Gary Weber, the man Marty Dixon was so eager to find, and there he stood at the cottage with the top-secret guest. Weber probably wouldn't want anyone to call attention to him, but I had told Dixon I'd give the man a message.

What was the harm?

I walked in his direction. Weber had ducked back into the SUV and came up holding two white sacks with the tops folded down. I recognized the take-out from McKetta's Barbeque.

He straightened and closed the car door.

His shoulders sagged when he saw me approach. He glanced at the cottage, as if judging the distance to see if he could make a getaway before I reached him.

"Are you Mr. Weber?" I said.

"Yes, ma'am." His tone didn't quite match the polite response.

"I'm Sabrina, the owner's niece, and I have a message for you."

"Me?" He juggled the white sacks and adjusted his huge belt buckle with his free hand. A diamond ring glittered on his pinky finger.

I smiled. "Yes, sir. A man showed up at the house not long ago looking for Gary Weber—and here you are."

"Who was it?"

"Marty Dixon," I said. "He wants to see you, actually. Very badly. He didn't leave a number, so I figured you were friends."

He shook his head. "Dixon is *not* a friend."

"Oh, I'm sorry, but I told him I'd pass on the message if I saw you, so now I have."

"Thanks," Weber said, "but if he shows up again you have my permission to tell him to vamoose."

I grinned at the word.

"What's so funny?" Weber said.

"Vamoose. Reminds me of a cartoon." I thought for a moment. "Might have been Yosemite Sam."

Weber smiled slightly. "I used to like watching him."

I noticed Hitchcock with his nose in the air, circling the man. Smelling barbequed meat.

"I don't want to keep you. Your dinner's getting cold."

"Yeah." He glanced down at the bags and held them higher, away from the cat. "I'm dead serious about Dixon. He's trouble."

"I believe you. I saw him in town earlier, promoting that singer."

My words struck a chord. Weber's complexion reddened. "Dixon has no business with Colt Jamison. If he claims he does, he's lying. You see him again, you can tell him I said so."

"Sure thing," I said. "C'mon, Hitchcock."

When I looked over my shoulder seconds later, Weber was already out of sight.

"I don't think he's going to contact Dixon." I looked down at Hitchcock. "Do you?"

"Mrreow," he said.

We continued our trek to the river, and I easily spotted my nephews. Matt stood a head taller than the other kids near him on the riverbank. Adam, the younger brother, was at the water's edge, where he had an up-close-and-personal view of tubers gliding by with the current. Matt appeared more interested in the girls.

One buxom young lady in a Colt Jamison T-shirt scurried to a picnic table set far from the water. She grabbed a bullhorn and climbed onto the tabletop.

"Listen up, Colt Jamison fans," she said.

Everyone in hearing distance turned to look, even the people floating by. My nephews saw me, waved, and headed my way.

"I have fan club applications for everyone," the girl announced, "and giveaways, too. Posters, bumper stickers, guitar picks. Sign up today for your very own Colt Jamison 'Broken Mirror' commemorative keychain."

I met the boys halfway, and we exchanged hugs and hellos. Adam noticed Hitchcock first. "Is this your cat?"

"Sure is. This is Hitchcock."

The boys knelt to pet the cat, and he happily rolled in the grass and batted at their fingers. The other Jamison fans crowded the giveaway table.

"Guys," I said, "if you want some swag you'd better hurry."

Matt shrugged.

"I do." Adam jumped up.

Matt cut his eyes toward bullhorn girl. "I'm not goin' over there."

"Why not?" I said.

"She has a thing for him," Adam said. "She's Tandee with a d-e-e."

"Shut up," Matt said.

I nodded at Adam. "Why don't you see what they have?"

He didn't have to be told twice.

"Tandee's probably a little old for you," I said to Matt. "You have a girlfriend at home?"

He shook his head. "Nope."

"Not for lack of interested girls, I'll bet."

A blush crept up his face, and he grinned.

Adam hurried back with posters and guitar picks for both of them. Matt seemed reluctant to show any kind of interest in the free stuff.

"Why don't we go back up to the house," I said. "Check out the posters and see if my prodigal brother has returned."

Before we reached Aunt Rowe's, I saw a black Suburban in the drive.

Matt said, "Dad's back."

We found Nick in the kitchen standing over the brownie pan and wearing a guilty expression.

"Hey, sis." Nick greeted me with a hug, then backed away to give me a once-over. "Lookin' good. Published author status agrees with you. I brought you something."

He turned to the counter behind him to pick up a bouquet of colorful flowers and handed it to me. "For you."

"Thanks. They're gorgeous." I took the flowers and sniffed them. "Where've you been?"

"Out picking up your surprise. And, oh boy, I smell those enchiladas." He crossed the kitchen to look in the oven window. "Glenda has outdone herself."

The boys entered the kitchen behind me, trailed by Hitchcock. They introduced their dad to the cat while I found a large jar in the cupboard to use as a vase. After Nick acknowledged Hitchcock with a good head scratch, the boys and cat moved into the living room with their freebies. I turned back to my brother.

"What's the occasion? I can't remember you ever bringing me flowers."

Meaning, what were you really doing in town that you don't want to talk about?

"Call it a congrats-on-your-new-book gift," he said. "I couldn't think of a better idea, so I took the easy way out. You know I suck at buying gifts."

"Right. You were never good at gift giving." I gave him a playful punch in the shoulder and we laughed. "It really *is* good to see you."

I took in Nick's tanned complexion, red T-shirt with cutoffs, and thong sandals. His hair was dark and curly like mine, but he wore it relatively short and manageable. He looked relaxed, and though Nick turned forty this year, I couldn't spot even one worry line on his face. That, in spite of having the two boys to keep up with. I had a feeling the concerns would escalate when girlfriends entered the picture.

"How's Melanie?" I said.

"Busy with work, as usual."

"And she didn't want to come visit."

He went to the sink and squirted soap on his hands. "Not especially. She says there's always too much drama here." He ran the water, lathered his hands, and leaned closer to the window. "She may be right. Is the sheriff still trying to pick up our aunt?"

"Why? What's going on?" I joined him at the window.

Sheriff Crawford, tall and handsome as ever in his uniform, stood on the lawn with Aunt Rowe. The door to his cruiser was open.

I heard slapping footsteps, and Adam burst into the room. "The cops are here."

"Take it easy," I said. "Sheriff Crawford is one of Aunt Rowe's good friends. And mine. I'm going to say hi."

"Can we check out his car?" Adam said.

Nick shook his head.

I went outside and greeted the sheriff with a wave.

"Sabrina," he said. "Just who I came to see."

"Jeb," Aunt Rowe said, exaggerating her tone, "here I thought you had a hankering to see me."

25

"I always do, Rowe." The sheriff gave her a smile so meaningful —
poignant might be the word — that I felt like I'd intruded.

He turned to me and said, "Too bad I'm here on business."

His words had an ominous ring, and I tried to make light of
them. "I don't suppose you're here for an autographed copy of my
new book."

"Not at this time," he said, "but I do have a copy at the office I
wouldn't mind you signing when you get a chance."

"I'd love to. But what's going on? Why are you here and giving
me that look?"

"I'm investigating an assault case," he said, "and I understand
you're an eye witness. What can you tell me about a fella named
Marty Dixon?"

Chapter 5

"I can't report much about Marty Dixon," I told Sheriff Crawford. "I never heard of the man before today. Did he file an assault charge?"

"This sounds interesting," Aunt Rowe said. "A piece of gossip that hasn't reached my ears yet."

"Sorry to disappoint, Rowe," the sheriff said without answering my question. "We're not in the spreading-the-story-around phase. Would you excuse us for a few minutes?"

"If I must." She jabbed his arm with a forefinger. "Spoilsport."

He grinned at her and watched as she turned away and walked into the house. She beckoned for the boys to follow her inside. The sheriff motioned for me to join him on a bench under the shade of a nearby oak tree. After we settled on the bench, he looked at me.

"I've been given a dozen different accounts of what happened outside the pizza shop. I need an unbiased witness."

"What have you been told?" I said.

"Doesn't work that way." He waggled a forefinger. "You first. Tell me what you saw."

"Okay." I closed my eyes for a few seconds to envision the course of events. "First of all, things seemed tense at the book club meeting to begin with. Did you know about the book club meeting at the pizza shop?"

"I did," he said.

"It was almost as if something happened before I arrived that set everyone's nerves on edge. No one mentioned that, though. I gave a talk, answered a few questions, then the man in the red Corvette showed up."

"Marty Dixon?"

"People called him Dixon. I didn't know him."

"What happened after he showed up?"

I hated to report on Tracey's bad behavior. She was the person who'd contacted me about coming to speak to the book club, and she'd been very pleasant. I didn't expect her to do anything rash like attacking a man the way she had today. But this was the sheriff asking for my truthful account, and he seemed of a mind to wring the details out of me one way or another.

"Tracey, one of the book club members, jumped up the second she saw him and ran outside." I paused for a moment. "You know, I'm surprised Dixon complained about an assault."

"Finish your story, please." His serious expression gave away nothing.

Had Dixon complained about Tracey?

"Honestly," I said, "the only people happy about Dixon's appearance were the kids who came for free pizza. At least Dixon claimed they could get it free, courtesy of Colt Jamison. I don't know if what he said was true or if the kids actually got free pizza."

"They did, according to my deputies," he said.

I straightened. "Speaking of deputies, it's obvious that Deputy Rosales knows Marty Dixon rather well. She wasn't happy to see him either."

"We're not going to talk about my deputy. Please, go back to the woman running outside after Dixon's arrival. Describe the scene for me."

I took a deep breath and told him everything. Well, nearly everything. I made a conscious decision to skip the part about Tracey bringing up ways to get away with murder, but I admitted that she was without a doubt the instigator of the fight.

"Dixon was partly defending himself and partly teasing Tracey," I said. "At least that was my take. She wasn't amused."

"No, she definitely was not," he said.

"Wait," I said. "Is Tracey the one complaining that she was assaulted by Dixon?"

The sheriff rubbed his chin as if checking how badly he needed a shave. "Now you're getting the picture."

"That's silly," I said. "Nobody who was there would believe that story."

"She has a friend backing her up," the sheriff said.

Elise, if I had to guess.

"You need to watch the video," I said.

The sheriff turned sharply. "What video?"

I gave him Jeff's name. "I'm not sure how good the video is, but it might help you. What does Dixon say about this?"

"Don't know yet," he said. "Haven't been able to locate him."

"Can't help you there," I said, "but he shouldn't be hard to find, driving around town in that red sports car. He came by here and asked about renting a cottage, but we're all filled up."

The sheriff frowned. "His mother hasn't heard from him."

"His mother lives in Lavender?"

"Sure does, but she didn't even know he was in town."

"Huh." I thought for a moment. "I don't know what Dixon will have to say about the fight. Something's up between him and Tracey. I'd guess something personal 'cause Tracey was running on pure emotion. In my opinion."

"There's a history," the sheriff said.

"Really?" I waited for him to say more, and he didn't disappoint.

"They grew up together. Tracey's the type of woman who holds a grudge, so there's no tellin' what she has stacked up against Marty Dixon. Maybe from before he moved to Nashville. Maybe something about his deciding to move in the first place. I'm speculating, you understand."

"You sound like me when I plot a book," I said.

"Right." The sheriff allowed me a small grin. "Anyone else in the pizza shop get involved in the altercation?"

"Tracey's friend, Elise, came outside and urged Tracey to stop, but she wouldn't listen."

"How about the pizza shop owners? Bruno? Charlotte? Her husband, Fritz?"

I shook my head. "I didn't see any of them outside. With all those kids pouring in for pizza, I'm sure they were overwhelmed with business."

The sheriff stood. "Thanks for the help. If you see Dixon, give me a call. I'd like to wrap this up tonight."

"You got it." I stood, too. "Please, don't mention my name to Tracey. If she holds grudges, I don't need her blackballing me or my book."

"Roger that," he said.

• • •

I tucked my curiosity about the problem between Tracey and Marty Dixon into a corner of my mind and enjoyed dinner with Nick, his boys, and Aunt Rowe. While Hitchcock wandered around our legs and batted at stray crumbs, the kids told us all about their escapades of the past school year and what they hoped to accomplish next semester.

Matthew aced all his classes and Adam struggled to keep up with his older brother's reputation. A natural progression, I decided, and nothing to worry about. I hoped it didn't bother Adam that Matt was much taller and a very handsome young man. I had no doubt Adam would catch up in terms of height and looks before long.

As we finished ample servings of lemon meringue pie, Nick pushed his chair back. "Whew. I don't think I could eat one more bite. That was great, Aunt Rowe. Thanks."

"I'm thrilled to have you boys here. Y'all remind me so much of Richard." She looked down, and I wondered if she was fighting tears as she remembered my late father, her brother.

"I'll bet this'll *really* remind you of Dad," Nick said.

Aunt Rowe looked up as he rubbed his belly and deepened his voice. "Meal of the month, Rowe," he said. "I'd better head on to bed before I crater here at the table."

Aunt Rowe and I burst into laughter. Nick had his Dad imitation down pat.

"Mrreow," Hitchcock said in what I took as his attempt to laugh along with us.

"You can't go to bed," Adam said, his voice more of a whine. "We're going to town now. You promised."

I looked at Nick and lifted my brows in question. He groaned.

"What's in town that you boys need to see before morning?" Aunt Rowe said.

"There's this place called the Wild Pony," Matt said.

"That's a dance hall," I said, "and you can't get in unless you're twenty-one."

"The fan club has a Colt Jamison booth outside," Matt said, "and they're giving away T-shirts. I saw a post about it."

Nick glanced at the wall clock. "It's after eight. Whatever they had to give away is probably gone by now."

"But you promised we could go to town," Adam said. "We might even *see* Colt Jamison. That'd be super cool."

Aunt Rowe and I exchanged a glance. Good Lord, what would

these boys do if they knew that Jamison was practically under their noses, staying in the Athens cottage?

"I thought singers usually roll into town shortly before the concert," I said, "and that's two days away."

Nick looked at his sons. "You two are lucky I'm in a good mood. Who's going with us? Sabrina? Aunt Rowe?"

"I'll stay put and keep Hitchcock company," Aunt Rowe said. "My Colt Jamison sighting will have to wait."

I gave her a look. *Don't push it.*

"Mrreow." Hitchcock rubbed up against Aunt Rowe's leg then jumped into her lap.

I grinned at them and got up. "Count me in."

Thirty minutes later, we cruised the main drag of downtown Lavender. I pointed out Knead to Read, my friend Tyanne's bookstore, and Sweet Stop, the local candy store—two places I knew the boys intended to visit. Tonight, they had the Wild Pony Saloon on their minds. They weren't the only ones. The sidewalks and streets near the saloon were crowded. Nick circled the block three times before finding a place to park on a side street.

Even before we climbed out of the car, we could hear the song 'Broken Mirror' coming from speakers affixed to streetlights. Groups of teens danced on and around the sidewalks. An older guy who might make it as a Willie Nelson impersonator sat on the Wild Pony's porch rail and strummed his guitar. I wondered if the sheriff had ever caught up with Marty Dixon and found myself searching the crowd for the blond man with the pointy goatee.

"There's your girlfriend, Tandee," Adam shouted, emphasizing the *dee*. "She's lookin' for you, Matt." He pointed to a row of folding tables set up in front of the Wild Pony. Piles of shirts filled the tables. A large sign proclaimed *Free Shirts for Colt Jamison Fans*. The girl I'd seen handing out giveaways earlier was in a fan T-shirt and a pair of cutoffs far shorter than anyone should wear in public.

"She's not my girlfriend," Matt grumbled, but he headed in the fan club president's direction.

"Stick close, guys," Nick said loudly.

He got a slight nod from his younger son, but Matt was already out of range.

Nick spoke directly into my ear as we neared the saloon. "I

remember this place from the good old days. Line dancing to 'Achy Breaky Heart.'"

"I couldn't believe you liked that song," I said. "Still can't."

My attention was drawn to a woman wearing snug jeans with the legs stuffed into tall turquoise boots that matched her tank top. Her sleek black hair was tied up in a high ponytail. When she turned to scan the crowd, I recognized Patricia Rosales and gasped.

"What's up?" Nick followed my gaze.

"That's *the deputy*," I said.

"You mean your nemesis?"

He'd heard plenty from me about Rosales's attitude over the past year or so, but she looked like a different woman now. The laid-back version, and maybe I'd like this persona better.

"She's never relaxed," I said, "and I don't necessarily believe she's here because she's a Colt Jamison fan. It's more likely she's on an undercover assignment."

"I doubt it," he said. "Who goes undercover in Lavender?"

"Good point." I turned toward the tables, ten yards away, and looked for the boys. Only Adam was in view. He slipped on his new T-shirt over his other shirt and beamed at us.

"Matt?" I mouthed and threw my hands in the air.

He shrugged as a blood-curdling scream cut through the music. The sound came from the direction of the woods behind the building. I didn't see Matt—or the girl named Tandee—anywhere.

Nick ran to Adam and grabbed his hand. Kids stampeded away from the frightening sound. With Matthew missing, I ran toward the tree line, scanning left and right as I moved. Rosales wasn't in sight, and I wondered if she'd heard the scream.

A figure, barely visible in the rapidly diminishing daylight, emerged from the shadows. Matthew.

"Dad," he hollered. "Come quick."

I sprinted and Nick caught up and overtook me. I looked back and saw Adam running after us.

"What is it?" Nick yelled when he reached Matt. "Are you all right?"

"Yes. Follow me."

Nick, always a quick thinker, had turned on his phone flashlight. I ran into the trees behind them, guided by the beam. Brambles and thorns caught at my clothes. I turned to make sure Adam was still with us and nearly bumped into Matt when he stopped abruptly.

A few feet in front of Matt, Tandee stood looking at the ground. Her scream had dissolved into whimpers.

I looked, too, and felt a jolt as I realized a body lay facedown on the ground near her feet.

Matt said, "We were walking, and I stepped on something, and I didn't know what it was, but it must have been his arm. Those shoe prints on his arm are mine."

The boy's voice quaked, and he shook visibly. Nick wrapped an arm around him. "You're okay. Stay calm."

"But it's not okay," Matt said. "The man might be dead."

"Don't touch anything," I said.

"We have to help him." Without warning, Matt crouched and rolled the body over. "I took CPR in school."

The thought was a noble one, but I had seen blood and could tell by looking it was too late to help. The man's throat had been cut by something sharp and jagged.

"Son, we can't do anything." Nick held Matt's arm and pulled him away.

I took a closer look at the man, then let my head fall back and looked heavenward for a few seconds. My heart raced.

After taking a few calming breaths, I said, "Let me make a call."

I wanted to take action before Rosales arrived on the scene, which would probably be any second now. I took out my phone and pulled up my contacts list. Punched the number for Sheriff Crawford's cell.

"Hi, Sheriff," I said when he answered.

"Sabrina." He sounded sleepy, and I got the impression he'd done what we should have done—gone straight to bed after dinner.

"I'm at the Wild Pony with my brother and his boys," I said. "See, they're giving away free T-shirts over here, and the boys knew all about the giveaway and they begged Nick to come to town for—"

"Sabrina, please," he said, "it's late. I don't think you called to tell me about the shirts, did you?"

"No, Sheriff." I swallowed hard. "My nephew just found Marty Dixon. Trouble is, he's dead."

Chapter 6

I ended my call to the sheriff and realized my hands were shaking badly. I stuffed them into my shorts pockets and tried to steady my breathing. There was no way to stay calm with a man's dead body lying in plain sight. We needed to move.

"The sheriff's team is on the way," I said. "Let's get out of these trees so they can spot us."

And to get these kids away from the body.

Nick gave me an appreciative nod and herded the boys back in the direction we'd come. I followed and glanced over my shoulder to make sure Tandee was with us.

She wasn't. I pivoted and saw the girl hadn't budged. With her arms wrapped tightly around her torso, she stood over the dead man. She rocked back and forth on her heels and appeared to be talking to herself. I couldn't hear what she said over the hammering of my heartbeat.

I gave Tandee credit for not racing out of the woods screaming the second she spotted the body. Her complexion appeared ghostly, and I worried that she would pass out. I walked toward her and could make out her words as I grew closer.

"It's not my fault, it's not my fault, not my fault."

Did she fear we'd think otherwise?

I looked her over and didn't see any blood. Whoever did this would have some blood spatter on them, wouldn't they? The thought brought another question. Where was the killer now? Another reason for us to move. Get out in the open where people would see us.

Safety in numbers.

I reached out and tapped Tandee's arm. She jumped as if I'd touched her with a hot poker. Her gaze flew to my face and back to the body.

"Tandee," I said. "C'mon with me. Let's go stand with Matt and Adam."

She chanted, "Not my fault, not my fault, not my fault."

I wondered if she'd had some part in what happened to Marty Dixon. Or maybe she felt she could have prevented the murder. No telling. Whatever the case, this young woman was traumatized.

"Tandee, please come with me. We need to move. It's best if we're not standing right here when the sheriff arrives."

Her head jerked toward me. "The sheriff?"

"Yes. He's on his way. He'll find out what happened here tonight."

"Good." She nodded. "That's good."

Guiding her by the arm, I urged the girl away from the grisly scene. When we cleared the trees, I spotted the guys hovering nearby. Nick's mouth was set in a grim line. Adam's eyes were red-rimmed. Matt paced beside the trees until he saw Tandee approaching with me. He practically leapt to close the distance between us.

"Are you okay?" he said to the girl.

She nodded and swept wispy bangs back from her face. "I, I'm shocked."

"Yeah." Matt looked at her more closely. "Did you know him?"

"Not well," she said.

Matt looked at me. "Did *you* know the guy, Aunt Sabrina?"

I shook my head. "I saw him earlier today and heard his name is Marty Dixon."

I thought again about Tracey's fight with the man and wondered about her motivation. I hoped she hadn't tracked him down and killed him in cold blood, but things were going to look very bad for her during the investigation into this murder.

"What do you think happened?" Matt said, interrupting my musing. In spite of his initial freaked-out reaction to having stepped on the body, the boy wanted details. I'd rather he didn't take too much interest in the crime. This was supposed to be a nice and relaxing family vacation with his dad and brother.

"We don't need to solve the case," I said. "The sheriff will handle everything."

I checked Tandee for a reaction. My reference to the sheriff didn't appear to faze her this time.

"But you solve mysteries," Matt said, "and you've solved murders before. You and Hitchcock."

I hadn't shared that information with the boy, and I wondered who had. Maybe Aunt Rowe.

"That's not my job, Matt. I'm sure the sheriff will warn us all to stay out of the investigation."

He always does.

Nick came over and looked at Matt and Tandee. "Investigators will want to know what you two were doing in the woods tonight. I wouldn't mind having the answer to that question myself. What's the story?"

Matt faced his father. "She wanted to talk about me helping with the Colt Jamison fan club."

Nick said, "That doesn't require going into the woods."

"I asked him to walk with me," Tandee said. "We could use a fan club rep in Houston."

"Uh-huh." Nick met her gaze head-on. "Did you know my son is fifteen years old?"

"Almost sixteen," Matt blurted.

Nick glanced at him and back to the girl. "He's going into the ninth grade, miss. I'm sorry, I didn't catch your last name."

"Cushing," she said. "Tandee Cushing."

"Miss Cushing," Nick went on, "I'm guessing you're a good bit older."

"Yes, sir," she said. "I'm eighteen."

Nick nodded. "I'm sure you can understand my concern as a parent—"

"Dad." Matt whined the word into four syllables, reminding me of his much younger self.

I held my hand up like a stop sign and looked at my brother. "Nick, please. We're all stressed. Let's give it a rest."

He sighed, then turned and went back to stand with Adam. The younger boy's complexion was reddened, and I guessed he was fighting off tears. Nick draped his arm across the boy's shoulders.

Sirens sounded in the distance, growing closer at a fast clip. I wished the sheriff could have taken action without alerting the entire town that something was going down. When the whole cadre of emergency personnel descended, everyone within miles would know. With the hordes of teens in the vicinity, the scene was about to turn wild and crazy. I wondered about Marty Dixon's connection to the singer and whether his murder would have any effect on the upcoming concert.

I wondered, too, why Patricia Rosales hadn't already rushed us. The emergency alert would have gone out to the entire sheriff's department. I would have expected Rosales to be on top of us within minutes. Not that I wanted to deal with her right now.

As we waited for the authorities to reach us, I comforted myself with the fact that Matt couldn't be blamed for the murder even if his shoe prints *were* on the body. We had arrived less than thirty minutes ago, and Aunt Rowe could vouch for Matt's whereabouts earlier in the evening. If only he hadn't walked off with Tandee. We'd have picked up our free T-shirts and happily gone home for the night. Someone else would have discovered the crime, but it was far too late to change the facts.

A few minutes later, an ambulance, a fire truck, and three sheriff's department cars pulled into the field near us. The sheriff hurried over, and we pointed out the path to where we'd seen the body. Paramedics followed him into the trees.

Deputy Brent Ainsley and the new guy, Denny Salazar, approached us with their notebooks at the ready. They asked me to step away from the others. They planned to question us separately, and I had the lucky number-one spot.

Ainsley wore his usual smirk and began the question-and-answer session with, "I suppose your cat found another body. How many does that make?"

My back stiffened. "My cat did no such thing."

"Yeah, right." Ainsley chuckled. "Heard that before." He looked at Salazar. "Her cat's the bad luck cat. You'll hear plenty about him while you're workin' in this town."

I sighed. "Hitchcock is *not* your legendary cat, and he does *not* cause bad luck."

"There's a dead guy in the woods, isn't there?" Ainsley said.

"Yes, there is," I said, "but my cat is at home."

Salazar cleared his throat. "Do you know the victim's name, ma'am?"

I appreciated the voice of sanity. "I believe his name is Marty Dixon."

"And how do, did, you know Mr. Dixon?"

"I didn't know him. I saw him earlier today, at the pizza shop."

Salazar looked up and studied me for a moment. "I remember. You were there with your cat. The black cat."

"See what I'm tellin' you," Ainsley said. "The bad luck cat saw Dixon at the pizza shop. Now he's dead."

"Oh, for the love of—" I almost wished Patricia Rosales were here to do the questioning instead of Ainsley, but I managed to get through the session and answered all of the deputies' questions.

An hour later, they had finished talking with my family members. Sheriff Crawford gave us the go-ahead to leave. He knew where to find us and would give us a call if he needed any further information. Ainsley was with Tandee. Salazar was questioning others from the crowd who'd stepped up to volunteer information.

"Let's get out of here," I said to Nick, "while the getting is good."

"Right behind you," he said. "C'mon, boys."

Matt turned to check on Tandee.

"She'll be fine," Nick said. "Does she have family in the area?"

Matt shrugged. "I don't know."

"Did she say anything to you about Marty Dixon when you first saw the body?" I said. "She seemed, what's a good word—frantic—about what happened."

"She screamed," Matt said. "She might have said something first. I only remember the scream."

We headed for the car and made a detour around the crowd of onlookers who stood on the periphery of the crime scene tape the deputies had strung up.

A few people snapped pictures of us with their phones.

"Cover your faces," Nick muttered. "Nosy jerks."

"Sabrina."

A boy's voice called to me from the crowd. I looked up and saw Ethan Brady, a bookstore employee who worked for my friend Tyanne.

"Ethan, hi."

He moved away from the others and hurried over to me.

"I heard there was a murder. Is that true?"

"Since you're not a reporter, and I trust you, I'll say yes. We're not supposed to talk about this. There's an ongoing investigation."

"I won't spread gossip," Ethan said, "but can you answer a question for me?"

"Depends," I said. "What's the question?"

"Was the victim wearing a green flowered Hawaiian shirt?"

I stopped walking and looked at him. "Why do you ask?"

"I saw him when I came to get a free T-shirt. Did the deputies say anything to you about Deputy Rosales?"

"No. Why?"

"The man in the Hawaiian shirt was with her. Across the street in that park by the flagpoles." He leaned closer and lowered his voice. "They were having a serious screaming match."

"About what?" I said.

"I couldn't hear, but they weren't happy. Matter of fact, I remember thinking the guy should walk away for his own good."

"What are you saying?"

"I didn't think he was safe staying anywhere near her. Whatever was going on between them, Rosales was ticked. I read a ton of books and live in a fictional world more often than not, but —"

"So do I, Ethan. I understand. What does that have to do with what happened here?"

"I don't want to blow what I saw out of proportion."

"Go ahead and tell me what's on your mind, and I'll decide what I think."

"I've seen Deputy Rosales in a bad mood before," he said. "This time — with that guy — she looked mad enough to kill."

Chapter 7

Deputy Patricia Rosales was an expert of the verbal tongue lashing. I had to believe this was what Ethan had witnessed between Rosales and Dixon. She would never physically hurt a person and certainly not commit murder. Even though I didn't like the woman, I was as convinced of her innocence as I was of my own.

Someone had killed Marty Dixon, though, and the murder was keeping me awake. Every time I closed my eyes vivid images flashed behind my lids.

Matt's stunned expression when he ran from the woods.

Tandee's frozen pose.

That awful pool of blood.

Marty Dixon's lifeless body.

I rolled to my other side. Hitchcock, lying on top of the covers, dipped and swayed with my jostling like a deckhand sailing rough waters. I caught a glimpse of the clock on the nightstand. Almost three in the morning. We'd all been up talking until nearly one.

"Mrr," Hitchcock complained on my third tug at the blanket.

I pulled out one hand and stroked his head. "Sorry, buddy. Bad night. So glad you weren't there with us."

He nuzzled against my side, and I tried to dwell on his comforting presence. The technique didn't work.

Why did I think anything would lull me into dreamland after what happened?

I remembered my first glimpse of Dixon driving up in his racy red Corvette. So carefree. Friendly. Happily offering the free pizza. Tracey and Rosales didn't care for the guy, and I could understand they had a personal opinion. But who would want a guy like Dixon dead?

Random foul play was always a possibility. The town didn't run background checks on the thousands of visitors who strolled the streets of Lavender. A good number of tourists spent hours drinking inside the Wild Pony each night. Dixon might have simply been in the wrong place at the wrong time. But I'd considered that notion before under other circumstances — and the simple solution rarely panned out.

"Tracey Powell and Deputy Rosales both had a beef with the dead man," I told Hitchcock.

"Mrreow," he said sleepily.

"I don't see those two women having a connection to each other, only to Dixon, and they're both too smart to leave a body where it could be easily found." Jeff Slade had answered Tracey's question at the book club meeting in no uncertain terms. Don't leave the body behind.

I wondered if Ethan had an opportunity to speak with Sheriff Crawford and whether the boy had told him everything about the argument he'd witnessed between the dead man and the deputy. I hadn't given him any advice on the subject and wasn't sure what I'd do in his shoes.

Hitchcock rolled, and I felt him stretch to his full length. He held the stretch for a long time, then relaxed.

"Wish I knew what Marty Dixon did to rile those women up," I muttered.

Hitchcock made a sound low in his throat, something close to a growl.

"I know. This isn't my case to solve. I told Matt the same thing, and I meant every word."

Another sleepless twenty minutes went by before I propped myself on my elbows. In the dim glow of a cat-shaped nightlight plugged into the bedroom wall, I saw Hitchcock lift his head and peer at me.

"I'm not going to fall asleep at this point," I said. "How about going with me to Aunt Rowe's to bake something?"

Hitchcock was off the bed in a flash.

I threw on shorts and a T-shirt and pulled on my tennis shoes. Five minutes later, Hitchcock trotted by my side on the way to Aunt Rowe's big perfect-for-baking kitchen. Her guest rooms were on the opposite end of the house, and I'd be extra quiet so I wouldn't wake anyone, especially my nephews. Those boys needed to get their rest after the traumatic evening.

I'd traveled the path from my place to Aunt Rowe's many times. With the help of a bright half-moon, I didn't need to switch on the flashlight I'd brought with me. We traipsed along, listening to the river and the singing of tree frogs. The sudden brilliance of headlights coming down the lane startled me.

Lavender doesn't have much of a night life, and the Wild Pony had closed over an hour ago. Of course, friends could visit with friends at any time, day or night. Still, I wondered who was out at this hour. We didn't have a through street, so whoever it was had either taken a wrong turn or was headed to one of the cottages.

I stopped in my tracks when the light-colored pickup pulled in and parked at the Athens cottage. The same truck I saw there before — one I'd assumed belonged to Jamison, the man who wanted his presence kept a secret.

Maybe the singer had a craving for a candy bar or a beer. Made a quick run to the convenience store and came right back. Floyd, the man who worked nights at the Stop-and-Shop, might not recognize the singer. Still, going out would be a risk for Jamison.

The headlights turned off and the dome light flicked on for three seconds as someone climbed from the truck. I could make out the tall shape of the person. He approached the cottage. I hoped it was Jamison rather than some thief casing the joint.

That was definitely mystery-writer-speak and probably language from the past. These days criminals hacked into everything they needed to know online and could do it from the comfort of their own homes. They didn't wander around in the dark on the off chance they'd find crimes to commit.

I turned my head to make a comment to my cat and realized Hitchcock was no longer beside me. I looked around frantically and saw his dark form halfway between me and the river. Good grief. What the heck was he doing?

I headed that way, then stopped again as a shadow moved near the cat. My heart lurched, but the person didn't appear to be after Hitchcock, or even aware of the nearby cat. I thought Jamison had gone inside, but one glance over my shoulder confirmed that the Athens cottage remained dark. One thing I knew for sure. Someone was heading in the direction of the river toward the place I first saw Tandee hawking the Colt Jamison fan club. If I knew Hitchcock — and I knew my cat pretty danged well — he'd go where the action was. That meant I was going after my wayward cat.

When I grew close to the picnic table where Tandee had perched to make her announcements, I stopped and stood behind a tree trunk where I had a good view of the clearing. I didn't see

Hitchcock, but two men came into view: an older man with straggly shoulder-length hair, the other one younger and with lighter hair. Colt Jamison. The straggly guy said something and changed position. He seemed familiar for some reason.

I felt like one of those sleazy photographers who endanger the lives of famous people by chasing them for a picture. Jamison didn't have to fear me taking any picture—I hadn't brought my phone with me—but he wouldn't want me out here at all given that I could potentially identify him and spread the word that he was here in Lavender.

My heartbeat thrummed in my ears so loud I feared the men could hear it from where they stood. They gave no indication that they knew I was present. Straggly guy held a manila envelope, and he beckoned Jamison to come over to the picnic table, where he dumped pages out onto the flat surface between them. Then he flicked a cigarette lighter. My breath caught as I expected him to burn the papers right then. But the men bent to study the pages by the glow of the flame. I realized where I'd seen the straggly guy before—playing a guitar on the porch of the Wild Pony before the discovery of the body.

The men were reading something, engrossed in whatever information the pages held. I heard snippets of conversation.

"All the words," straggly guy said.

"Original mat—?"

"You betcha."

"Swear? Nobody'll come after me?" Jamison ran his hands through his short hair.

Straggly guy shook his head as he stuffed the papers back into the envelope. "Never happen."

Jamison took something from his pocket and handed it to the other man. Then he snatched the envelope, turned on his heel, and came my way.

Drat.

There was no chance he'd miss seeing me, so I began my best "crazy cat lady searching for her missing pet" performance. Not totally an act, because I dearly wanted to find Hitchcock and take him to safety.

"Psst, Hitchcock. Where are you? Kitty, kitty?" I looked under bushes and turned on my flashlight, patting myself on the back for bringing it along.

"Lose something?"

The deep voice behind me made me jump even though I expected the man's approach.

I turned to find myself face-to-face with the singer.

"My cat ran this way," I said. "It's just like him to roam and forget the time or the fact that I'm home worrying myself silly about him getting lost, and—" I paused and cocked my head as I looked at Jamison while trying not to stare. He sure was handsome.

"Isn't that what cats do?" he said. "Roam around at night?"

"Well, sure—" I stopped talking and waited for him to laugh. I had a feeling he didn't believe one word of my cat story.

"How'd you know he was gone?" he said, deadpan.

"I, what?"

"Most people are asleep now, so why were you up to realize your cat was gone?"

"I have insomnia. We were going to bake at my Aunt Rowe's."

Even in the near dark, I could tell he was frowning.

"We?" he said.

"Me and my cat, but then I lost sight of him and here I am."

"Your Aunt Rowe?"

"I live here in the Monte Carlo cottage. My aunt owns the properties." Ordinarily, I would introduce myself at this point, but that would put us in the awkward position of him knowing my name and not wanting to tell me his.

"Oh, I get it now." He looked at a point past me. "Is that your cat over there?"

I turned and saw Hitchcock sitting on a stump like the most well-behaved cat in the world.

"That's him," I said. "Thank you for your help. Have a good night now."

I hurried over to Hitchcock and picked him up.

"Mrreow," he said.

"Hush. Not one more word."

I headed straight to Aunt Rowe's house while questions raced through my head.

What was inside that envelope clutched in Colt Jamison's hand?

Had he made a trade for something or had he handed the older man cash?

Why did this transaction occur in the dead of night?

Who *was* that scraggly guy?

And here was the biggest question of all. Had Colt Jamison been out to make a quick run to the convenience store or was he in town at the time of Marty Dixon's murder?

Chapter 8

I snagged a few hours of sleep after my bake-a-thon during the wee hours. Hitchcock was gone when I squinted at my bedside clock and made out the digits 9:10. The cat was often out and about before me, and I usually found him at Aunt Rowe's house. I dressed quickly and headed that way. I wanted to keep Matt and Adam occupied today to take their minds off the murder even though it was front and center in mine.

The mystery writer in me hated waiting for answers to the *why, how, who, and when* questions related to a crime. My imagination felt like a merry-go-round, and I wished the spinning would stop and solutions would spill out.

Not so easy.

The area around the cottages appeared deserted. No sign of Colt Jamison—whom I still couldn't believe I'd talked to last night—or anyone else for that matter. The Thursday morning calm before the weekend storm.

I predictably found Hitchcock in the kitchen at Glenda's feet.

"There you are, you little scamp." I bent to scratch the cat's head. "You know I can smell that leftover chicken on your breath, right?"

"Mrreow." Hitchcock leaned into the scratch and didn't look the least bit guilty.

"Surprised to see you up so early after all this." Glenda swept her arm over the counter holding the German chocolate cake, four dozen peanut butter cookies, and two pies I'd baked.

"Wouldn't be fair to have you doing all the work," I said. "Keeping my guys in dessert is a challenging task."

"You couldn't sleep for thinking about the murder." She gave me a knowing look.

"You have me pegged." I headed for the coffeepot. "Figured you'd heard about what happened."

"The story's all over town, and on the news, too." She pulled a skillet from a cabinet and placed it on the cooktop.

"Any names mentioned?"

Glenda shook her head. "No, thank the Lord, but Rowe told me about Matthew and that girl finding the body."

"Are the boys up?"

"Not yet, but they'll be out here as soon as the smell of fryin' bacon hits 'em."

I grinned. "Is Aunt Rowe in her office?"

"No. She's out with Violet."

I paused with the coffeepot poised over my cup. "Violet, the life coach?"

"Yes, ma'am." Glenda took a sealed package of bacon from the refrigerator. I struggle with the "easy open" packages, but she skillfully peeled the plastic back in a split second.

"It's kind of early in the day to talk *life strategies* if you ask me." I poured my coffee and added creamer. "Where'd they go?"

Glenda turned on the burner and began lining the skillet with bacon strips. "I heard something about getting together with Twila Baxter."

I choked on my first sip of coffee, and after a few seconds managed to swallow the hot liquid without incident. "What on earth do they have planned with Twila?"

"Maybe they're going antiquing," Glenda said.

Twila owned a local antiques store and would be in the know about the best places to shop.

"I hope that's what they're doing. Every time I see Twila she dwells on saving her late husband's soul."

Glenda didn't appear surprised. "Lucky you."

"She continues to say Hitchcock and I have special powers."

"Do you?" she said with a smirk.

"Mrreow," Hitchcock said, and we laughed.

The meat began to sizzle. I turned to Glenda, all laughing aside.

"Is Aunt Rowe okay?" I paused to consider how to best voice my concern. "I mean, is there some reason she thinks her life is not all right as is? That she feels she needs help?"

"I'm sure Rowe wants to make the most of her years," she said. "We all do."

"I don't like the implications," I said. "I'd almost rather they're off to hold a séance with Twila."

"Drink your coffee and quit worrying," Glenda said.

"You must be talking to my sister." Nick appeared as if by magic and stood poised over the skillet. "The queen of worry."

Glenda grinned at me as Nick sniffed the air. "Gets 'em every time."

Nick looked from Glenda to me and back. "Will someone tell me what's going on?"

"Nothing important," I said. "Get you some coffee?"

"I'll help myself," he said with a big yawn. "Need an extra-large cup since I barely slept. Any news?"

My thoughts returned to the murder. "I haven't heard anything."

"Lloyd had the local news on at home this morning," Glenda said. "They made a slight mention of finding the man, name withheld pending notification of next of kin. You know how they do."

"Right," Nick said as he filled a coffee mug.

I took the sweet cream from the refrigerator and handed it to him. "Did they connect Colt Jamison to the story?"

"Don't think so." Glenda turned the bacon strips with a pair of tongs.

I heard movement coming from the direction of the bedrooms.

"The lure of food," I said.

After a quick glance in that direction, Nick said, "What's on the agenda today?"

"Whatever will keep their minds occupied," I said. "They enjoyed visiting Tyanne's bookstore last time they were in town, so we could go there for a bit. Luke plans to meet us for lunch, if that still works for you."

"Are you kidding?" Nick said. "I'm not passing up the chance to interrogate your new guy."

"Ha ha," I said. "Seriously, I don't want to make all the decisions. We'll see what the boys want to do."

Hitchcock looked up as Matt and Adam barreled into the room and headed straight for the orange juice Glenda had placed on the counter.

"Morning, boys," I said.

"Morning, Aunt Sabrina," Adam said. "Hey, can we go to that bookstore today? The one with the cats?"

"Mrreow," Hitchcock said.

• • •

Later in the morning, Ethan Brady led Matt and Adam to the section of Knead to Read that he'd decorated to resemble the solar system with stars and planets cut from shimmery cardboard hung from the ceiling by fishing line. Hitchcock, always mesmerized by the movement of the stars that hung near the air-conditioning vent, followed the guys. Zelda, Ty's orange female, and Willis, her tabby tomcat, leapt off the front windowsill and zipped after Hitchcock.

Nick, Tyanne, and I sat in a reading nook where Ty could keep an eye on the front of the store. For the moment, customers were scarce. One woman—an avid reader that I'd seen before—studied books thoroughly before adding them to her pile on the counter near the cash register.

"Great to see you again, Tyanne," Nick said. "You're looking good."

Nick had, of course, spent some time at Aunt Rowe's house as a kid—not as much as I had—and knew Tyanne from his summer visits.

"Thanks, Nick." She cast a concerned glance toward the boys. "Are they doing okay?"

"They haven't mentioned last night," he said. "Yet."

"I'm glad you called ahead," Tyanne told me. "Ethan has a row of books to show them. He's over the top about one new author. Says he's the next Rick Riordan."

"I wouldn't mind reading that book," I said.

Tyanne faced my brother. "How's everything in Houston? Your practice growing?"

"Baby boomers are busy preparing for their deaths," he said. "Business as usual."

I'd never heard my brother describe his estate planning law practice in quite that way.

He turned his attention to the store. "Have you remodeled since the last time I was here?"

"You mean since the nineties?" Ty said. "Yes."

"Very funny. It hasn't been that long." He paused. "Has it?"

Before Tyanne responded, a woman outside on the sidewalk caught my attention. Elise Lister glanced at the ads affixed to the windows, and for a moment I thought she meant to come in. When she continued on her way, I jumped up.

"Excuse me a minute. Be right back."

I hurried out of the store and quick-stepped to catch up with her. "Elise?"

The woman, a few yards in front of me, heard my call. Her straight blonde hair lifted off her shoulders as she whirled around.

"Sabrina." She smiled and glanced at the store behind me. "Are you doing another author event today?"

Her tone insinuated that she'd eagerly hurry into the bookstore if that were the case even though I had signed her copy of my book and spoken to her group yesterday.

"Just visiting," I said. "My brother and his boys are in from Houston, and Tyanne's bookstore is one of their favorite spots."

"That's nice," she said. "I'm sure you'll enjoy your time with them."

"I'd enjoy it more if we weren't shaken up about the murder."

Her smile dimmed. "I heard about that."

"What did you hear?" I said.

"You know, that a couple of kids found a body."

"My nephew was one of them."

She blanched. "Oh, I'm so sorry."

"Thanks. I'm hopeful the authorities can solve this murder quickly. We'll all feel a bit better when the culprit is behind bars."

"For sure," Elise said.

I decided to jump right into the questions I wanted answered. "How well did you know Marty Dixon?"

She frowned and shook her head. "I didn't."

The answer surprised me. "I assumed you did from the way you tried to stop Tracey when she bolted out of the pizza shop after him. Sure looked like you knew trouble was coming."

"Oh, that." She adjusted her purse straps on the shoulder of her pink T-shirt and didn't meet my eyes. "Tracey overreacts. Always has, ever since I first met her in the fourth grade."

I raised my brows. "You know her pretty well then. What was she overreacting to this time?"

Elise shrugged, and one of the purse straps slipped down to her elbow. "I'm not sure."

Right.

"Does she often get so riled up for no apparent reason?"

Another shrug. "She lets her emotions get the best of her."

"And you don't know why she was upset with Marty Dixon yesterday?"

"I think they had a little squabble. Honestly, I don't know the details." She fiddled with the purse strap again.

Her answer didn't seem honest, but I let it go.

"Have you talked to Tracey today?"

"Gee, today? No, as a matter of fact I haven't." She glanced at her watch, then over her shoulder with an expression that said I was keeping her from something oh-so-important.

"Do you know if Tracey's been interviewed?"

"About what?"

"The murder."

"Oh, they have no cause to talk with her," Elise said in a tone so casual you'd think she was discussing the weather. "Tracey was home all last night with her kids startin' at five in the evening."

She knew exactly why I was asking, and I wondered why she thought everyone would take her or Tracey's word for the woman's whereabouts the night before. I had the distinct feeling the two of them had discussed how best to handle the question of alibis.

"Were you at her house with them?" I said.

"No, I wasn't." Her mouth set in a grim line. "What are you getting at, Sabrina? Maybe you should spit out whatever's on your mind."

"I don't mean to upset you, Elise, but there were a lot of witnesses to Tracey's fight with a man who's been murdered. Naturally, the authorities will want to talk with her personally."

She'd asked what I had on my mind, but Elise didn't look any happier now that she knew.

"Have the authorities interviewed *you*?" I said.

She jumped back as if I'd moved to strike her. "No. Why would they?"

"I'm sure you're on the video."

"What video?" Panic flashed in her expression.

"The scene was videotaped," I said calmly. "The authorities will likely gain access to that video and proceed to interview everyone. Unless they can solve the murder quickly, in which case they may not go to such lengths."

"Well, they can start by talking to their own Deputy Rosales,"

Elise said, all bluster. "She was there, and I mean to tell you Marty Dixon was pushing all of that woman's buttons."

"I'm not asking about her, Elise. I'm asking about your friend. Tracey. Why was she so ticked off with Marty Dixon?" I softened my tone. "I'm hoping to help her head off trouble, not trying to hurt her. Or you."

Elise's expression seemed to collapse, and she hung her head for a few seconds. When she looked up, she appeared to have made a decision.

"Tracey is a fierce defender of family," she said. "I don't have a brother myself, but you do, Sabrina. It's not my place to tell her story, but I'd like you to promise me one thing."

"What's that?" I said.

"Before you form an opinion about Tracey, ask yourself what you'd do if someone was hell-bent on destroying your brother."

Chapter 9

I walked back to the bookstore without learning the name of Tracey's brother or the reason anyone thought Marty Dixon had been out to destroy him. Elise had probably said more than she intended to before cutting off the conversation. She must feel sure of Tracey's innocence when it came to the murder or she wouldn't have told me anything. Tyanne might be able to fill in details about Tracey's family, so I didn't protest when Elise said goodbye and hurried down the sidewalk.

Inside, I found Ty busy ringing up her customer's purchases. The woman had added at least a dozen books to her stack, and several other customers had entered the store. Not a good time to pick my friend's brain about details surrounding a murder.

My own brother wasn't in the chair where I'd left him. I walked down the center aisle and heard him in the back, talking with Adam and Ethan. Halfway there, I spotted Matt sitting cross-legged in an aisle. The bookshelf in front of him was marked *Mysteries & Thrillers* and held half a dozen copies of my book. He looked up as I approached, and I sat on the floor beside him.

"Looking for something special?"

"Nope." He turned to me. "It's super cool to see your book on the shelf."

I nodded. "Finally. Seemed like the day would never come."

"What did that woman say about the murder?" he said, in an abrupt change of topic.

I didn't realize Elise and I had an audience. "What makes you ask such a thing?"

"Y'all's body language," he said. "You looked serious, and she was avoiding your questions."

I raised my brows. "You're a student of body language now?"

"I read a book. That lady didn't want anything to do with whatever you were saying."

"You got that part right." I studied his serious expression and the way he picked at the carpet by his right leg—a nervous tick. "Are you okay, bud?"

Matt nodded quickly, but he didn't answer my question.

"What happened to you last night would traumatize anyone."

"I'm not traumatized," he said. "Did that lady know anything about the dead guy?"

"Matt, I'm not having this conversation with you. We'll go to lunch, then do something, whatever it takes, to put last night out of your mind."

He shook his head. "Not possible. I see the man every time I close my eyes."

I put a hand on his arm. "I'm so sorry, but you'll be okay. Give it some time."

"I'm not a baby like Adam. He'd have nightmares for a month. I'm glad he didn't see the body."

"Me, too."

"I'll be better after we figure out what happened," Matt said.

I knew *I'd* feel better, but I didn't want Matt involved. I glanced over my shoulder to make sure no one else was nearby and lowered my voice. "*We* aren't going to figure out anything. First of all, your dad wouldn't approve. Plus, Sheriff Crawford doesn't like people nosing into official business."

"Bet that won't stop *you*."

I was glad when Hitchcock picked that moment to stroll into the aisle. The cat inserted himself between us. "Mrreow."

I stroked his head. "You want to throw in your two cents, huh?"

Matt said, "I know they call Hitchcock the bad luck cat because of some legend, but I'd never believe such a stupid thing."

Hitchcock plopped onto his side and stretched, demonstrating how little the ridiculous legend affected him.

Matt scratched the cat's head. "He can help us solve the case."

I sighed. "He's not Super Cat, and did you hear what I said about staying out of the investigation?"

Matt reached out and ran a finger down the spine of a copy of *Scarlet's Run*. "You can pretend you're Carly Pierce."

As if pretending made everything okay.

I resisted the urge to ruffle his hair the way I did when he was younger. "I do make believe I'm Carly when I solve a crime on the page. Reality is off-limits."

"I'll play the profiler."

The fact he knew the term intrigued me. "A profiler, huh?"

"Yeah. We'll interview the victim. Learning more about him will lead us to the killer."

"Where'd you learn that?"

"Reading books," he said. "Now, Mr. —" He paused. "What's the victim's name again?"

"Dixon, so I'm told."

"Right, Mr. Dixon," Matt said, "what brought you to Lavender? You here for the Colt Jamison show?"

"Why would you ask him that?" I said.

"Tons of people will come for the show," Matt said. "Maybe he's one of them."

"Logical," I said.

"Then again, Tandee acted like she knew him, so maybe Dixon lived here, like she does."

I frowned. "How do you know where Tandee lives?"

Matt looked at the floor for a second before he answered. "She told me."

"You haven't been to her house, have you?"

"No. I just got here last night."

More like three in the afternoon, but that wasn't the point. "When did you find out where she lives?"

"We chatted online."

"Before this week?"

He nodded.

"What did you chat about?"

"Jamison. His songs. The fan club. It's not a big deal."

I thought differently, and Nick would agree with me. "Have you chatted with Tandee since last night?"

"Nope."

"Swear?"

"Swear."

"Good. Don't."

Matt's forehead creased, and he looked away for a second before turning back to me. "Why are you so freaked out?"

I leaned closer and spoke barely above a whisper. "As the pretend profiler in this case, you've learned that a young woman pulled an unsuspecting bystander into some trees where they discovered a man's body. She seemed to walk straight to the spot.

Why did she go to that specific place, on that evening, at that time?"

Matt's complexion paled. "Do you think Tandee knew the guy was in there? Dead?"

"I don't know, Matt, but investigators don't assume anything. Everyone who was there last night is a suspect."

"Even us?"

I nodded soberly. "I'm afraid so, and that's why I'd feel better if you kept your distance from Tandee."

He swallowed. "I get it."

I clapped him on the knee. "You're supposed to be on vacation, having some fun. It'll be lunchtime soon. Why don't you go check on your brother."

Matt jumped up and was out of sight before I got to my feet. I sighed and went to find Tyanne. She remained behind the cash register, without customers for the moment.

I propped my elbows on the counter in front of her.

"I don't know how you do it," I said.

"Run the store?"

"No, raise three kids and keep your sanity."

She gave me a lopsided grin. "You think I'm sane?"

"I'm serious. Matt just told me something worrisome."

I filled her in about Tandee and the fact that she'd befriended Matt online.

"Does Melanie monitor the boys' social media accounts?" Ty said.

"I have no idea."

"What did she say about the murder?"

I shrugged. "I don't know if anyone told her what happened."

Tyanne put a hand on her chest. "A mom needs to know these things. No question."

"You think I'm gonna tell her?" I said. "You know Melanie and I aren't that chummy. I wouldn't be one bit surprised if the guys are purposely keeping the news to themselves."

"Why would they?" she said.

"So she doesn't try to convince them to come home before the Colt Jamison show."

"That's not a good excuse," Ty said, "but I understand the logic. Did you know we're expecting upwards of fifty thousand tourists this weekend for that concert?"

56

I felt my jaw drop. "Where will they all go?"

"We have a lot of wide-open spaces. Especially around the winery that's hosting the show. People may camp out along every road, the way fishermen do on the night before fishing season opens."

I couldn't believe fifty thousand fishermen showed up in Lavender once a year—I'd have noticed. Outside, a group of tourists neared the bookstore.

"Hey, before you get busy again, I wanted to ask you something. Do you know a woman named Tracey Powell?"

Ty nodded. "Sure. She's a customer."

"Good. Do you know who her brother is?"

"It's, um." Ty snapped her fingers a few times. "That guy, he's, um, got it. Chester, the guy who owns the Wild Pony."

"Really?" I'd met Chester briefly on my first visit to the dance hall. I especially remembered how extremely drunk he was that day.

"Yup, that's her brother. And speaking of brothers, I have a question about yours." Ty glanced toward the back of the store, then turned to me. "I've never seen Nick like this."

I leaned closer. "Like what?"

"He's so different, so casual, but uncomfortable with it. Unfocused."

"Maybe he's starting to take after me."

She laughed at the comment and sobered quickly. "No, I mean he seems troubled."

"Maybe about what happened last night?"

"Seems like something else," she said, "and I started thinking. When does Nick turn forty?"

"He already did," I said, "back in June."

Ty pointed at me. "That's it then. Bryan went through the same thing after his fortieth."

"Is this something you and I will experience in the not-distant-enough future?" I said.

She shook her head. "It hits men worse. They start to question who they are, every decision they ever made. Lots of wondering what life is all about, where to find the meaning. I can see it in Nick's expression."

"Guess I missed the signs," I said. "Are you saying this is a common thing in men?"

"Sure is," she said as the bell over the door rang and a new group of customers flowed in. "I call it the midlife crazies."

Chapter 10

My discussion with Tyanne ended abruptly when a group of chattering women closed the bookstore door behind them. She greeted the customers while Nick and I gathered the boys and Hitchcock and headed out. While we had been inside, the street had taken on the carnival-like atmosphere common during the last few weeks of summer vacation. I didn't feel comfortable walking Hitchcock on his leash among so many pedestrians.

"Into the tote for now," I told the cat and paused in front of the bookstore to slide him in feet-first. After I hung the tote on my shoulder, Hitchcock poked his head out so he could take in the sights.

From the spot where I stood, I saw a face painter, a hot pretzel cart, and a balloon artist who had a lineup of children waiting to place orders. On the nearest corner, a woman who resembled a young Wynonna strummed her guitar and sang a catchy tune I didn't recognize. Farther down the street, a duo performed for passersby. We didn't typically have street singers, and I wondered if these people had come in hopes of being discovered by someone with Colt Jamison's entourage.

"This is so cool," Adam said. "Dad, can I have a hot pretzel?"

"We're having lunch soon," Nick said. "Maybe later."

Adam looked around eagerly. "Maybe we'll see Colt Jamison out here."

"Duh," Matt said. "He's not gonna play for free when everybody's paying to see his show on Saturday."

"Singers have been known to pop in at places they're least expected," Nick said, "and he's a local Texas boy. I'd keep my eyes open if I were you."

Adam shot his brother a smug grin and took the lead as we proceeded down the sidewalk. I kept an eye on the pedestrians and hoped we would not run into Tandee Cushing again. I felt sure Matt understood my concerns about his female friend leading him straight to the crime scene, but that didn't guarantee he'd stay away from her. I was ready to run interference if need be—if such a thing was possible with a teenage boy.

Adam and Matt drifted closer to the singing duo. Nick paused to look in a shop window, and I wondered why it had taken Tyanne to alert me that something was going on with my own brother. He was wearing docksiders without socks, for crying out loud. Talk about a red flag. Nick *never* wore shoes without socks. I checked his face. What was with that three-day scruff? I remembered clearly when he started shaving and refused to skip a single day. Maybe he was trying to relax and let go for the guys-only road trip with his boys.

Nick saw me watching him in the reflection of the shop window.

"What?" he said.

"Oh, it's the fiction writer in me taking in character traits."

"You putting me in a book now?"

"Maybe. You never know."

I thought about the heart-to-heart I wanted to have with my brother, but this wasn't the right time. Nick liked his privacy, always had, and I'd have to tread carefully and without uttering the words *midlife crisis*. Best-case scenario, all he needed was time away to play for a change. Coming to Lavender was the best way I knew of to shake off the effects of the big-city rat race.

My phone buzzed, and I pulled it out to see a text message from Luke.

Twelve thirty okay for lunch? Barbeque, subs, or pizza?

"Lunch in an hour." I turned my phone so Nick could read the screen. "Should we ask the boys what they want?"

"No need," he said. "They'll choose pizza."

I responded to Luke's text, and we agreed to meet at Tower of Pizza.

"How about a prelunch coffee?" Nick said. "I'm draggin'."

"I know the feeling. Follow me."

I led Nick and the boys to Hot Stuff, my favorite away-from-home writing spot. The steamy weather didn't keep the customers away. For those who didn't like drinking hot stuff in the sweltering heat, the owner, my friend Max, had added flavored iced coffees to his menu.

One of the bistro tables outside freed up, and I snagged the shaded spot before anyone else could. Prince belted out "1999" from the speakers mounted under the building's eaves. Nick didn't want to wait for someone to come out and take our order and headed inside. Matt and Adam weren't interested in coffee, but they had spotted the flashing red-and-silver jukebox through the window and went in to take a closer look.

I placed my tote on the ground, attached Hitchcock's leash to his harness, and he jumped out. Two older women seated nearby smiled and pointed at the cat.

Hitchcock strutted as far as the leash would allow, showing off at the attention, then came back and rubbed against my leg. "Mrreow."

I stroked his back. "Handsome boy, you might get to see your friend Noah again. How'd you like that?" The four-year-old had behaved surprisingly well with the cat the day before, and I was glad we were meeting Luke at a place Hitchcock would be welcome.

I considered the upcoming lunch with a mixture of excitement and trepidation. I'd looked forward to introducing Luke to Nick for a long time. Now that the meeting was about to happen, butterflies danced in my stomach. I wanted the guys to like each other in spite of the fact that they were very different types. Luke was rugged and outdoorsy, Nick bookish and formal.

Usually.

The shop door opened. Max bopped out in time to the music, balancing coffee cups on his tray. He went to the foursome seated near me and deposited the cups on their table before coming my way.

"Good to see you, Sabrina." He stooped to peer under the table. "And you, Hitchcock."

"Mrr," Hitchcock said.

"No writing today?" Max asked.

I shook my head. "I'm on a short break. My brother's visiting. He and my nephews are inside."

"Breaks are good, time to time," he said. "Matter of fact, I'm going to take one right now."

He signaled one of his employees to cover for him, then pulled out the chair across from me. "You mind?"

"Not at all."

Max tugged a white napkin from his apron pocket and mopped his forehead. "I'll give you one piece of advice."

"What's that?"

"Don't abandon your writing for a career in film."

I'd expected him to make a comment about the heat. Stay

hydrated, or something to that effect. "What are you talking about?"

"YouTube," he said. "I saw y'all captured on film. You and Hitchcock."

I frowned. "You saw us *where*?"

He motioned at the coffee shop. "Everybody's watching. The video might go viral."

My pulse kicked up. "The video taken outside the pizza shop?" I couldn't imagine any other possibility.

"That's the one," he said. "You're not the star of the show, but you're there in the background."

"Yeah, I remember." I wondered if Jeff had posted his video before or after Dixon turned up dead. Or maybe it wasn't Jeff's video. The fact that he'd recorded one didn't mean he'd posted it online. Any one of those teens who'd piled into the pizza shop could have filmed the fight between Tracey and Marty Dixon.

"Darn shame what happened to that Dixon fella," Max said.

I nodded my agreement.

"City council's trying to sweep the whole thing under the rug," Max said. "Bad for tourism if word gets out, and they don't want any trouble with the concert."

"Are they expecting trouble?"

"They don't want Jamison to cancel. His people might tell him to stay away from Lavender so there's no risk of the press connecting his name to the murder."

I thought of the man staying in Aunt Rowe's Athens cottage. "I don't think he'll back out."

Max leaned closer. "Fritz is the one I'd have expected to lash out at Dixon, but he's not on the video. Was he working yesterday?"

"Fritz?" I thought back to the couple who both worked with Bruno. Fritz and Charlotte. Noah's parents.

"Right," he said. "Dark-haired guy. Works the pizza ovens."

I thought for a moment, pictured the scene. "Yeah, he was working." I wondered what Max knew about Fritz that I didn't.

Max looked down, shaking his head. "Dixon had no friends here. He should have known better than coming back, even if he did work for Colt Jamison."

According to Gary Weber, Dixon didn't work for the singer, but I didn't want to discuss Jamison. "Why would Fritz lash out?"

"Aunt Sabrina," Adam called to me as he came through the door. "You're on YouTube."

I sighed. "So I heard."

Adam reached us, with Nick and Matt close behind. I introduced them to Max. Nick handed me my coffee to free up a hand so he could shake Max's.

"Great place you have here, man," Nick said. "Love the music."

I felt sure the song playing—"Right Place, Wrong Time"—was one chosen by Nick on the jukebox.

"Thanks," Max said. "We do a good business and Sabrina's one of my best customers."

"The two Cs," I said. "Caffeine and creativity go together."

Nick turned his back to Max and met my eye. "Could I have a word with you?"

Max noticed my brother's serious tone and stood. "Need to get back to the customers. Enjoy your visit."

Nick focused on me. Without looking at the boys, he said, "Kids, why don't you go check out that singer?"

I glanced toward the direction he indicated. A man with hair past his shoulders and a glittery red guitar hanging from a strap stood with one foot propped on a bench near the street. He intrigued the boys enough that they walked toward him without questioning their dad. I studied guitar man for a moment and felt frown lines scoring my forehead. He was the guy Jamison had met with by the river.

"Listen." Nick drew my attention back to him. "What have you gotten yourself into?"

"Huh?" I turned to look at him. "What?"

"When was that video taken?"

"Yesterday, I guess. I haven't seen it, and I haven't gotten myself into anything."

"This is serious. You were right there, practically in the fight, the same day as the murder." He pulled the chair vacated by Max away from the table and dropped onto the seat. "You *looked* involved."

"I was an innocent bystander who came from a book club meeting. Reminds me of the song."

"What song?" he said.

I pointed toward a speaker. "This one. I was there at the right place, but the wrong time."

He ran a hand through his hair. "Is that crazy woman a friend of yours?"

"No. I mean, she's in the book club. That's how we met, but I don't really *know* her."

Nick glanced around us to see if anyone appeared to be listening to our conversation. He lowered his voice. "The man was murdered, Sabrina."

"I know that."

"You think she went after him?"

"I hope not."

Hitchcock heard the whine in my voice and jumped up on my lap. "Mrreow."

I stroked his head and wondered if Nick would balk when he realized we were going to the scene of the video for today's lunch.

"I'd have been better off not seeing that video," Nick said. "First my son finds a body, now I'm worried about you. We should go—"

I stood, holding Hitchcock in my arms. "If you're about to say that you and the boys need to head home, please don't."

He shook his head. "We're not leaving, but I'm concerned about your situation."

"Look," I said, "if it's bothering you so much we can pay a visit to the sheriff. He can assure you I'm only a random witness."

I turned to check on the boys, who stood near the corner watching the singer. The man swung his head to flip his long hair behind his shoulders.

I looked at Nick. "Who is that guy?"

"I don't know. Why?"

I didn't want to share the story of seeing Colt Jamison's clandestine meeting with the scruffy guy.

"I'm getting a bad vibe for some reason. Let's get the boys out of here."

Nick agreed and walked in their direction.

Max was serving a table near me as I played back my conversation with him and came up with a question. I waved a hand to grab his attention.

"What's up?" he said. "Your brother okay?"

"He's fine." I nodded. "Question for you. You mentioned Dixon had no friends in this town. Any idea why? Did he do something awful?"

Max rubbed his chin, thinking. "Got too big for his britches is what I've heard. Nobody likes a name-dropping braggart, and that's what he'd become."

That change in Dixon's personality most likely came after his move to Nashville, but I'd been wondering about Dixon's pre-Nashville days. Max wasn't a native of Lavender, though, and probably didn't know the Dixon family history. I asked my next question anyway.

"Sheriff Crawford mentioned Dixon's mother lives here," I said. "You know if that's true?"

"Oh, yeah, Wanda lives here all right. Her next-door neighbor came by earlier. Says Wanda was crying her eyes out before she even learned about the murder. Marty didn't tell her he was coming to Lavender. Didn't come see her, not even a phone call. Hurt her feelings big-time. And get the biggest news —"

He paused for effect, but I wasn't in a patient mood.

"What news?"

"She says her Marty wrote that hit song — 'Broken Mirror' — the one Colt Jamison is claiming as his own."

Chapter 11

As we headed for our lunch with Luke, I vowed to keep the gossip I'd heard to myself. My nephews would be crushed if there was any shred of truth to the rumor that their idol, Colt Jamison, had lied about writing his number-one hit song. I envisioned an even worse scenario. What if the man really hadn't written "Broken Mirror" and had decided to make sure Marty Dixon would never tell the truth about the song's origin?

Don't be ridiculous, Sabrina.

Colt Jamison obviously did well in his career. The singer was talented and popular. Too smart to commit murder and end up in jail. He had associates, though, with a stake in the music business. Men like Gary Weber who rented the Athens cottage because he wanted Jamison to write more number-one hits.

Maybe Weber got wind of the fact that Dixon was going to make false claims about the song and that's why he didn't like the guy. I had no idea how much a man in Weber's position got paid — whether he had a set salary or worked on some type of commission. Either way, his income was tied to Jamison's success. Damage to his client's reputation would hit Weber where it hurt — in the wallet.

Then again, there might be no truth to the rumor. Marty Dixon might have never written a song in his too-short life. Could be he liked to talk big, and Lord knew what he might have told his mother. This could quickly become a whisper-down-the-alley situation with an ending that no one could predict.

Hitchcock poked his head out of my tote and nudged my arm as if he knew I needed to stop obsessing.

"Okay, you're right," I whispered. "Time to rein in the overactive imagination."

"Mrreow," he said.

Nick, lagging a few steps behind me with the boys, said, "You talking to us?"

I slowed and turned to my brother. "Just telling Hitchcock how excited I am about our lunch meeting."

Nick didn't comment, and we arrived at the pizzeria a few minutes later. I spotted Luke waiting on a bench near the front door and felt the warm rush that I always experience when I see him.

Luke stood to greet me with a quick hug and a kiss on the cheek before turning to the guys. The scent of his citrusy aftershave lingered as I made introductions and they all shook hands.

I noticed Matt's and Adam's interest in Luke's uniform. Adam eyed the sidearm Luke carried.

"Have you ever shot anybody?" Adam asked.

"Not lately," Luke said, straight-faced.

I popped him in the arm. "C'mon, don't scare them."

"Sorry about that," Luke said, grinning. "Y'all have had enough stress in the past day."

"More than enough," Nick said.

"Seriously, though." Luke put a hand on his Glock. "I shoot this several times a week, but only at target practice."

"Man, I'd like to try that." Adam's brown eyes glistened with excitement.

Nick didn't look happy at the prospect. Luke noticed my brother's reaction and shook his head. "We have strict regulations about our duty weapons. I can take you on a day-in-the-life tour instead. Show you what being a Texas game warden is all about. If I can tear you away from your Aunt Sabrina for a few hours." He looked at me.

I smiled. "It'd be great for you to have a guys day out. Get to know each other better."

"Cool," Adam said. "Can we, Dad?"

"Sure." Nick nodded. "If I chaperone."

His tone insinuated he thought Luke needed watching, but Luke didn't react to the comment.

"We can decide on a day and time after we eat," Luke said. "They have awesome pizza here."

I turned to the entrance, where a large poster proclaimed the coming weekend as a *Colt Jamison Extravaganza* and featured a head shot of Jamison in a cowboy hat pulled low over his brow and a sly glint in his eye. Inside, the usual Italian pizzeria music had been replaced by country music.

Adam looked at Matt. "They're playing Colt's new album."

"Nice," Matt said. He'd usually respond with something like "I know that, you dumbhead," and I assumed he was playing the cool customer for Luke's benefit.

I led the way to the screened porch, where Hitchcock would be free to escape the tote bag for a little while. I breathed a sigh of relief at the relative calm of the place compared to the day before. A group of four older women occupied a table in the corner. I didn't see anyone watching YouTube videos, and Matt's admirer Tandee was nowhere in sight. All good signs.

We took our seats and Bruno immediately came out with his order pad. He smoothed his dark hair back, then adjusted the bib of his white apron.

"Good to see you again, Sabrina. Sorry I didn't get to say goodbye yesterday, but we enjoyed having you speak to the book club." He glanced around the table and nodded to the others. "Gentlemen. Are y'all ready?"

We placed our order, and I let Hitchcock out of the tote, keeping his leash attached to the harness. The cat appeared to be looking for Noah, so I asked Bruno if the boy was here.

"He's out with his dad at the moment," Bruno said. "I expect them back soon."

"Hitchcock," I said, "maybe you can play with your friend a little later. We'll see." The cat ignored me and walked under the table out of my line of vision.

Hitchcock was acting aloof, but I need not have worried about Luke getting along with my brother. After a few minutes of polite chitchatting and inquiries about each other's work and the boys' school, Luke began telling stories of wild water rescues and tracking deer poachers. The boys were enthralled and even Nick seemed engrossed in the conversation.

I noticed the women at the other table looking at us and pointing to Hitchcock, who had sprawled near my chair.

"Excuse me," one of them called. The woman had stick-straight gray hair and wore shimmery fish-shaped earrings at least three inches long. She seemed to focus on me, so I stood and looped the end of Hitchcock's leash over the ladder-back chair post. When I approached the woman, I realized they all wore Colt Jamison T-shirts.

"Yes, ma'am?" I wondered if she'd heard Bruno's comment about the book club and meant to ask about my book.

She jiggled her right earring with an index finger. "I saw you in that fight video. Are you with the Colt Jamison fan club?"

"No, I'm not in the club, but y'all look like fans yourselves," I said, hoping to change the subject.

"Yes, we're certainly Jamison supporters," she said, and the woman to her right nodded in agreement. "We heard the big fight yesterday had a connection to him, and we're worried about poor Colt."

"He wasn't there," I said. "I think he's probably fine."

"But why did that woman start the fight?" she said. "Was it connected to the concert?"

"I have no idea."

"But she's your friend."

"She's a passing acquaintance, no more."

"If you say so." The woman's brows lifted. She and her friends exchanged glances, and I had the feeling none of them believed me.

"Sorry I can't be of more help," I said. "Enjoy the Jamison extravaganza."

"We will." Ms. Fish Earrings straightened as she glanced toward the back door. "I think you'd better go after your cat."

I followed her gaze and saw Hitchcock dash out the exit. I glanced toward our table, where Bruno was delivering our drinks. Hitchcock had taken advantage of the diversion to slip away.

His specialty.

"Thanks for the alert," I told the woman and hurried after him.

I found the cat quickly, thank goodness, in the small backyard, where Bruno's grandson was playing on a tire swing that hung horizontally from three pieces of rope. I walked to them and grabbed the end of the cat's leash.

"Well, Hitchcock, I see you've found your friend."

He gave me a kitty smirk, and I turned to the boy. "Hi, Noah."

The four-year-old lay across the tire on his belly with his head hanging over the edge. His fine blond hair swayed as the tire drifted back and forth. "Hi."

I looked around and didn't see anyone with the child, though I heard a man's voice on the other side of the gate.

"We came here for lunch," I told Noah, "but Hitchcock must have seen you and decided he'd rather play."

The boy pushed off the dirt with his little blue Nike sneakers and sent the tire swinging.

The man's voice grew louder, and I had no trouble making out his words. "You're right. I am *not* one bit sorry."

"Shhh," a woman said. "He can hear."

"So what? Hears only the truth coming from me but never from you."

Sounded like a husband-and-wife spat to me. Noah's parents?

"What's the truth about last night," the woman said, "if you're so perfect?"

"I went out to walk off some steam, like I said."

"Didn't do such a good job, seeing how you're still worked up." Her words dropped to a whisper, and I couldn't make out anything else.

I glanced through the doors into the pizzeria and saw Luke motioning to me. Our pizza had arrived. A dark-haired woman in khaki shorts and a red shirt stood near our table with her back to me. A waitress?

Noah giggled, and I looked down to see Hitchcock had jumped onto the tire and was nosing him in the neck.

"That tickles," he said. "Can you push us? I wanna swing with the cat."

"I think it's time for us to go have lunch," I said.

"Pleeeaaassse," Noah whined.

The gate creaked, and a woman in a white apron splotched with tomato sauce came through. I caught a glimpse of a man behind her before the gate swung shut. The guy who worked the pizza oven, if I wasn't mistaken. Fritz. "Mama, look at the cat," Noah called. "Come push us."

Hitchcock jumped to the ground, and I stooped to pick him up before turning to Noah's mother. Tears streaked her face. Angry tears, judging by the fire in her eyes and the firm set of her lips.

"Are you okay?" I said.

"Fine." She snapped the word, then turned away. "I need to get back to work. Noah, come along." She reached toward him, and the boy reluctantly jumped off the swing and put his hand in hers.

"My cat escaped," I explained so she wouldn't think I came outside with the intention of eavesdropping, even though that's what I'd done. "I see our lunch is served now. See you later."

The boy waved. His mother ignored me and tugged him through

a door that I assumed went straight into the kitchen. I returned to the screened porch. The second I was out of the sun's glare, I recognized the woman in the red shirt. What the heck was Deputy Patricia Rosales doing here, besides interrupting our lunch?

My nephews were busy attacking their pizza and barely noticed me as I approached.

Luke smiled at me as I took the chair next to his and settled Hitchcock by my feet. Then he held out a palm toward Rosales. "Look who came to say hello."

"Deputy." I nodded to Rosales, who stood between Nick and Adam. "Have you met my brother and his boys?"

"I have." She stood with her thumbs hooked in her shorts pockets and glanced at each of us seated around the table. "Yes, I see y'all are like one big happy family." Her voice practically dripped with what I took for jealousy.

Oh, boy.

I had complained about Rosales to my brother often enough that I'm sure he realized her snarkiness was directed at me for being here with Luke. Nick finished chewing a bite of pizza then turned to the deputy.

"This is our first time meeting Sabrina's friend Luke. And you must be Deputy Rosales. Sabrina has mentioned both of you often, and it's a pleasure to finally meet her friends." He grinned at Rosales, then Luke, then me.

I didn't want Rosales to ask what I might have mentioned about her to my brother.

"You're out of uniform again," I said. "Last night, and now today. You on vacation?"

She shook her head. "I worked security last night, doing some interviews today." She fixed her gaze on Matthew. "I have some questions for you, young man."

Matt's brows shot up. "Who, me?"

"He already talked to you people last night," Nick said.

Rosales tipped her head toward him. "He hasn't talked to *me*."

"You weren't part of the investigation," I said, "which seemed odd, especially since you were working security. We saw you out there."

"Patricia," Luke said, "c'mon, we're having lunch here."

"You don't get it," she said. "I *need* some answers."

Nick wiped his mouth then slapped his napkin down beside his plate. "My son already told everything he knows. He walked into the woods, tripped over a dead body, and that's it. There's not a helluva lot to tell."

His tone drew the attention of the busybody women who appeared to be straining to hear more. I put a cautioning hand on Nick's arm to quiet him down. Hitchcock rubbed up against my legs, and I felt the vibration of his nervous purr.

Rosales didn't back-talk Nick, which seemed almost more scary than her usual behavior. I still didn't know if she had come here purposely to see us, because she was hungry and we happened to run into her, or something else entirely.

I was curious about her relationship with the victim. "Marty Dixon was a friend of yours, wasn't he?" I watched closely for her reaction. Her exchange with Dixon had not sounded one bit friendly, and Ethan had told me Rosales looked mad enough to kill when he saw her with the guy. Of course, sometimes the most heated discussions occur between friends.

"We knew each other as kids," she said.

"So, this is personal." I lifted my soft drink and took a sip.

Rosales met my gaze. "You might say that."

Nick cleared his throat and spoke softly. "Sorry for your loss."

I wondered if Rosales *was* sorry about Dixon's murder. If she was in the mood to discuss him, I wanted to hear what she had to say. "Have you had lunch?"

The deputy's brows rose. "No, I haven't."

"Why don't you join us? If these two pizza monsters need more, we'll order more." I indicated the boys, who were completely immersed in their pizza.

Luke looked at me as if I'd suddenly grown a second nose. I'd surprised myself with the invitation, but Rosales one-upped me when she accepted.

Nick gave me an I-hope-you-know-what-you're-doing glance and stood to pull over a chair from a nearby table. He slid it in beside his own and Rosales took the seat hesitantly.

Adam came up for air and swiped at his mouth with the back of a hand. "Did you go to school with the guy who died?"

Nick said, "Adam, that's not—"

"It's okay," Rosales interrupted. "We weren't in the same school, but I knew him when we were both in high school. Later, Marty moved to Nashville."

I picked up a slice of pizza and took a bite. Bruno, having noticed that we'd added another person to the table, came out and took Rosales's drink order and handed her a plate.

"Was that man—Marty—a singer?" Matt said.

"Not that I knew," Rosales said. "Are you boys performers?"

"We're fans," Adam said. "We came here for the Colt Jamison concert."

"And to visit your Aunt Sabrina," Nick said.

"The concert is drawing lots of people," Rosales said. "Town is about to get very crowded."

"Dixon was promoting the concert," I said in between bites, "but I guess his death won't stop the show."

Rosales shook her head. "Won't even cause a kink in the schedule."

"That's rather sad," I said. "What kind of kid was Marty?"

Rosales looked up. "What do you mean?"

"Was he musical? I mean, he went to Nashville, so it stands to reason he has a musical connection."

"He wanted away from here for one thing," Rosales said. "Might have known people in Nashville. More likely, he wanted to tag along on the coattails of someone famous. Marty wasn't into working."

"Was he the daydreaming creative type?" The rumored claim that Dixon had written a hit country song nagged at me.

"I didn't keep close tabs on the guy," Rosales said. "I knew him as a kid, that's it. He was closer to my brother."

"What does your brother think about what happened?" I said. "Assuming you talked to him."

Rosales's face fell. She dropped her pizza slice onto her plate. "I haven't told him anything. My brother died when he was seventeen."

Chapter 12

Later that afternoon, I helped Glenda fold guest towels for the cottages. "I didn't ask Rosales one more question after she said she'd lost her brother at seventeen," I told her.

Nick and the boys had gone tubing, and I opted out. I needed to work on the problematic scene I had pulled up on my laptop back in the Monte Carlo cottage, but my thoughts were too unfocused to write a coherent sentence.

"Did Rosales end up asking Matthew what he saw last night?" Glenda said.

"No, and that's weird in and of itself. She said that's what she wanted, but I don't think it's what she wanted at all." I placed a folded towel on top of the pile of clean laundry and picked up another. "It's like she wanted to hash over everything, get our take on what happened, but she didn't want to come out and ask us to help."

Glenda fluffed a towel out, ready to fold, then stopped and stared at me. "Rosales asking you for help? That's a good one."

"I know, right?"

My curiosity was stuck on the fact that the deputy was arguing with Dixon. Now Dixon was dead and Rosales "had to know" what happened. She didn't appear to be on duty. Rosales loved to flaunt her authority, and it wouldn't surprise me to learn she slept in the darned uniform. Was she on an undercover assignment? Vacation? On leave while this "personal" case was investigated? Something was definitely going on with her.

Glenda stepped closer to look me in the eye. "After the way that woman has treated you, please tell me you aren't thinking about jumping into the middle of whatever mind game she's playing."

"No, of course not." I forced what I hoped would pass for a sincere expression.

I needed to steer clear of the deputy, but I'd still love to know the reason for her personality shift. In a totally out-of-character move, she'd invited us into her personal space. If she simply needed a friend to talk to, why pick us?

The murder of Marty Dixon had naturally brought up sad

memories of her brother. Still, I'd have expected the murder of their old friend to fire her up and have her beating the bushes for clues. I'd bet Laurel, my dispatcher friend, could shed some light on the situation.

Glenda was still giving me the eye, as if reading my thoughts, so I changed the subject.

"Any sightings of our top-secret guest?"

She shook her head. "Far as I know, he hasn't set foot outside of the cottage door."

"Smart man," I said, keeping the exchange I'd witnessed at the river to myself. "Anything from his manager?"

"Not to my knowledge." Glenda folded the last towel and closed the dryer door. "You know, I sure feel awful about being rude to that man who was killed."

"I know, but he wasn't nice to us. He pushed for information we had no business giving out."

"I guess you're right."

"And we didn't have a free cottage to rent to him."

"True."

"I don't know why he needed to rent a place at all. I heard his mother lives here in Lavender."

"Is that so?" Glenda took a fresh apron from a laundry room cabinet and looped it over her neck.

I moved closer and took the apron sashes to tie the bow for her.

"Her name's Wanda Dixon," I said. "Do you know her?"

Glenda shook her head. "Don't think so, but Rowe might." We moved into the kitchen, where I scanned an assortment of baking supplies out on the counter. Icebox layer cake if I had to guess from the ingredients assembled.

"Where is Aunt Rowe anyway? Still out with that woman? The life coach?"

"Oh, they came back a couple of hours ago." Glenda unwrapped a stick of butter and cut off the portion she needed for a crust. "Looked like they went on a shopping spree, came back all loaded down with packages. Now they're having some kind of 'mini conference.'" She lifted her eyebrows and made air quotes.

"A conference? Where?"

"In the storeroom. They had Thomas rearrange the cartons of

supplies to make room for tables and chairs. No idea what they're up to, and I'm keeping my distance."

"This deserves further investigation," I said.

Glenda opened the flour cannister and grabbed a measuring cup. "Rather you than me."

• • •

Hitchcock caught up with me outside, coming from Lord knew where. He trotted along as I walked at a fast clip toward what we called the storage room even though it was actually a separate building almost as large as the cottages. The sun bore down on us, and grass tickled my toes as I crossed the lawn in flip-flops.

"I was focused on the murder," I told the cat, "but you know how it's good to check up on Aunt Rowe from time to time."

"Mrrreeooow," Hitchcock said with emphasis.

I giggled. "Exactly."

I heard music playing inside the storage room when we grew closer. Thomas sat on a camp stool parked next to the door. "Password?" he said.

I frowned. "What?"

He crossed his arms over his chest and shook his head. "That's not getting you in."

"What are you talking about?"

He shrugged. "Rowena said no one gets into the clubhouse without the password."

"Oh, stop it." I waved a dismissive hand at him. "This isn't a clubhouse."

Hitchcock jumped up on a windowsill and peered into the building. I walked over to join the cat and shaded my eyes with a hand. The glare from the sun kept me from seeing a thing.

I turned to Thomas. "What's going on in there?"

He took a handkerchief from his pants pocket and wiped his brow. "Beats me. Group of ladies and lots of laughing."

"Is that a Colt Jamison song I hear?" I said.

"Don't know for a fact, but since that's the password—Colt Jamison—you're probably right." He stood, opened the door, and waved a hand for me to enter. "Go right on in."

Hitchcock slipped by me and ran inside. Frigid air-conditioning hit me, raising goose bumps on my arms. I paused for a moment to listen and wondered if Aunt Rowe had managed to spirit Jamison over here to perform live for a select audience. Then the song cut off abruptly, replaced by a woman's voice. "And there you have a prime example of a person who charted his course. I'd say things are going pretty well for him, wouldn't you?" A chorus of positive cheers followed the question.

I crept past the section of the building that stored lawn maintenance equipment, not wanting to call attention to my presence. My phone vibrated in my pocket, and I stopped to slip it out and check the screen. Guilt washed over me as I read the text from my agent, Kree Vanderpool.

Looking forward to your book three proposal. How's it coming?

Good Lord. Book two was still a rough draft, and I had no idea how to answer her question.

Later.

I dropped the phone back into my pocket, then heard Aunt Rowe speaking in the next room.

"Now, Violet," she said, "you can hardly compare us to Colt Jamison. He's forty years younger, give or take, and has those moneymaking pipes."

I inched ahead until I could peer into the main room, where three tables were set up conference style with chairs facing away from me. Aunt Rowe and her friend Helen sat in the front row. Adele, another of her friends, sat at the second table with Daisy McKetta, co-owner of the local barbeque restaurant. I didn't recognize the two women in the back, though one of them seemed familiar for some reason.

Violet Howe, the life coach, stood before the others, her attention focused on a poster that read *Chart Your Course* in large purple caps. She wore a pink-and-white polka-dotted tunic over white capris. She'd braided the purple streak in her hair and her pink feather jutted out from an ear.

"Jamison charted his own course," Violet said. "That's the point. Your course is different from his and from each other's. And don't forget that sometimes you have to step out of your comfort zone to achieve your goals."

Oh, jeez. I didn't want to get caught up in this.

"Give yourself permission to change," Violet added.

Hitchcock picked that moment to bound into the room. He'd spotted Aunt Rowe and ran straight up to her chair. Violet's gaze traveled from the cat to me. "Welcome, Ms. Sabrina, and your precious cat. How about you? Have you charted your course?"

I shook my head. "Thanks, but I'm good."

Aunt Rowe turned around. "Sabrina is another fine example of achievement. She chased her dream and her published book is doing very well."

"Wonderful." Violet beamed at me. "When's your second book coming out?"

"Umm," I said. "Next year. Probably."

Luckily for me, Hitchcock distracted everyone by jumping up on Aunt Rowe's table and strutting across the top with his tail held high as he stepped on and around opened binders. He paused to bat a pen off the table.

His actions didn't deter Violet. She approached me with an arm outstretched. "Come, dear, you may need some encouragement from one of my success stories." She put a hand on my elbow and gently urged me toward an attendee in the back row—the one who'd seemed familiar.

When the woman turned toward me, our eyes met and my jaw dropped. The usual black clothes had been exchanged for a sunny yellow top and jeans. Her gray hair had been dyed blonde with subtle highlights.

"Twila?" I said. "What on earth?"

"I'm ready for a new image," the elderly antiques store owner said in her quavery voice. "Your aunt graciously helped me with the easy parts." She patted her new hairdo, then put a hand on her chest. "Inside, I need a lot more work."

"You look awesome," Daisy said.

"We'll help you, Twila," Helen said, "and then there's someone else who needs our help more than anyone I ever knew. We might oughta load ourselves up in the Suburban right now and head on over to help this woman."

Curiosity pulled me farther into the room. "Who's that, Helen?"

"Tracey Powell," she said. "Poor thing has been the driving force behind turning her brother's life around, but now she's gone too far and attacked the man who ended up dead. On video, no less. She needs to chart her own course and stop worrying about her sorry brother if you ask me."

"I saw that video," Daisy said. "You're on it, too, Sabrina."

"Yes, I know." I wasn't surprised that Daisy, a major link in Lavender's gossip chain, knew about the video.

Aunt Rowe looked at Helen. "What on earth was Tracey thinking?"

"Some people are saying she killed the man for cheating her brother Chester," Daisy said, "but being charged with murder is not what she's worried about."

No one else was biting, so I did. "What *is* she worried about, in your opinion?"

"Keep in mind I got this from a customer," Daisy said, "and he got it from a neighbor's daughter's best friend."

Aunt Rowe rolled her eyes. "A reliable source, I'm sure."

Daisy shot a glare in Aunt Rowe's direction before continuing. "Chester can't account for his whereabouts at the time of the murder. Makes sense to me that Tracey's worried he got drunk, wandered into the woods, and killed the man himself."

Chapter 13

The life coach managed to get her conference attendees back on the Chart Your Course path. I wouldn't have minded hanging around if that meant I could learn the reason Aunt Rowe felt she needed to work with Violet. The way I saw it, Twila Baxter had an obvious reason to seek guidance. She used to look like a woman living in the same era as the antiques she sold in her store. Now she was reinventing herself—moving into the current day and age. I felt proud of the woman for making a change.

Violet started her class on a written exercise, so I picked up Hitchcock and slipped out before she could start working on me.

I headed toward the Monte Carlo cottage, thinking about Tracey and her brother Chester. Could he really not account for his whereabouts at the time of the murder? Gossip could easily derail an investigation, and if I knew Daisy, she wouldn't keep any juicy details to herself. Yes, the video proved Tracey had a bone to pick with Marty Dixon. She had reacted with emotion rather than logic when she saw him. However, her actions didn't prove she or her brother were connected to the man's murder.

My obvious goal for the afternoon should have been to go home and craft a succinct and positive response to my agent's question about the proposal for my third novel. Since Nick and the boys were on the river, I'd have time to do some editing on the draft of my second book.

When we reached our cottage, though, Hitchcock veered off toward my car. He ran to the passenger side door, sat down, and looked at me.

"Mrreow."

I caught up with him and stopped, hands propped on my hips. "What is it?"

"Mrreow," he said again.

I sighed. "You're right. I did want to go over and have a little chat with our friend Laurel."

What did it mean that Hitchcock seemed to pick up on my intentions without my saying a word aloud? I'd always thought the term *crazy cat lady* referred to someone who had a huge number of cats rather than someone who became crazy due to association with one cat. I paused, considering the issue, and decided people could call me crazy if they wanted to.

"Hold on a second and let me grab my tote," I told Hitchcock. Was it my imagination that he smiled?

Twenty minutes later, I turned into the parking lot at the sheriff's office. A pretty blonde woman in a royal blue dress and black heels stood outside the entrance and raised a microphone to her mouth. A man near her lifted a video camera marked *KTSU Austin*, and the woman began speaking. This looked interesting.

I parked quickly and attached Hitchcock's leash. We jumped out of the car and joined a small group congregated around the reporter.

". . . here in Lavender, up until last evening the summer's biggest news was the upcoming Colt Jamison concert to be held this Saturday on the grounds of Beckman Vineyards. That was before last night's brutal murder of Jamison's dear friend, Marty Dixon. Though Dixon was a trusted member of Jamison's public relations team, the fact that he was stabbed with a piece of a broken mirror is no P.R. stunt. Jamison's hit song 'Broken Mirror' is a tale of loss and sorrow — a sad story magnified by what happened to Marty Dixon last night. Law enforcement is using all resources to find Dixon's killer. We have not yet reached Colt Jamison for comment. Reporting from Lavender, Texas, this is Kendra Steele, KTSU Austin."

A patrol car pulled into the lot with Deputy Ainsley behind the wheel. Kendra Steele motioned for the videographer to follow her in that direction, no doubt in hopes of dragging information about the case out of Ainsley.

I didn't see anyone I knew outside and was about to go in when the door opened and Gary Weber nearly bowled me over. Jamison's manager pulled up short, looked from me to Hitchcock, then at the other group of people huddled nearby as if they meant to wait right there until the next news update.

Weber turned back to me and spoke in a low voice. "What's going on out here?"

"There's a reporter." I nodded toward Deputy Ainsley, now waylaid by Kendra Steele. "Over there in the blue dress. She just filmed a short segment about Marty Dixon's murder."

"Glad I missed it," he said.

"You probably wouldn't have wanted to hear her description of

Dixon as a friend and trusted P.R. guy on Colt Jamison's team."

He frowned. "She *said* that?"

I nodded. "A *dear* friend—that's how she described him. Were they dear friends?"

"Hardly." He stepped off the curb and headed toward the black SUV I'd seen him driving the day before.

I glanced back at the building, then fell into step with Weber. Hitchcock hurried to keep up with the man's long strides. "Were you here to see the sheriff?" I said.

"Here to be grilled is more like it." He looked me up and down without slowing his pace. "You're not in cahoots with that reporter, are you?"

"No. I'm Sabrina, from Around-the-World Cottages. We met yesterday."

He glanced down at Hitchcock trotting between us. "Oh, yeah. You and the cat."

"What does Sheriff Crawford have to say about the murder?" I said.

"They're working the case day and night. You ask me, he doesn't have a clue what happened."

"Maybe not yet," I said, "but he'll figure it out. Did he say anything about the murder weapon?"

"Nope. He said they're not releasing any details."

Apparently, Kendra Steele had sources—or she had lied about the broken mirror to give her story some pizazz.

"Why didn't you like Marty Dixon?" I said.

Weber rounded the front of his SUV, putting the vehicle between himself and the reporter before he stopped walking. "I never told you that, and I know anything I say can be used against me, so I'm keeping my mouth shut."

"The sheriff Mirandized you?"

"No, but everybody who ever watched TV knows that line. Why are you badgering me anyway? I have work to do." He pulled his key ring from a pocket and punched the key fob to unlock his door.

"With Colt Jamison?" I said.

"I work *for* him, yes."

"I'm not planning to use anything against you," I said, "and I promise I would never share anything with the reporter. I write mystery fiction, so I can't help getting curious about real-life mysteries. You and I are on the same side."

"How's that?" he said.

"I live within a stone's throw of the Athens cottage. I'm extremely observant, but also very good at keeping any secrets if you catch my drift." I gave him a knowing grin.

His shoulders dropped, and I figured he realized that I knew Jamison was staying in that cottage.

"You'd *better* be good at keeping secrets," he said with a frown. "We don't need any reporters milling around."

"Or any fans," I said.

"Or them," he agreed. "You wanna know why I didn't like Dixon? Hell, I didn't know the man well enough to like him or not like him. We had a business interest, and he was a screwup."

"How so?"

"Why do you care anyway?"

"I want the mystery solved. We don't need reporters in Lavender talking about murder and warning people to steer clear. My aunt makes her living from the tourist business."

Hitchcock brushed up against my leg, but his gaze was focused on Weber as though he was eager to hear what the man said next. I picked my cat up so he'd have a better vantage point.

"Look," Weber said, "Dixon was a scammer and a cheater. He did what was good for Dixon, and that's it. Only helpful thing he did for Colt was nix him getting mixed up with that club."

"You mean the Wild Pony?"

"Yeah. We talked about setting up the concert on their property. They wanted Colt to make a personal appearance the night before. Drum up business. The plans were going full steam ahead, but Dixon got a bad vibe about the owner. Recommended we avoid dealing with the dude, so we changed the venue."

I nodded. This might have been the first in a row of events that set Tracey off.

"Now that I've seen both locations, that was a good call," he said. "Beckman Vineyards is classy, gives the right image."

"But now Dixon is dead, and that's a big blot on the Jamison brand."

"Shouldn't be." Weber rubbed the back of his neck hard. I

imagined he wished he could wipe away the whole problem of Dixon and the murder as easily.

"Did Colt feel the same about Dixon as you did?"

"Absolutely." He paused and stared at me for a moment before going on. "None of this is for the reporter's ears, right?"

"I understand, and I see no reason she'd even speak with me."

"Good," Weber said. "So Colt and I agreed to fire Dixon last week. Next thing we know, here he is. Claimed he has family in town. I said fine, visit your mom. Leave us the hell alone. Dude wouldn't listen. I've told all this to the sheriff."

"Maybe Dixon wanted to keep up the pretense of working for a star. Didn't want to lose his bragging rights just yet."

"Could be," Weber said.

"How did Colt take the news about the murder?"

"I don't know. Look, I have to get out of here before that woman—"

We glanced at the reporter, who was still with Ainsley. "Looks like Deputy Ainsley enjoys the limelight," I said. "She might be with him a while."

"There's a time and place for publicity, and my time is *not* now," Weber said.

"Is the concert still going on as planned?" I said.

Weber's eyes widened. "Hell, yes, it's going on. We have too much sunk into this to change plans now."

"Good, because my nephews would be heartbroken if it canceled. They came in from Houston."

"They have their tickets?" Weber pulled the left side of his sport coat away from his chest and reached into a pocket.

"Yes, they stood in line for hours to get them."

"Bet these are better." He pulled a white envelope from his pocket. "Tickets for four prime seats—front row, center. They're all yours. All you have to do is help me keep that secret."

The man wanted to assure I'd keep quiet about Jamison's whereabouts and probably everything else he'd said to me about his and Jamison's association with Dixon. I accepted the bribe for the boys' sake.

Weber opened the SUV door.

"Another quick question," I said.

He had one leg in and twisted to look at me. "What?"

"Was Marty Dixon a songwriter?"

His smile faltered. "Why do you ask?"

"Lots of rumors flying around town," I said. "One of them is that Dixon wrote the song 'Broken Mirror.'"

"That's insane," he said, maybe too quickly. "I never knew Marty Dixon to sing a note or pick up a guitar, either."

"I don't pay much attention to rumors," I said, "but I thought you'd want to be aware."

"In that case, I thank you," Weber said, "but I assure you that 'Broken Mirror' is Colt Jamison's own heartfelt tale of sin, sorrow, and heartache rolled into song. Colt writes his own material, and you can take that all the way to the bank."

Deputy Ainsley broke away from Kendra Steele and paused to retrieve something from his car. Steele turned in our direction.

"Time to vamoose," Weber said, using the term we'd laughed about the day before. He got into his SUV and sped away.

Hitchcock and I looked at each other. "Did he seem overly offended when I mentioned the possibility someone else might have written that song?" I said.

"Mrreow," Hitchcock said.

"I thought so, too."

I slipped into the cool building lobby and wondered whether anything I'd heard would place Gary Weber on the suspect list running through my head.

Chapter 14

I paused to secure the tickets Weber had handed over into the zippered pocket of my tote. The tickets would likely be the most exciting thing I'd given Matt and Adam since the battery-operated car I bought when they were five and three. I smiled at the memory of those boys motoring around their backyard in that little red car. Then I walked into the sheriff's department to see what I could find out about Deputy Rosales and her recent uncharacteristic behavior.

Laurel was on a call when she spotted us. She waved as she explained to the caller that a dog having puppies was not usually considered a nine-one-one emergency. She provided contact information for our local vet and ended the call. Then she motioned for a coworker to cover the phones and approached us.

She'd made a dramatic change to her hair, which was usually light brown. Today it was tinted a pale pink. One side was cut into short layers while the other hit at chin length. Her visible ear had a row of piercings I decided were new.

"Hey there, Hitchcock. How's my favorite cat?" Laurel bent to give him a welcoming head scratch before she stood to address me. "What brings y'all here?"

"We were in the vicinity, and I knew you'd be disappointed if I didn't bring Hitchcock by to say hello."

"Yeah, uh-huh. Nothing whatsoever to do with the murder." She tipped her head and gave me the eye.

"We haven't talked in a while, and I *do* consider you a friend." I paused and smiled. "Also, I wouldn't be opposed to discussing the case."

"Okay, friend, you know that's against policy, but how about joining me for a coffee break?"

"Deal," I said.

As we walked down the hall, I noticed a trail of cat hair Hitchcock had left on Laurel's pants. The price of befriending a cat. The deep rumble of Sheriff Crawford's voice came from behind his closed office door, and I wondered who he was talking to. The other offices we passed were empty.

We got our coffees in the break room and went outside to a table under a shade tree by the back door. Hitchcock had been here with me before and jumped up to sit beside me on the familiar bench. One of the gang, here to hang out and chat.

"New hairstyle," I said to Laurel after we laughed at the cat. "I like it."

"Thanks, I needed an update."

"You're the second person I've seen today who's had a makeover. Nice earrings, too. What's the occasion?"

Looking at her row of piercings, I wondered how long it took to get all those earrings in place. And did she sleep with the backs of them poking into the side of her head?

"I'm going to the concert with some girlfriends," Laurel said. "We want to look a little less like the grandma types we are when we start acting like star-struck teenagers."

I laughed. "C'mon, you're not that old, but I wouldn't have pegged you for a Colt Jamison groupie, either."

"Have you heard his new album?" she said.

"Parts of it."

"He's a fabulous singer and sexy as all get out. Look at this." She slid her phone from a pocket and touched the screen. A picture of Jamison I'd seen before, with the cowboy hat tipped low over his brows, appeared. After stabbing the screen a few more times, Laurel turned the phone to me and hit Start on a video. The camera zoomed in for a close-up of the singer's handsome face as he performed a ballad about lifelong love while staring straight into the camera with mesmerizing brown eyes.

I rubbed my arms as a chill ran over me.

Laurel noticed and grinned. "Got you, didn't he?"

"He's a good singer," I admitted.

Given her excitement, I figured Laurel was exactly the type of fan Jamison was hiding out from in the Athens cottage. I nodded toward the building. "Where's everybody today?"

"Sheriff is here. Interviewing witnesses all day long. One after another."

"He has that many?"

"Everybody who was nearby," she said, "in case someone saw something, you know."

"Right." I nodded. "I noticed Deputy Ainsley outside. Where's Rosales? She working today?"

"Nope."

"She on vacation?"

Laurel shook her head. "Not exactly."

"What does that mean?"

"Why are you asking about her? Normally you'd thank your lucky stars you missed her, so let's leave it at that. Okay?"

I must have hit a nerve, which only made me more curious about Rosales. "Okay. You know, it's fine to say 'none of your business, Sabrina.'"

"It's none of your business, Sabrina."

"Fine. I'll stop asking questions and share something you might find interesting. I saw Rosales earlier today, had lunch with her as a matter of fact. Me and Luke, my brother, and his boys."

Laurel's brows rose. "You did?"

"Yup," I said. "She saw us at Tower of Pizza and came over to say hi."

"Really?" By her facial expression, you'd think I'd told Laurel that Santa Claus and his reindeer landed in the town square—today, in the August heat.

She leaned closer to me. "She took a couple personal days, that's all. First time I've ever known her to take time off for no apparent reason."

"Good for her."

"Not the best choice, taking off during a murder investigation. Not like her at all."

"Especially not when she knew the victim personally," I said.

She sat back and straightened. "She did?"

I nodded again. "Since they were teenagers."

Laurel looked down at the tabletop and shook her head. "I wonder if the sheriff knows that."

"New subject," I said. "You'll probably see Nick come in at some point. He wanted to have words with the sheriff."

"I didn't know he was in town," she said. "How's he doing?"

"He was better before his older son and another teenager found the body last night."

Laurel groaned. "I didn't realize who the boy was. That's a bad break."

"Yeah, and then Nick saw me on the video of Tracey Powell

fighting with the dead man. Nick's freaked about the whole thing."

"He's not alone," she said. "We're getting a lot of bad press."

"The reporter out front gave a live report—said Dixon was stabbed with a piece of broken mirror."

"Good Lord." Laurel stood and picked up her cup. "Guess the sheriff hasn't heard that one yet, or we'd have heard him yelling. He's been swamped with the witness interviews. I'd better get back to my desk."

"Is it true? About the mirror?"

Laurel glanced toward the building. "You know I can't share facts about the investigation with you."

I sipped my coffee and waited.

"It's no secret, though," she continued, "that the city sanitation department's asking for extra help to clean up after some moron who thinks it's a grand idea—maybe some sort of tribute to Colt Jamison's dead friend—to throw around pieces of smashed mirrors."

"That's a dumb thing to do."

"Yeah, the shards are making a big mess and causing a safety hazard. I'm not sayin' Dixon was stabbed with a piece of glass, you understand."

"Okay, I get it. With glass bits lying around, it's possible a killer randomly picked up a piece and decided to use it."

She looked down at Hitchcock. "One thing's for sure. I wouldn't let your sweet boy walk around out there and risk getting glass splinters in a paw."

"Mrreow," Hitchcock said.

I picked him up. "I'll let you get back to work. If you don't mind, I'm making a pit stop inside before we get on our way."

"Help yourself," she said. "Good to see y'all."

I took Hitchcock with me into the ladies' room. Two minutes later, I hurried toward the exit. Sheriff Crawford's office door opened and a dark-haired woman stepped out. I stopped abruptly to avoid running into her.

"Mrreow," Hitchcock said, and the woman turned around.

"Oh, I'm so sorry." She met my eyes, and I could see hers were red-rimmed and puffy.

"No worries." I noticed she clutched a tissue in one fist. "You're Charlotte."

She seemed to panic, as if my knowing her name was a catastrophe of huge proportions.

"No, I mean yes, I am. How do you know me?"

She had a very short memory if she didn't recall seeing me and Hitchcock at Tower of Pizza. Maybe her anger had kept her from logging in the details of that moment.

"All pizza lovers in Lavender know you," I said. "You're the pizza pie lady."

A wan smile flickered across her lips. "You're a customer."

"That's right. And Hitchcock, my cat, loves to play with Noah. In fact, we were there yesterday *and* today."

She seemed to notice for the first time that I held a cat in my arms. She reached out to touch the top of Hitchcock's head. "Yes, Noah talks of the cat all the time. Very nice to see you, but I must get back to work."

She ducked her head and practically ran out the door.

Behind me, the sheriff cleared his throat. "I see you're acquainted with Charlotte Hansen."

"Only through the pizzeria," I said. "Why was she here?"

"I'm interviewing witnesses," he said.

"I didn't realize she was at the scene of the murder."

"Didn't say she was," he said.

"The interview upset her for some reason," I said.

"And you'd love for me to explain why," he said, "though you know I'm not going to do so."

"Can't blame a girl for wondering." I smiled. "So I'll take my cat, and we'll go."

"Not so fast," he said. "I'm interviewing everyone who was at the scene of the fight and/or the discovery of the body. Your name made both lists, so I'm glad you're here. Please step into my office."

Chapter 15

"You already asked me what I knew about Marty Dixon." I entered the sheriff's office and took a seat in a visitor chair. Hitchcock batted at dust motes on the wood floor.

Sheriff Crawford closed the door and went around his desk.

"Our discussion occurred before the man turned up dead. I'm working on a timeline." He let out a loud sigh as he dropped into his chair. A half-eaten package of peanut butter crackers sat on the desk next to a cup of coffee, and I wondered if he'd had an actual meal since the murder.

"How can I help?" I leaned forward slightly and tried to read the upside-down scribbles on his notepad.

He folded his large hands over the page and focused his no-nonsense gaze on me. If we didn't have what I considered a relatively close and congenial friendship, that expression might have scared the bejeebers out of me.

"What time did you last see the victim?" he said.

"Late yesterday afternoon, as I mentioned, when he came by and asked about renting a cottage. Then immediately after the teenagers discovered his body. Eight thirty or so last night."

"And where were you between those hours?" he said.

I straightened and put my hand on my chest. "Me? I hardly think I need an alibi when I didn't even know the man, and—"

He patted the air with a hand. "Sabrina, Sabrina, wait, that's not what I'm saying."

I slumped in the chair and puffed out a breath. "Thank goodness, but what *are* you saying?"

"I understand you didn't know him, but you always have your ear to the ground. You notice things. You ask questions. *Lots* of questions. While you were about your business between those hours you observed people."

"That sounds like a compliment." I allowed myself a small smile. "Are you consulting with me on your investigation?"

"Not exactly," he said. "I'm counting on the fact that after you found out about the murder you didn't go into hibernation."

"And you think I'm nosy."

"That, too."

I said, "Have you already talked with witnesses who saw Dixon between four and eight yesterday?"

"This isn't about who else I've talked to."

Hitchcock jumped up on my lap, purring as he bumped his head into my hand. Trying to keep me in line. I stroked his back.

"I have heard some things, like the fact that Dixon's mother lives here in Lavender."

"That's not helpful," he said, "Since I'm the one who told you his mother lives here."

"Oh, right." I chewed my bottom lip for a second. "He might have gone to see her during those hours."

"He didn't. She hadn't seen Marty since two Mother's Days ago."

"That's so sad," I said, even though I wasn't the best at keeping in touch with my own mother. "Does he have other family here?"

"His stepfather," Crawford said.

"Siblings?"

"None."

"Was he married?"

"Nope."

"Far as I know, nobody has anything good to say about Dixon. The reporter said he's a dear friend of Colt Jamison's, but I don't believe that, either."

The sheriff lifted one brow. "You heard a news report?"

"Yeah, right out here." I pointed. "Kendra Steele reporting live from your parking lot."

He slapped the desk with an open palm. "That's what I get for staying cooped up in here and avoiding her calls. Missed the chance to run her off."

"That wouldn't have played well, assuming her videographer had caught you in the act."

"No, I guess not." He shook his head, jotted something on his notepad, then looked at me. "Tell me about these people who have nothing good to say."

"Well, you already know Gary Weber's story."

"How are you acquainted with Weber?"

"I saw him outside a few minutes ago, and he's renting the Athens cottage."

"Any other Jamison people staying out at the cottages?"

"I don't think so." It wasn't literally a lie, but it felt like one. I plowed ahead in a different direction. "You know Tracey Powell didn't have any warm and fuzzies for Dixon, and her friend Elise didn't like him any better."

"I'm familiar with those two." The sheriff tapped his notepad with the tip of his pen. "Who else?"

I didn't want to discuss Deputy Rosales. If she wanted her boss to know her personal business, she'd tell him.

"The pizza shop owners probably weren't Dixon fans, since he caused the fight that broke out on their front lawn," I said. "That can't be good for sales. But I don't think Charlotte's tears were about business. Did she know Dixon personally?"

"I'm the one asking the questions." He pulled a cracker from the open package, and Hitchcock perked up at the sound of the crinkly wrapper. His whiskers twitched. The sheriff shook a no-you-don't finger at my cat and popped the cracker into his mouth. He chewed and swallowed before answering. "Charlotte's very tenderhearted. Some people cry when they watch the news."

"Do you suspect her?"

He sipped the coffee that had to be cold by now, then set the mug back down with a clunk. "Do I need to remind you —"

"No, you don't. The investigation is yours, not mine. I'm only a pawn in your game."

"Quit being dramatic," he said.

"This is a dramatic situation, and I'm only trying to help."

"Maybe you still can," he said. "I need to know if you were with your nephew Matt continuously between four and eight yesterday."

I knew better than to freak out at the question — or to lie. I petted Hitchcock for comfort and looked up at the ceiling as I recalled the day before. "I got home, and the boys were at the river. I went down there, saw the gang of fan club kids, then we came to the house for dinner. Afterward, we went to the Wild Pony for the free T-shirts, and I think you know the rest. Yes, I was with Matt the whole time. Except for if he went to the bathroom, which I'm sure he must have done at some point."

"You mentioned the fan club," he said. "What do you know about Tandee Cushing?"

"She's a flirt," I said, "and she's too old for Matt."

"How long has he known her?"

I didn't want to bring up their online relationship. "I couldn't tell you. I don't know."

"Is Matt interested in her?"

"He's fifteen," I said. "She's a cute girl. He probably feels like hot stuff because she's paying attention to him. What do you think?"

The sheriff grinned. "I remember being in similar situations back in the day." His grin faded. "Do you think Matt would do something for Ms. Cushing if she asked him to?"

My face heated instantly. "He would help with the fan club, yes. He's an avid Colt Jamison fan. If you're asking what I think you're asking, then absolutely not. He's a good boy, Sheriff, and he's not going to commit a crime for some girl he barely knows."

I thought he was going to call me on the discrepancy in my comments about how long Matt knew Tandee. Instead, he said, "How long is your brother staying here in town with his boys?"

"They planned to stay a week, but with everything that's happened, Nick might decide to clear out after the concert."

He nodded, thinking, and took another swig of coffee.

"You know, Sheriff, the killer's hands must be cut to pieces if he or she used a piece of a broken mirror to kill Dixon. So check Matt's hands, but he's out on the river at the moment, and he wouldn't be out there with open wounds on his hands. Think of the bacteria." I cringed.

"Back up. What did you say about a broken mirror?"

"Your pal Kendra Steele said that's the murder weapon."

"Lord have mercy," the sheriff said. "She doesn't know jack about any murder weapon. We're still waiting on the medical examiner over in Emerald Springs to make a ruling."

"I was serious about checking Matt's hands. Do you want me to send him over here to talk with you later? I'll do it."

"Calm down, Sabrina. I'm planning to meet with your brother and Matt later."

"Today?" My heart rate kicked up a notch.

"Yes."

"Do they need to bring a lawyer?"

The sheriff stared at me. "I thought your brother *was* a lawyer."

"Right, but I mean, you know what I mean."

He shook his head with a what-did-I-do-to-deserve-this expression. "Matt called me before they went out on the river. The boy started asking me questions the same way you do. I could barely get a word in edgewise. I'm thinking disregard for authority must run in the family. He wanted to come over straightaway. I told him my first opening was at six. Now that I squeezed you in unexpectedly, I'm runnin' behind, but we're about done here."

I checked my watch as the sheriff stood and walked around his desk. Four thirty.

"I'm glad we had this talk," he said, "and you *have* been a big help. I'll be in touch if I need any more information."

I left his office and didn't see anyone waiting for a meeting with the sheriff. Had he lied to get rid of me? In my opinion, we were nowhere near finished with our conversation, but maybe saying less was more under the circumstances.

Hitchcock tried to tug me toward Laurel's desk, but the dispatcher was on the phone and not looking in our direction. I picked up my cat and went to the hot car.

We got in, and I started the engine and flipped the AC to high. "I had so many more details I could have shared if he'd given me more time to talk through everything. Now I feel guilty for keeping too much to myself, even though it's his own fault in a way for cutting the meeting short. I had so many more questions for him, too."

"Mrreow," Hitchcock said.

"Like what's the real reason Charlotte was crying? What's up with Deputy Rosales? Is Gary Weber simply a nice guy who handed over front-row seats out of the goodness of his heart or is he trying to throw me off? Did Tandee have a reason to want Dixon out of the way? And what about other possible enemies of the dead man? Life is like fiction, isn't it? The possibilities are honestly endless."

I stopped rambling and looked at Hitchcock. He'd tucked his legs underneath his body and assumed his meat loaf position. He was purring. Totally unperturbed.

I should be so lucky.

Chapter 16

I sat in the parking lot and watched the door for a while, hoping for a glimpse of the next witness coming in to meet with the sheriff. I wondered if that person would be someone I recognized. I also wondered what Matt had asked the sheriff that led to them setting up their six o'clock appointment. The thought of my nephew becoming involved with a criminal investigation made me feel edgy and overheated. I adjusted the AC vent, then tried Matt's cell phone and Nick's, with no response. They were probably still out on the river.

After fifteen minutes of seeing no one come or go, I decided the sheriff could be conducting interviews by phone. I had too much work at home to justify this colossal waste of time, so I headed back to the cottages.

A few minutes later I pulled into Aunt Rowe's driveway and parked next to her car, the only vehicle in sight. I wanted to snag some alone time with her, and this might be my chance. The kitchen was unusually quiet when I walked in. No Glenda. No signs of dinner preparation. Hitchcock went straight to his water bowl. I walked through the living room and down the hallway. Aunt Rowe's door was cracked.

I knocked on the door trim. "Anybody home?"

I poked my head in and saw Aunt Rowe on the chaise in the corner. She was barefoot and wearing stretchy black shorts with a magenta V-neck tee. A floor lamp cast its glow over her shoulder and onto a notebook in her lap. She held a pen poised over a page.

She looked up at me and smiled. "What a nice surprise."

She stuck her pen in the book to keep her page and tucked the notebook beside her. She pulled her legs in to sit cross-legged and patted the end of the chaise. "Come. Sit. I'm surprised you're not out solving the murder."

"I would if I could, but I can't make heads or tails of what happened." I went to the bed, plopped backward onto the mattress, and stretched my arms over my head.

"Not like you to give up on a mystery," she said.

"The details are spinning around in here." I tapped my head

with an index finger. "Something useful may spill out given enough time. How's your special guest doing?"

"Fine as a fiddle," Aunt Rowe said. "Haven't heard a peep out of him."

"Are you sure he's still in the cottage?"

"Of course, he's there. Sends requests for clean towels and coffee fixin's on a regular basis."

"Good to know. I ran into Gary Weber in town. He told me he and Jamison fired the murder victim last week, or tried to. They didn't want him here, but he came anyway."

"Lord, don't tell me poor Colt is a suspect."

I sat up. "No, Aunt Rowe, I'm not going to tell you that."

Should he be a suspect?

I decided to change the subject. "This reminds me, I wanted to ask if you know the victim's mother. A lady named Wanda. I heard she lives here in town."

"Wanda?" Aunt Rowe closed her eyes as she thought about the name. "There was a Wanda who worked at the drugstore back when she was a teenager. I'm guessing she'd be in her fifties by now."

"That's probably about the right age. Know where I could find her?"

"And why would you want to do that?" she teased.

"To pay my respects," I said. "Maybe see if she knows whether her son had any enemies."

"That's my girl," Aunt Rowe said. "She might live in her family's old place off of Pike Creek Road. When do you plan to see her?"

"Maybe tomorrow. Nick and the boys are going out with Luke to experience the life of a game warden."

I slid my phone from my pocket to see if they'd responded to my phone calls.

Nothing.

"Have you heard from Nick since they headed to the river?" I said.

"Not a word," she said. "He's relaxing for a change."

I doubted that, especially with the sheriff meeting looming. I thought about the changes in my brother that Ty pointed out. The ones I'd noticed myself. I turned to Aunt Rowe. "Does Nick seem different to you?"

"Different how?"

"I don't know. Like something's bothering him?"

She thought for a moment before answering. "Not especially. Seems like his normal self to me."

"Is that good or bad?"

She shrugged. "Neither. You know Nick. He contemplates everything to death."

"Yeah. I can relate to that." I checked Aunt Rowe's straight-backed position, with her legs still crossed and hands resting on her knees. "You're going to get cramped up sitting that way." I crossed my own legs in a weak attempt to copy her.

"No, I won't," she said. "I've been practicing the Lotus pose, and I'm close to getting it right."

Each of her feet was tucked into the opposite thigh, not up on top of her legs the way I thought the pose was supposed to look. "You're doing way better than me. When did you start practicing yoga?"

"Yesterday," she said. "I'm going to achieve the flexibility of a thirty-year-old. Twenty would be a stretch, but thirty is doable."

Aunt Rowe had plenty of spunk, and I'd be impressed but not terribly surprised if she met her goal. Yoga was a lot safer than some of the other things she'd tried since I moved to Lavender. I wholeheartedly approved of yoga.

"Sounds like a good idea, Aunt Rowe. Did Violet get you started with yoga?"

She nodded. "Violet gave me the shove I needed to start. Without flexibility I wouldn't be able to achieve my other goals." She grabbed a foot and attempted to pull it up and over the top of the opposite thigh.

"What *are* your other goals?"

Aunt Rowe gave up on the stretch and looked at me. "Some of them are private. I'll just say that when you get to be my age you think a lot about the things you haven't done."

"I already have a list."

"But you're on the brink of a successful writing career. You'll hit your stride and soon have a whole row of bestsellers. You have a good man and a bright future with him unless I miss my guess." Her expression seemed wistful.

"Is that what you want?" I said. "A good man?"

Aunt Rowe had been married several times already, and I'd never had the impression she wanted to try marriage again.

She sniffed. "There aren't enough good ones left."

"You only need one," I said. "What's wrong with Sheriff Crawford?"

She frowned. "He's always working. If a man doesn't have enough sense to retire when it's time, or at least take some days off, how would we ever go on that cruise around the world together?"

I sat back. "Whoa, that's your measuring stick for a man's worth?"

She shrugged. "The cruise is on my list."

"You're not exactly retired yourself," I said.

"These cottages could run smoothly with Thomas's and Glenda's help while I take some time off. No problem."

"If you're interested in going on a world cruise with the sheriff, then why do you reject every advance he ever makes?"

"Not every one." Her eyes sparkled, and I wondered what she was keeping to herself.

I grinned. "Now you've piqued my curiosity."

She picked up her book. "I need to get back to Violet's homework assignment. Then I'm off to another yoga session."

"What's the dinner plan for tonight?"

"We have plenty of leftovers, if you want them. Nick and the boys are going to visit his fraternity brother tonight, so Glenda took some time off. We're free to do whatever we want, and I chose yoga."

She was gently pushing me out the door, so I headed to my place. When I arrived, I found Hitchcock stretched out on the sofa.

"Mrreow," he said when I came in.

"I'm going to do some work," I said as I opened my laptop.

He gave me a sidelong glance.

"Don't believe me, huh? I'm responding to Kree's message about my book proposal."

I sat and checked my files to remind myself where I'd left off the last time I worked on the proposal for book three. My mind wandered to thoughts of Aunt Rowe and the sheriff. She could have snagged the handsome widower years ago, and I was glad to hear she was finally showing an interest. I thought about Luke and wondered if he and I would ever decide to cruise the world together. I couldn't picture the two of us lounging on the deck of an ocean liner.

Thinking of Luke, I pulled out my phone and sent him a text message.

Thanks for lunch. The boys enjoyed spending time with you, and so did I.

I put my phone down and pulled up an email to craft my reply to Kree. Another solid couple of days to work on the proposal and I'd be ready to send it off to her. I gave myself some leeway and told her I was aiming for mid-September.

My phone buzzed with a response to my text.

Lunch was great. Hey, there's something weird going on with D.R.

Code for Deputy Rosales.

Something besides how she acted at lunch?

Yeah. Where are you?

Home.

I waited for another text, but the phone rang instead. Luke. I answered quickly.

"Hi there," I said. "What's going on?"

"Still working," he said. "Went by the Wild Pony to track down a guy who left his boat parked in a fire lane at the grocery store. Saw Rosales there."

"At the grocery store?"

"No. The Wild Pony. She's at the bar."

I paused. "What's she doing?"

"Looks like she's drinking. Sitting there by herself and out of uniform. She saw me and didn't react. Like she didn't know me."

"You're worried."

"More like suspicious."

"Of what, exactly?"

"I'm not sure."

"I saw Laurel today. She told me Rosales is taking some personal days off."

"Yeah, right," he said. "There's a *murder* to solve and she *knew* the guy. She's working it."

"How's she working the case at the bar?"

"Not sure, but mark my words, the woman is on the case."

"I believe you," I told him. "Maybe she suspects a tourist, someone who won't recognize her as law enforcement without her uniform."

"That's one possibility," he said.

"What are you going to do?"

"There's nothing to do," he said. "Guess your curious streak rubbed off on me, that's all. I gotta get back to work."

"Late night?"

"Probably. I'll be by at six in the morning to pick up Nick and the boys. See you then, if you're up."

We ended the call, and I noticed Hitchcock staring at me. "That was Luke. Deputy Rosales might be tying one on at the Wild Pony. Could be thinking about her late brother and his friend Marty Dixon."

"Mrreow," Hitchcock said.

"I don't believe she's there to drink. I agree with Luke. She's working the case. She's there for a reason. Maybe watching Chester. Or Tracey. She probably thinks they have a good motive, and she may be right. But why's she doing this unofficially? That's the part I don't get."

Hitchcock blinked at me, his eyes heavy.

"Will she accuse me of invading her privacy if I go over there?"

"Mrr," he said.

"I'm going anyway."

Chapter 17

On my way to the Wild Pony I noticed work crews were out in force, as if someone had designated this as Clean Up Lavender Day. The crews picked up debris along the roadways and swept gutters and sidewalks. The shiny flashes of light I spotted in the debris confirmed the story Laurel had told me: someone truly *was* flinging pieces of broken mirrors around town. This was one time I wouldn't mind folks being a bit *more* superstitious. Whoever was behind this craziness apparently wasn't worried about seven years of bad luck. My thoughts turned to Rosales and what might be going on with her. Was she mulling over the facts of the case as she sat and drank? Drowning her sorrows over some personal problem? Luke didn't think that was the case, and neither did I. Maybe she suspected Chester and wanted to give him the willies by staring him down until he broke and confessed to a crime.

It was early evening when I parked across the street from the saloon, but the sun was still bright, the humidity high. As I crossed the hot asphalt lot, perspiration trickled down my back. I could tell by the number of cars that tourist season was still in full swing. When school started in a couple of weeks, the crowds would thin. I realized as I looked around the lot that I had no idea what Patricia Rosales drove when she wasn't on duty.

As I approached the entrance, which was plastered with bumper stickers, I spotted a new one, bright yellow with the words *Colt* and *Texas* separated by a red heart. I went inside to the hum of conversation, clacking of billiard balls, and someone in the other room singing "Mamas, Don't Let Your Babies Grow Up to Be Cowboys." I decided it must be a live performance since the voice faltered on some of the notes.

I squeezed through the people milling around near the entrance and scanned those seated at the bar. No Patricia Rosales. I slid onto a stool next to an older man who was so intent on shelling and eating peanuts he didn't seem to notice me. The tall, blond bartender was probably one of the many college students working part-time in Lavender for the summer. He came over to me with a towel slung over his shoulder, and I ordered a bottle of Corona that I didn't necessarily intend to drink.

I glanced up at the TV mounted behind the bar, then lowered my gaze and checked the reflections in the mirrored wall to see if I could spot Rosales that way. By the time the bartender came back with my beer, I'd decided neither Rosales nor Chester was in the room. I picked up the bottle and slid off my stool, then walked into the back room filled with pool tables.

Some men looked up and leered as I passed, possibly mistaking me for a woman on the prowl as I scanned the room. I quickly determined that Rosales wasn't in here either, and coming alone had not been my brightest idea. I was thinking about leaving when a door on the far side of the room opened and Tracey Powell came out. She was dressed in black slacks and a white shirt and wore her hair pulled up into a messy bun on top of her head. She carried an armload of supplies — packaged napkins and sacks of peanuts.

Tracey might have barreled by without noticing me, but I stepped into her path. She slowed and her expression registered surprise at seeing me.

She focused on the beer bottle in my hand. "Are congratulations in order?"

I frowned. "For what?"

"You told us at book club you'd come and lift a cold one with me when you finished your manuscript."

I waved off the comment. "False alarm. I'm nowhere near the celebration stage."

"Well, hell," Tracey said. "Let's lift one anyway. I could use another drink. C'mon with me."

Her words slurred a bit, and I wondered how much she'd already had. I followed her out of the room and to the bar, where she stashed the peanuts and napkins under a counter. She looked at my bottle.

"Get you another?"

I shook my head. "No, thanks. I'm good."

She grabbed a tall mug and filled it with beer from a tap, then motioned when a couple vacated a table against the far wall. "You have a minute to sit?"

"A few," I said.

We went to the table, and I took the seat that gave me the best view of the room.

Tracey noticed me scanning the place. "You meeting someone?"

"No." Coming here to look for Rosales didn't qualify as "meeting." "Luke's working tonight."

Tracey leaned in. "You'd better not bring up that danged video, 'cause I'm about sick up to here of being harassed about that fiasco." She made a slicing motion over her head.

Having fought with the murder victim, I didn't think she should act like she was the person wronged, but maybe that was just me. "I'd rather pretend that whole scene never happened."

"You and me both," Tracey said in a blustery tone before her expression turned sheepish. "Look, Sabrina, sorry for busting up the book club meeting like I did. I didn't even get a chance to thank you for coming, so thanks."

"You're welcome."

Her words were definitely slurred. She picked up her mug with a shaky hand and took a swig of beer. I hoped she wasn't following in her brother's footsteps when it came to drinking. That could be the reason Aunt Rowe's friend Helen had said Tracey needed help with her life.

I took a tiny sip from my bottle, then said, "How's Chester? Is he here tonight?"

She shook her head quickly. "His ulcer's acting up. I told him to get some rest."

"Sorry to hear that." My inner skeptic wondered if that was the truth or if she intended to keep Chester hidden away. "I've been concerned about y'all."

"Why? 'Cause my being such a hothead put me and Chester on the sheriff's suspect list?"

"Well, there's that. I was talking about the concert venue change."

"Yeah, that was a blow to the bank account," Tracey said. "They canceled the personal appearance, too." She shook her head as if a more tragic story could never be told.

"Sorry things didn't work out."

"We'll have to pick ourselves up by our bootstraps and line up something better. Business will improve."

If it were true that Chester couldn't account for his whereabouts at the time of the murder, I feared she'd have bigger things to worry about.

Tracey said, "At least the video gave us some free publicity. They were playing it in here earlier."

"Is that why you were hiding in the back room?"

She grinned. "You got it."

I took advantage of her decent mood and asked, "How long had you known Marty Dixon?"

She looked away and didn't answer for a full minute before turning back to me. "Most of my life. I thought he was a friend."

I hoped she didn't handle all her friends the way she had Dixon.

"Marty didn't come around often," she said. "A quick stop every now and then when he was on his way to somewhere else. He's the one who approached us about having the show here."

"Then you got your hopes up," I said.

"Of course we did." Her tone grew sharp. "Who wouldn't?"

"I'm not blaming you."

"Marty didn't have the decency to tell us himself that plans had changed," she went on. "We had to hear it from some Nashville muckety-muck."

"And then you saw Marty outside the pizza shop and—" I paused.

"I went ballistic," she said. "Doesn't mean I killed him."

"I never said you did. I have no idea what happened to Marty Dixon."

"But you're not crossing us off the suspect list."

"I don't have a list," I said.

"Bull. You're little miss let's-solve-the-murder, and not only in fiction. You've jumped right into more than one murder investigation around here."

"You don't have to get nasty," I said.

She pinned me with a glare. "Why are you really here? Did the sheriff send you?"

"The sheriff wouldn't send me to investigate squat for him even if I wanted to," I said. "I came to talk to Deputy Rosales."

"What?" Tracey sat back, and her jaw dropped. "Rosales is here?"

"I heard she was," I said, "but I haven't spotted her yet."

"Oh, Lordy." Tracey began rocking back and forth in her seat. "She's after us. I knew this would happen."

Oh, brother.

"I'm sure you have an alibi," I said. "You'll be fine."

"She won't believe anything I say, and what about Chester? What if we're each other's alibi? What if she's here to haul us in?"

"You're blowing this out of proportion. I heard she was here having a drink, that's all. I'm not sure how you missed her."

"I was on the computer most of the afternoon," Tracey said. "I don't keep up with everyone who walks in, but I don't trust that woman. If she's here—"

I made a cut-it-out motion with my hand. "Maybe she's not, so chill." The singer in the other room was attempting "Take This Job and Shove It" without the pizzazz of the original version, and the crowd joined in on the chorus.

"You have a rowdy bunch in there," I said to change the subject.

"Including Jamison's road crew." Tracey raised her voice to be heard over the ruckus. "They piled in about an hour ago. Said it'll take them three days to set up everything for the show."

Jamison's road crew probably knew Marty Dixon. I wondered if Rosales was interested in watching someone in that crew.

"At least you're getting some business from them," I said.

"Better'n nothing." Tracey gulped more beer, then stood. "They probably don't think much of Zeke's singing if they're used to listening to Colt. But hey, he's local, and he doesn't renege on his deals to sing when we need him. I'm going back to the office."

We parted ways, and I walked into the room where Aunt Rowe and I had once taken a brief line-dancing class with a group of her friends. My eyes needed a minute to adjust to the dim lighting, so I leaned against the wall and turned to the well-lit stage. The group performing had three members in addition to the lead singer, who had a guitar strapped over his shoulder and long braided hair. When he faced the audience, I recognized him as the man I saw playing guitar on the street corner earlier. And last night in the clandestine meeting with Colt Jamison.

"Not too good, are they?" said a woman standing to my right.

I turned to her and spotted the reason I'd come here in the first place. Patricia Rosales sat at a table for six. She was easy to pick out in the same red shirt she'd been wearing at lunchtime. If I had to guess, I'd say the men at the table were members of the group who worked for Jamison. They wore jeans with matching Colt Jamison T-shirts and work boots. One of them lifted a beer mug, said something, and laughed. Then he lifted his mug higher in a toast, and everyone at the table, including Rosales, joined in.

She leaned into the man next to her, and I watched as she slugged back her beer like there was no tomorrow.

Chapter 18

I belatedly answered the woman beside me who'd commented on the music. "They're not the best band I ever heard, but they seem to fit in here at the Wild Pony."

The woman wasn't listening. Her attention had turned to a man who approached her with an outstretched hand. They walked together toward the dance floor, drawn by the next song in the set—"Livin' on Love." The musicians, I decided, were better than the singer.

I turned my attention back to Rosales. She was either nuzzling the neck of the man next to her or whispering in his ear. She appeared loose and unguarded, so unlike her usual self that I could hardly believe this was the same Patricia Rosales. But then she'd always been on duty when I saw her. The woman had a personal life, of course, but I knew nothing about that side of her.

Rosales would likely spot me if I kept standing here, so I strolled the room's perimeter to find a less conspicuous vantage point. My intuition said her true purpose in hanging with the Jamison crew was to fish for information related to Marty Dixon's death. I scanned the crowd as I walked, though I didn't expect to run into any acquaintances. No one I knew well frequented the Wild Pony, and I'd guess the majority of the people in the room tonight were tourists.

The thought had barely crossed my mind when I saw Jeff Slade seated ten feet in front of me at a pub table. It seemed like a week had passed since I'd met the fellow writer at the book club meeting. A cute redheaded waitress in snug jeans delivered a refill of what looked like whiskey, gave Jeff a big smile, and removed his empty glass. He leaned into the aisle to watch her walk away, then saw me when he straightened.

"Sabrina." He gave me a two-finger salute and glanced at the bottle in my hand. "I didn't figure you as the beer type."

I lifted my bottle in greeting. "I'm not, usually."

"What brings you out?" he said. "The great band?"

"Um, no. I stopped by to see Tracey." I responded with the first thing that popped in my head, and I *had* seen Tracey, so it worked.

Jeff picked up his glass and sipped. I glanced toward Rosales. She was still with that guy. I repositioned myself so I could easily check on her without looking suspicious. Then I turned back to Jeff, noticing that he'd spiffed up for tonight. His coral golf shirt was more attractive than the frayed T-shirt he wore to the book club meeting. His face was clean-shaven, his wavy brown hair gelled into submission.

"You left the bad luck at home tonight?" he said.

"What?" I said, even though I'd heard him perfectly.

"Your cat, what's-his-name?"

I lasered a glare at the man. "His *name* is Hitchcock, and hearing that reference makes me feel like walking away and *never* speaking to you again, except then you might continue to tell other people what you think, which is *not* acceptable. So, please, don't ever say those words about my cat. Ever. Again."

Jeff had pulled back from me, his brows drawn together. "What words?"

I lowered my voice. "Are you serious right now?"

He grinned. "No, but jeez, you sure are edgy. I was kidding."

I took a swig of my beer. "That wasn't funny."

He twirled his glass on the table. "You want to sit?"

I didn't want to deal with him any longer, but I had some questions. Not to mention, my feet could use a break. I pulled the chair out and sat. "You have no idea what Hitchcock and I have been through because of that stupid superstition."

"Sorry, I don't want to alienate a writer that I admire."

I looked at him. "Are you serious *now*?"

"I am. Started reading your book, and it's great."

"Thanks." Much as I enjoyed hearing compliments about my writing, I moved on to my questions. "Have you talked to Tracey?"

"Since she became a video star?" he said with a smirk.

This guy could be really annoying. "No. Since you got here."

"Nuh-uh." He took another sip of his drink.

"If you do, don't mention the video. It's a sore spot."

"No wonder."

"Are you the one who uploaded the video to YouTube?"

"Nah. I think somebody beat me to it."

You think?

I decided to drop the topic for now. "Do you come to the Wild Pony often?"

"Not too, until recently," Jeff said. "My buddy Fritz grabs me sometimes to come out when he needs a break. He's the one introduced me to the place. Now I have a renewed interest of my own."

He tipped his head toward a nearby table, where the redhead was serving drinks.

"Ah, I get it. Were you here last night?"

He screwed up his mouth, thinking. "Last night? No."

"When's the last time you were here?"

He shrugged. "A week? I don't know."

I thought back to what he'd said about his friend. "Do I know Fritz? The name sounds familiar."

"You know his kid," Jeff said. "At the pizza shop. Your cat—" He paused and enunciated, "*Hitchcock* was playing with him yesterday."

"Right, Noah's a cute kid."

Jeff snapped his fingers and pointed at me. "Noah. That's him."

"Yesterday was crazy when Marty Dixon showed up," I said. "Did you know Dixon?"

"Nope."

"Know anything about him?"

"Only what Tracey spouted off right before you arrived at book club. She wants to get a lawyer to sue Jamison's people for changing the concert site. I didn't catch everything she was sayin'. A lot of blah, blah, blah."

"I can understand why she disliked Dixon," I said.

"She's not alone there," Jeff said. "Bruno wasn't a fan of the guy."

I frowned. "Why not?"

"I don't remember what his deal was." Jeff picked up his glass and took a drink, and I reminded myself he'd already finished one drink and might not be the most reliable person to get details from.

"Thing is," Jeff went on, "we were there to talk about your book, so I was glad to see you. Shut them up about that other garbage."

Garbage that had new importance given the murder.

"Have you ever seen Marty Dixon here at the Wild Pony?"

"Can't answer that. Since I didn't know the guy, I wouldn't have recognized him if he walked right up to me. And I'm kinda focused on the ladies when I'm here."

Of course you are.

The band was finishing up their rendition of "The Dance," and Rosales was deep in conversation with her friend.

When the song ended, Zeke cleared his throat and said, "Thank y'all for comin' out to the Wild Pony. We'll take a short break, and y'all can listen to some Colt Jamison. When we come back, we'll take your requests."

The band members descended the steps from the stage and recorded music began playing. I recognized the smooth tone of Jamison's voice as he sang something about lonely nights and memories. Jeff watched the redhead as she headed out with a tray of empties. I turned and started when I realized Rosales was no longer in her chair. I scanned the room. No red shirt.

Dang it.

I slipped off my stool. "I need to run, Jeff. Good seeing you."

He gave me another two-finger salute. "See ya around."

I hurried from the room, looking for Rosales. She wasn't in the bar area, and I decided she might have headed for the ladies' room. I turned in that direction and found myself facing Jeff's redhead. She focused on my empty hands.

"Hi, there. Bring you a drink?"

"No, thank you."

"Are you a friend of Jeff's?" she said.

I shrugged. "I first met him yesterday. I'm not interested in him, if that's what you mean." I was probably ten years older than Jeff, and even older than her, so I was hardly competition.

"Thought I'd warn you," she said. "I'd steer clear if I were you. He can be a jerk."

"I've noticed," I said.

"Okay." She smiled. "Sure I can't get you something?"

"No, but wait. Would you say Jeff is a regular here?"

She nodded. "Too regular for me, but we're supposed to play nice with the customers."

"Before tonight," I said, "when's the last time you saw him?"

"Last night," she said.

"Are you sure?"

"Positive. He's a good tipper. Might want more than excellent service, but that's all he's gettin'."

She grinned, and I smiled in understanding. "Thank you."

The waitress turned back to the bar, and I walked toward the ladies' room. I wondered why Jeff had lied about not being here last night, and the obvious answer was he didn't want to admit to being on the premises near the site of a murder. He claimed he didn't know Marty Dixon. Was that a lie as well?

Something to consider.

The back exit connected a breezeway to a separate smaller building that housed the restrooms. The waiting line snaked out and back into the main building.

This was dumb. I wasn't going to accost Rosales in the ladies' room—back her into a corner and demand to know what she was doing here. I disentangled myself from the women joining the line and went outside to the patio. Thought about calling it a night. The guys might be home from visiting Nick's friend by now, and I was eager to hear about their meeting with the sheriff.

The pub tables on the patio were filled with patrons. No Rosales. Music streamed through speakers mounted to the side of the building, and I recognized the by-now well-known song "Broken Mirror." Across the patio, I saw a black cat that looked a lot like Hitchcock sitting atop a decorative rail fence.

Good Lord, I hoped it wasn't Hitchcock. I hurried in that direction. The cat jumped down, ran around and under the pub tables, and sped out of sight. This was exactly like something Hitchcock would do. I felt compelled to make sure this wasn't my cat and followed in the direction the cat had gone.

The sun was starting to set as I walked around to a side of the building I'd never seen before. Lots of trees over here. A cat could easily have run straight up any one of them. I should stop this nonsense and make a simple call home to see if Hitchcock was there. Except I lived alone. If he'd stayed at home in the Monte Carlo cottage—and I hoped he had—no one would have seen him.

I kept walking until a strident voice interrupted my musing about the cat.

"What the hell do you think you're doing following me around?"

Shocked, I jumped back before noticing Patricia Rosales leaning against the fat trunk of an oak tree.

"I wasn't, I mean I didn't—"

"Don't give me that." She pushed away from the tree and walked toward me. "I saw you in there watching me, trying to figure out what I'm doing."

I straightened defensively. "I came out here after a cat."

"Oh, right." She put one fist on a hip.

"I really did. I saw it on the patio, then I worried it could be Hitchcock, and I wanted to make sure it wasn't him."

"Save it," Rosales said. "If you're tryin' to prove I'm guilty, you can give that up, 'cause I didn't do anything."

"What?"

She threw her hands up and turned around, walked a few feet away, then dropped her chin to her chest as if the accusatory, blustery side of her had run out of steam.

"You should be on vacation," I said, "or at least taking it easy."

She whirled to look at me. "Where do you get off tryin' to tell me what to do?"

"That's what people usually do when they take personal time off work. Relax. Have some fun."

"Well, that's not what I'm doing," Rosales said.

"No. I think you're on the hunt for clues. You want to find Marty Dixon's killer, but I can't figure out why you took off from work to do it. Seems like you could investigate and get paid for the time you're spending."

"This is none of your damn business," she said harshly, "so you should get out of here and leave me alone." Her voice cracked with those last words.

I had come here curious about Rosales's actions, but now I was beginning to feel something completely different. Compassion. For the woman who was never anything but mean when she talked to me.

Go figure.

I processed what she'd said about not being guilty. Was she talking about Marty Dixon? As if I thought she'd killed him? I was afraid to put that into so many words. I walked closer to the woman.

"Do you need help?"

"No." One clipped word. I guess she figured that's all I was worth.

"I'm serious. If there's something you need, I'll see what I can do. If you have a problem, you shouldn't face it alone."

No response.

I'd never seen Rosales with a friend. I hoped she had someone to turn to. But if she did, then why was she alone tonight? Tyanne was often my go-to person, plus I had family, other friends, and now Luke, too. If Rosales didn't have anyone, I couldn't simply walk away.

I tried a different tack. "Have you learned anything useful here tonight?"

"Not much," she said. "There's a whole town full of suspects who might have done it."

She didn't deny working the case—that was something. I remembered seeing Rosales here at the Wild Pony the night before, and I wondered whether she had a solid alibi. I didn't have the courage to put my thoughts into those exact words. Instead I said, "Are you afraid someone will pin the murder on you?"

Rosales grimaced. "That's about the size of it."

Chapter 19

When I got back to Aunt Rowe's house, I saw Hitchcock in the kitchen window over the sink. I breathed a sigh of relief that he was not the cat I'd seen prancing around at the Wild Pony. He wouldn't have had time to make it back here this fast.

I had enough to worry about with thinking about Rosales. The deputy had a skeleton or two in her closet. She wanted the murder resolved before anyone dug too far into her past. Sounded risky to me, but I couldn't convince her to come clean with the sheriff.

To Rosales the facts were simple: she knew she didn't have anything to do with the murder, and investigating her was unnecessary and off-limits. Everything else was fair game. She was all in favor of me snooping around to figure out who killed Dixon and why. That sure was a change from her usual attitude about my sleuthing.

Before we parted, Rosales made me promise to keep everything we talked about to myself. For the life of me, I couldn't explain why I'd agreed to something so impossible. I wasn't the greatest at keeping my mouth shut, but I sure didn't want to be the one to cause the rumor mill to start spinning. If that happened, the press could report something crazy—they might call Rosales a vigilante local deputy who murdered Colt Jamison's P.R. guy. Better to keep my lips zipped when it came to Rosales.

I walked into the kitchen and found the boys sitting with Aunt Rowe at the table. They each had heaping bowls of Blue Bell vanilla ice cream topped with chocolate syrup and chopped peanuts. A fourth untouched bowl sat in front of an empty chair. Matt looked like he'd just come from a shower with his wet hair slicked back and wearing a fresh T-shirt. Adam had the appearance of a boy who'd traveled through a windstorm and wrestled a dirty dog since I'd last seen him.

We exchanged greetings, and I walked by the window to give Hitchcock a chin scratch before joining the others at the table. The ice cream called out to my sweet tooth.

"Perfect treat for a hot August night." I looked around and didn't see Nick. "Where's your dad?"

"On the phone with Mom," Adam said.

Matt looked up. "He's out on the deck."

I met his gaze. "You holding up okay?"

"I'm good," Matt said.

They continued to eat and seemed oddly silent. After a few seconds Aunt Rowe put her spoon down and looked at Matt.

"Why don't you fill your Aunt Sabrina in about your talk with the sheriff," she said. "That way your father won't have to rehash the story yet again after he's finished telling your mother."

My heart thudded. "What's this about? Did something bad happen?"

"Could be worse," Aunt Rowe said. "You might want to go ahead and get yourself a bowl of ice cream, though. We decided it would make us feel a bit better, and I think it's doing the trick."

"Tell me. I can get ice cream later." I looked at the bowl in front of me. "Better yet, I'll eat Nick's before it melts."

Aunt Rowe nodded at Matt, encouraging him to speak.

Matt looked up from his bowl. "Remember how I knew Tandee before?"

"Before you came to Lavender? From social media."

"Yeah," he said. "Turns out she hooked up with lotsa kids that way. From all over the place."

"Her purpose being—?" I paused for him to complete the thought.

Adam's head lifted. "She told 'em she needed money for the fan club, and some rich kids gave her the money, but it didn't—"

"Shut up," Matt said. "You don't know anything."

Aunt Rowe reached out and put her hand on Matt's forearm. She shook her head, and he heaved a sigh.

After a moment, he said, "She took money from kids. Said it was a VIP membership fee, but she didn't use it for the fan club. Sheriff says she used it to buy drugs."

My jaw dropped. "Oh. I didn't see that coming."

"No one did," Aunt Rowe said, "especially Matt here."

"You're not involved with the drugs, though." I'd be shocked if he was, but I had to check.

"No way," Matt said quickly. "Scout's honor."

"We believe you," Aunt Rowe said.

I took my time to process this new information and began eating the ice cream in front of me. Hitchcock jumped down from his perch and came over to sit beside me and stare as I ate. If the cat expected me to offer him some ice cream, he had a long wait coming.

"So the sheriff just up and shared this information about the drugs in the meeting?"

"Kind of. After he asked me a bunch of questions about Tandee, Dad started asking *him* stuff, like those lawyers do on TV."

I could imagine how fired up Nick would be under these circumstances.

"Did Tandee ever ask *you* for money?" I said.

Matt finished a bite of ice cream, then said, "Once. Somehow she knew Dad's a lawyer. I never told her, but I guess she thought I'd have cash. I said my dad handles all the bills. He's like my business manager."

"You don't have a business," Adam said.

Matt glared at his younger brother.

"You handled the situation very well," Aunt Rowe said. "You know how to steer clear of trouble."

"Does the sheriff think Tandee was taking drugs—or selling them?"

Matt lifted his shoulders. "Don't know. He said he's in the fact-finding stage."

Otherwise known as the trying to decide if he had enough to make an arrest stage. "I'm glad you didn't give her money."

Matt scooped up another bite. "I knew something was up."

"Your common sense at work." I thought over the events of the past two days. "Do we know if Tandee knew Marty Dixon?"

"They both did stuff for Colt Jamison," Matt said. "I figure they knew each other."

"I'm sure the sheriff will have plenty of questions for her to answer." I sat back in my chair and stretched my arms over my head. It had been a long day.

"Deputy Salazar talked to me and Tandee last night," Matt said. "I guess somebody told the sheriff about the money, then he figured everything out."

"And he put it all together today?"

Matt nodded miserably. "Yeah. The sheriff checked my phone to go through all my messages."

"Did you know anything about the drug connection?"

He hung his head. I looked at Aunt Rowe, who nodded in confirmation.

"Oh, Matt, you know better," I said.

"I kinda guessed, but I didn't know anything for sure until I heard some kids talking about drugs yesterday."

"That sounds like she might be selling," I said.

We ate ice cream for a while, until the scraping of spoons against ceramic bowls broke the silence.

Aunt Rowe cleared her throat. "Are you gonna tell her the rest, or should I?"

"You can," Matt said.

I turned to Aunt Rowe. "What else?"

"Jeb went to see Tandee this afternoon to discuss the whole mess," Aunt Rowe said. "She's been staying with a brother, off and on. Parents have been out of the picture for years."

"Okay," I said. "And?"

"The brother hasn't seen Tandee in days. Doesn't know where to find her. She's not answering her phone." Aunt Rowe lifted her brows. "Jeb thinks she got wind of him coming for her and left town."

Adam's spoon clattered into his empty bowl. "But she's president of the fan club. She wouldn't leave before the show."

Aunt Rowe and I exchanged a look. If the girl thought she was about to be arrested, she might have run without giving that concert one bit of thought.

"I may be the queen of jumping to conclusions," I said, "but we should give Tandee the benefit of the doubt."

Nick walked into the kitchen as the words left my mouth. "You're feeling more generous toward that girl than I am." He held his phone out to Matt. "Your mother wants to talk to you."

The boy's shoulders slumped, but he took the phone and got up. He strode toward the living room. "Hi, Mom."

Nick looked down at the table. "Where's mine?"

"Oops." I jumped up. "Sit down and I'll fix you another dish."

Adam said, "Can I have more?"

Aunt Rowe stood and gathered the empty bowls. "You already had enough for three people. I think you should grab a shower now. Don't you have a big day tomorrow with the game warden?"

Adam looked at Nick. "We're still going with Luke, right, Dad?"

"Yes." Nick shook his head as if he'd made a decision against his better judgment. "Early start. Six a.m."

Adam brightened and shot out of the room.

"You're staying for the Jamison concert, too, aren't you?" I remembered the special tickets Gary Weber had handed me, but this probably wasn't the best time to bring them up.

"We'll stay." Nick sounded reluctant. "I promised Mel I'd keep the boys in my sight at all times."

Aunt Rowe smirked. "I'll get started fixin' you a pallet on the floor in their bedroom."

"That's a little beyond the call," Nick said. "Appreciate the offer."

"How about I go and keep your youngest on task?" she said.

"Now that's a good idea." Nick nodded. "Thanks."

Hitchcock trotted out of the room behind Aunt Rowe. I drizzled chocolate syrup over Nick's ice cream, sprinkled on the peanuts, and took the bowl to him.

I sat in the chair across the table. "You know, the fact that Tandee isn't where the sheriff looked for her doesn't mean she ran to escape the law. She might be staying with a friend or anyone who came for the concert and has room to put her up."

"She's a criminal," Nick said, "one way or another."

I shrugged. "Sounds like it."

Nick dug into the ice cream, and I thought about Tandee. Up until yesterday, she'd been buzzing around town advertising for Colt Jamison. Now she'd allegedly taken off, the fan club and upcoming show be damned. On the face of things, it seemed the girl had somehow been alerted that her requests for money and a possible drug connection were common knowledge that would reach the sheriff sooner than later.

She'd asked Matt for money, so we knew that part of the story was true.

I snapped out of a fog when I realized Nick was tapping his spoon on his bowl. "You're zoned out over there. Not listening to a word I say."

"I'm sorry. What?"

"My speech ended with 'Matt should have come to me with this way before now,'" Nick said.

119

"Perfect judgment doesn't switch on when a kid turns fifteen," I said.

"What turns on is hormones, and that's part of the problem."

"Matt will be fine," I said. "I think he's handling this horrible situation quite well, don't you?"

"He says he's fine. Seems to be taking this in stride, tell you the truth. Kid may end up working in law enforcement. Me? I may die young of heart failure from worrying about those boys." He put his spoon down and looked at me. "You know, sometimes I envy your freedom."

"I may not have kids to worry about, but I have Hitchcock. He can be a handful."

"You're comparing my kids to a cat?"

"Not really. Honestly, I think you're handling this situation remarkably well. And Melanie didn't demand that y'all come straight back home. That's good."

"Well, she tried, but I said no."

"At least the sheriff didn't tell Matt not to leave town."

Nick paused with a spoonful of ice cream in midair. "Not in so many words, but he knew we planned to see the concert. His parting comment didn't leave me feeling warm and fuzzy."

"What'd he say?"

"Don't leave town without checking in with me first."

• • •

I tried to sleep that night but I couldn't get comfortable. The cottage's air conditioner fought hard to cool the humid air. My gown stuck to my clammy skin. After the first dozen times I flopped around and switched sides, Hitchcock gave up on me and left the bed.

I had missed a call from Luke earlier, and I wanted to be awake when he came to pick up the guys in the morning. That was looking less and less likely the longer I went without sleep, but I couldn't quit thinking about Marty Dixon. What had he done to make someone decide to kill him? Who had the opportunity to do such a thing?

Gary Weber, for instance. Where was he at the time of the murder? I felt sure he had a lot of money at stake, as did Colt Jamison. Dixon might have had something up his sleeve—something that would harm Jamison's reputation and Weber's wallet.

And what about Charlotte from the pizza shop? Why was she crying as she left the sheriff's office? Had he accused her of something or did she, like Rosales, have some unfounded fear that someone *might* accuse her?

I couldn't forget Tracey. Did she honestly think her brother had wandered into the woods and killed a man? Then there was that scruffy singer—Zeke—who'd met Jamison down by the river. There had to be a country music lyric in there. *Down by the river . . .*

I flipped over again and yanked the sheet with me. Ten seconds later I knew it was no use. I got up and threw on some clothes, then slid my feet into flip-flops. I dragged myself into the living room and turned on a lamp.

"Hey, Hitchcock?" He wasn't on the sofa where I expected to find him. I turned in a circle, scanning the room. "I'm going to bake. Wanna come?"

No answering meow.

I sighed. One day Hitchcock and I might have our own house with our very own kitchen. Baking at Aunt Rowe's during the night was an awkward habit, one that kept her from having complete privacy in her own home. Not that she minded me taking advantage of the space. Still, a woman should be free to run out to the kitchen in her underwear if she wanted to. That wouldn't happen so long as I popped in at odd times of the day or night.

I didn't see Hitchcock and decided he must already be out and scouting around. I opened the door and the heat of the night enveloped me. Using the flashlight app on my phone to guide me, I checked around my cottage for Hitchcock and didn't find him. His feline instinct would probably guide him to Aunt Rowe's house before I finished. We'd done this many times before.

I hadn't made it very far when I heard music. I stopped walking. Someone was singing. I waited for a few seconds, then walked in the direction of the sound. I spotted the outline of a man seated on the rock where I often go to sit and think. The boulder jutted out of the riverbank and made a perfect place to ponder life's challenges.

I grew closer and realized the man held a pad and pencil. But that wasn't all he held—he had a cat in his lap.

Hitchcock.

The man—Colt Jamison, I realized—wore shorts and tennies with a dark-colored shirt and cap. I didn't think he could hear me because of the rushing water, and I didn't want him to fall into the river if I took him by surprise. I paused for a few moments and thought about the man who wrote songs like I wrote books. He seemed ordinary, not a person interested in all the hoopla. Not like an untouchable country superstar.

Enough of that, Sabrina.

I took a few steps forward and made kitty-calling noises. Hitchcock looked in my direction. The man turned toward me as I neared.

"Hi there," I said. "Sorry to interrupt. I was missing my cat. Again."

"Seems like he gives you a lot of trouble," Jamison said.

"Who, Hitchcock? Nah. He's a special cat, and I'm willing to put up with a lot when it comes to him." Hitchcock looked up into Jamison's face as the man stroked his back. "Look at him," I said. "He's like an adoring fan."

"Yeah."

"You're sitting on my thinking rock."

"Excuse me?"

"I call it the thinking rock, and it works real well when I'm stuck and staring at a blank page. That's when I come out here and sit and think. Eventually the words flow."

"What words?" he said.

"Oh, in my novels." I felt a momentary flush of shyness. "I write mysteries."

"Then I've picked a good place," he said. "Maybe your thinkin' rock can work some magic for me."

"Having trouble with a song?"

"Yes, ma'am," Colt said. "Words aren't flowin' like they should."

"Not yet," I said. "Give it some time, and you'll probably get them perfect."

"Thanks for believin' in me."

I paused and thought about how this opportunity might not come again. "You're probably stressed like everyone else about what happened to Marty Dixon."

"Absolutely," he said in what sounded like a sincere tone. "They find what happened to him yet?"

I shook my head. "No, and I can't help wondering if he had trouble with someone lately. Just because this happened here in Lavender doesn't mean that a local person is guilty. Maybe trouble followed him here."

"I'm sure that's possible," he said.

"Do you know of any trouble Dixon had in Nashville? Any enemies? Fights with anyone that you know of?"

"Sorry, but there's nothin' I can say to help figure that out. I'm off on my own most of the time. Writin' songs, practicing, on the road."

"Did you hear the rumor about Marty writing a song?" I said, playing this by ear.

"No, ma'am, I didn't."

I was pushing my luck with this man—a celebrity many people would be fawning over right now, and here I was interrogating the poor guy.

"I understand his mother lives here in Lavender," I said. "Did he happen to say anything about family to you?"

Colt snapped his fingers. "Now that you mention it, he did say something about his mom. He didn't want to see her. Didn't plan to go by the house to say hey. Nothing."

"Do you have any idea why that was?"

"Nope." He thought for a moment, continuing to stroke Hitchcock's back. "The girlfriend was a different story."

"Girlfriend?" I hadn't heard one thing about a woman.

"Yes, ma'am. Marty had a girl here. Didn't catch her name, but his face lit up whenever he talked about her. He couldn't wait to come and see her again. I got the feeling it had been a while."

"How long?" I said.

"Don't know, but I'm sure she's the reason he pushed so hard to bring the tour to the Hill Country and right to her back door here in Lavender."

Chapter 20

In spite of my restless night, I was up, showered, and dressed early. When Luke's pickup rolled into Aunt Rowe's driveway a little before six, I was there to greet him. He slid out of the truck and gathered me into his arms. I inhaled the scent of his citrusy cologne and minty toothpaste and was happy I'd gotten out of bed.

"I *like* this welcoming committee," he said. "What got you up and at 'em so early?"

"You," I said.

And the fact that I can't quit thinking about a dead man and his mystery girlfriend who might have had a reason to commit murder.

Luke took my face in his hands, dipped his head, and gave me a deep kiss. When he backed away, he said, "I've missed you. After your relatives head home, we should make plans to spend more time together."

"I like that idea." I grinned.

Luke looked at the dark house. "Are the guys up?"

"I think I heard some rumbling around." I took his arm and moved toward the door. "While you wait, how about a piece of the blueberry coffee cake I made last night?"

More like in the wee hours of this morning.

"Wouldn't risk hurting your feelings by saying no," he said.

We walked into the quiet kitchen. The sounds of someone moving around drifted out from the bedrooms. Hitchcock was at his dish, crunching on his breakfast, and glanced up at us briefly. I took out a dessert plate and cut Luke a piece of cake while he helped himself to a cup of coffee.

"What do you hear about the murder investigation?" he said.

"The latest thing is about the girl who was with Matt when they found the body," I said. "Sheriff says she's missing."

"Missing?" Luke turned away from the coffeepot, holding his cup. "Any idea what happened to her?"

I told him what the guys had reported from their meeting with the sheriff. "When I saw Tandee, she had every appearance of a woman intent on attracting more Colt Jamison fans to cheer him on this weekend."

"She may return to do that. She could be off running an errand or back home with her brother by now."

"True." I wondered if the sheriff had solid evidence to arrest Tandee on a drug-related charge. "The other news is that Marty Dixon had a girlfriend here in Lavender. I have no clue who she is."

"Where'd you hear about her?"

I wanted to tell Luke about Jamison in spite of Aunt Rowe's instructions to keep the singer's presence a secret, but not now when the boys might burst into the room at any moment.

"Some men from the concert crew were at the Wild Pony last night."

A true statement.

"You went over there looking for Rosales." Luke looked down, shaking his head. "One second after telling you I saw her, I wished I hadn't. At the very least, I could have offered to meet you there."

Luke had once rescued me from an aggressive guy trying to put a move on me at the Wild Pony, and he didn't like my going to that place by myself.

"I went and made it back intact," I said. "Nothing to worry about. I saw Rosales, and she was working the case as you thought. I talked to a couple of people who were at that book club meeting the other day, then came home."

"Uh-huh." He took a forkful of the cake. "Will you do me a favor?"

"What is it?" I said.

He paused as though choosing his next words carefully, then settled on, "Take advantage of the day and write while the guys are out with me? Hitchcock would be happy to sit by your computer and supervise. Wouldn't you, Hitchcock?"

The cat looked up at us. "Mrreow."

"See?" Luke said with a smile.

"I do need to get some writing done."

I grabbed another plate and cut myself a piece of cake. Today *would* be a perfect day to concentrate on my work. I hadn't given my manuscript one thought, though, not with all of the questions flying around in my head, the biggest being who was Marty Dixon's mystery girlfriend? I tried a bite of the coffee cake.

"This is pretty good, don't you think?" I said, changing the subject.

"Yes, ma'am," Luke said. "Say, about how many words would you say you can write in an average day?"

"Depends." I put my fork down on my plate. "Why do you ask?"

"When I drop the guys off this evening, I'll check back. See how you did with your word count."

A jolt of panic zipped through me. I forced a smile. "Just what I need. An enforcer."

"That sounds harsh," he said. "I'd rather be called an encourager."

• • •

I walked into Hot Stuff at seven and sat at my usual table. Opened my laptop. "Stayin' Alive" by the Bee Gees played over the sound system, and I bopped my head in time with the music. A list of questions ran in a continuous loop through my head. It was early, though, and much of the world was still in bed. My questions about the murder of Marty Dixon could hold for the next hour or two as I reacquainted myself with the plot outline for my third Carly Pierce novel.

Max knew that when I brought my laptop with me I was off-limits for idle chitchat. He didn't tarry when he brought me a steaming cup of coffee. I sat with my back toward the majority of the tables and slipped into writer mode.

I had decided to work on my proposal for Kree rather than revisions to my draft of *Grave Pursuit*, my second Carly Pierce book. I needed a long block of time for that project, and this morning was better suited to a simpler and shorter task. Plot points for book three had simmered in my head for a good month now, and I hoped for words to spill out onto the page once I got started. Best case, I'd have something concrete to satisfy Luke's question about word count.

An hour into my work, a threesome of teenage girls sat at the table nearest me. I could hardly remember what it felt like to be their age, all giggly and concerned about appearances. They wore shorts and shirts that had the fit of expensive clothes, along with brand-name shoes that I'd guess had set their parents back a pretty penny. One of the girls wore pink-framed glasses with a Kate Spade logo on the earpiece. I turned my attention back to my laptop and added pink glasses as a tag for one of the characters in my story.

"I'm staking out my spot in line tonight," Pink Glasses said to her friends.

"The show's not for another thirty-six hours," the girl to her left said in a squeaky voice. "You'll freakin' melt. It's like a hundred degrees out."

"The forecast says a high of ninety-two," Pink Glasses said, "and they have shade trees over there."

"I'll go with you," the third chimed in. "I'll go crazy if you get a better seat than I do."

"Our seats are together, silly." This from Squeaky. "It won't matter. The show won't start for at least an hour after we get in the gate."

"I hope we're close enough for Colt to see me," Girl Three said in a dreamy tone.

"Like he'll care," Squeaky said. "He'll probably bring his girl-friend with him."

A possibility, but he's all by himself for now.

"Bet he likes blondes with long legs, and no braces," Squeaky said.

I stole a glance at the dreamy-voiced girl, a short brunette with braces. She stared daggers at Squeaky, and I wondered why many young girls acted so mean, even to their own friends.

"Well, I'm going to win the backstage meeting," Dreamy Girl said, "and you'll go crazy jealous."

"*I'm* going to win," Pink Glasses said.

"No way," Squeaky said. "I bought three tickets." She held up three fingers stacked with rings. "Count 'em. *Three.*"

"That doesn't guarantee you're the winner," Dreamy Girl said in a whine. "It only means you're the one who had three hundred dollars cash when we didn't. We have as good a chance of that personal meeting with Colt as you do."

They had succeeded in stealing my focus, so I turned to them.

"Excuse me," I said.

The girls turned toward me in unison.

"Yeah?" Pink Glasses said.

"I couldn't help but hear you discussing tickets. Were there tickets other than the concert ticket itself up for sale?"

Blank stares.

"My nephews are Jamison fans," I said, "but I don't think they knew about these special tickets. Winning a personal meeting would put them over the moon."

They exchanged glances with each other, like the last thing in the world they wanted was more competition in the contest of who might get to meet their idol face-to-face. "It's more of a thing for girls," Pink Glasses said.

"Is that a rule of the contest?" I said. "Girls only?"

Dreamy Girl shook her head. "Anyone can buy a ticket."

"Anyone with cash," Squeaky said. "They don't take credit cards, and they're a hundred bucks a ticket."

"Where can I buy these tickets?" I said.

"The fan club president sold them to us," she said.

I might have guessed. I wondered if there would be a real contest, or if Tandee was selling these supposed tickets for additional drug money.

"Any idea where I might find this president?" I said.

"If she's not at the Wild Pony," Squeaky said, "she might be out at Beckman Vineyards. That's where we saw her."

"When did you see her there?"

Another exchanged glance. "Like yesterday," Squeaky said. "In the afternoon."

"Are there other things she's selling?" I said, thinking of Tandee's alleged drug issue.

Squeaky exchanged a glance with Pink Glasses that seemed a bit furtive, but maybe I was reading too much into it.

"She has bumper stickers and keychains," Dreamy Girl said. "They're free."

I wondered if these girls knew anything about Marty Dixon, or if they would care. Probably not. Their biggest problems in life were getting a good position in line for the show and winning the contest. I decided I'd rather not prolong the discussion with them.

"Thanks for the info," I said and turned back to my laptop. Matt hadn't mentioned the hundred-dollar tickets, and I didn't think he would have kept that information to himself. Maybe Tandee had walked him away from the crowd the other night to make her pitch about his buying a ticket for the personal meeting with Colt Jamison contest. Then she saw the body and the tickets were never mentioned.

My focus on my story was totally broken, so I packed up my laptop. I sent a text to the sheriff to let him know about my possible tip that Tandee might be found at the winery. I couldn't see her sitting out there waiting to be found, but stranger things had happened. I might make a trip out there myself to talk to the workers I'd seen with Rosales the night before.

On my way out of the shop I spotted Violet Howe in a booth near the door. The life coach wore a purple and hot pink floral dress that coordinated nicely with the purple streak and pink feather in her hair. She caught my eye, and I couldn't be rude and leave without acknowledging her.

I stopped by her booth and noticed the teal folder on the table — one of her "discovery packets."

"Hi, Violet. You're out and about early."

"So are you," she said. "I'm here to meet with a client. If you want to work with me while I'm in town, you should reserve a spot. They're filling up fast."

"I've been so busy," I said.

She tipped her head. "We don't need to discuss your cat in our sessions. People come to me for all sorts of things, personal, business, family issues, anything at all they need coaching on. Don't you believe you could benefit from working with me?"

"I'm a believer," I said. "If you can turn Twila Baxter around, you can help anyone, only I'm not feeling the need—"

I paused because Violet was looking at a spot over my shoulder. I turned to see Bruno Krause standing behind me and holding two cups of coffee.

"Hello, Sabrina." He looked at my tote. "Are you here writing this morning?"

"I was, but it's getting a little too loud to focus." Most of the seats in the shop were filled and "Billie Jean" came over the speakers, playing a couple notches too loud.

"I'm surprised you're not out discussing the murder case with the sheriff," Bruno said.

"We did that yesterday," I said. "I'm sure he'd like to see less of me." I had mentioned to the book club that talking with the sheriff helped me with plotting. Bruno didn't need to know how much time I spent dwelling on actual cases. "I'm surprised you're not at your shop selling pizza."

"Everybody needs a little downtime." Bruno smiled at Violet, and I realized he was the person meeting with her. I was blocking his path to the booth, so I backed up.

He placed the coffee cups on the table. "Do you know my friend Violet?"

"I do. She's staying at the cottages." His description of Violet as a friend didn't escape me, and I took that to mean he didn't want to advertise his meeting with a life coach.

I looked at Bruno. "I believe this is the first time I've ever seen you away from the pizza shop."

"I've practically been wasting my life away there," he said. "Today I decided Charlotte and Fritz can handle things."

"Good for you," I said. "Fritz is your son-in-law?"

He nodded. "Right."

"Noah's father."

"That's right." He slid into the booth and took the lid off his cup.

My phone buzzed, and I pulled it from my pocket to see that Tyanne was calling.

"Excuse me, I need to get this," I told Violet and Bruno. "Y'all have a nice day."

I opened the door and was outside when I answered. "Hi there. I was thinking about dropping in this morning."

"Weren't you already here?" she said.

"This morning? No."

"Oh, I thought you came by to drop Hitchcock off."

"No. He's at home."

"Think again, Sabrina. I'm looking at him as we speak."

Chapter 21

I felt naïve for believing that Hitchcock had abandoned his habit of hitching rides into town when I turned my back. I'd had many conversations with the cat about being a bad boy. I'd told him a thousand times how dangerous it was for him to go off on his own, all to no avail. I wondered if Violet was the person he'd hitched a ride with this time.

No need to go back and question the woman about the cat. He was so good at slipping into cars unnoticed that she probably didn't realize she had a hitchhiker. If she was the person he rode into town with I'd probably never know. I hurried over to Knead to Read. When I walked into the bookstore, Ethan pointed to the front windowsill, where Hitchcock sat with Zelda and Willis.

I walked over to the cats. Willis was busy kneading the multicolored knotted rag rug they loved to lay on. Hitchcock gave me his most innocent look through slitted eyes. "If you wanted a playdate with your friends you should have asked me."

"Mrreow."

"Well, it's a little late at this point." I turned around and blew out a breath. "I swear."

Ethan laughed. "My mom says males don't change. What you see is what you get."

I grinned. "And you think this goes for cats, too?"

"Seems like it does," Ethan said. "Anyway, I'm glad he came here, 'cause I wanted to ask you something."

"About what?" I went over and leaned against the counter.

"You know how I saw Deputy Rosales arguing with Marty Dixon the other night?"

I straightened, wary about this line of conversation. "I remember."

"Well, she's not at work," he said. "Don't you think that's really weird? I mean, she's always working."

"I know."

"What's going on with her? You don't think—" He paused and lowered his voice. "Do you think she did something to that guy?"

Tyanne came around the counter, wearing a lime green sundress with turquoise accents and matching turquoise Crocs sandals.

She focused her stern expression on Ethan. "Don't ever forget I have the bionic hearing of a mom."

"Yes, ma'am," he said, "I mean no, ma'am."

"Of course, Deputy Rosales didn't commit a crime," she continued. "She's a law enforcement officer, and I don't know that I've ever seen one more fierce about upholding the law."

"I have to agree with Tyanne," I said. "Rosales is a straight arrow."

Ethan shook his head and muttered, "You didn't hear her. She had a personal beef with that guy. What if the sheriff figured that out and, I don't know, maybe fired her?"

I glanced at Tyanne and back to Ethan. "She's not fired. She took a few personal days off."

"That would be a relief to know," he said, "if that's true."

"I wouldn't repeat any of this to anyone," I said. "I don't think Sheriff Crawford would appreciate us talking about his people, and I sure don't want us to get on Deputy Rosales's bad side."

"Yes, ma'am," Ethan said, "I mean, no, whatever, you know what I mean."

The bell over the door jingled, and Billie Spengler whooshed in with the light scent of a fragrance that reminded me of vanilla. "Reporting for duty," she said. "Hello, Sabrina."

"Hi, Billie."

Tyanne's grandmotherly employee was the cheeriest senior I knew. She had a pretty head of snow white curls and wore a simple white shirt over light blue slacks. Tyanne and Ethan greeted Billie, and she walked behind the counter to stash her purse.

"I heard some troubling news this morning," she said with an uncharacteristic frown.

Tyanne looked up from book order notes she was making on a tablet. "What's that, Billie?"

"Deputy Salazar—the new guy—is questioning my neighbor's girl, Elise, about the murder. Called her up and told her to come over to the sheriff's office this morning."

"Billie," I said, "Don't worry about this. Elise was there the morning that Marty Dixon drove up to the pizza shop and a fight broke out. She's a witness."

"Yeah," Ethan said. "She made it into the video."

"What video?" Ty said.

Ethan pulled out his phone. "I can show you."

Oh, Lord. We didn't need to see that right now.

I made a slashing motion with my hand, and he put the phone away.

"Elise is only one of the dozens of witnesses that Sheriff Crawford is talking to," I said.

Unless she happens to be Marty Dixon's girlfriend.

Once the idea came to me, I couldn't turn it loose. Elise was about the right age for Dixon. She had acted like she wanted Tracey to stop fighting with him, and I had assumed she'd wanted to save Tracey from getting in trouble. She might have been trying to save her boyfriend from getting beat up by Tracey. Did that make sense?

Where did that leave me when considering the girlfriend as the killer? If Elise had wanted to save Dixon in the afternoon, something drastic would have had to change to make her want to kill him that same night. Then again, maybe she wasn't the girlfriend at all. I hadn't seen any kind of connection between the two—no furtive glance, no words exchanged. Not a smile or a wink. I would have noticed, wouldn't I?

"I'm sure Sheriff Crawford will do the right thing," Tyanne told Billie. "Don't worry."

The bell over the door sounded, and this time a group of shoppers entered. I picked up Hitchcock and took him with me to the store's break room. He lapped at the cats' water bowl. I helped myself to a bottled water, cracked it open, and took a long swallow.

Elise had never made the suspect list I had running in my head. Tracey had, along with her brother Chester, and Gary Weber. Maybe Jamison, but I didn't see the singer venturing far from the Athens cottage. I had seen his truck returning from somewhere, though. Where had he gone? For a short ride, just to get out? Even a short trip to the nearest convenience store could result in a mass invasion of fans if he was spotted. I didn't think he would risk it, nor could I imagine the soft-spoken man killing for any reason.

Elise might be a different story—but I didn't know if she was a girlfriend, much less a person with a motive to kill.

Tyanne came in and pulled a chair out from the kitchen table. She plopped down and looked at me. "So now everybody is worrying about a different suspect. For Ethan it's Rosales, and Billie has Elise. Who're you worrying about?"

I pulled out my own chair and sat across from her. "Definitely not Rosales."

She raised her brows. "As many times as she's picked on you, I'd think you'd be glad to throw her under the bus."

I shook my head. "She had a history with Marty Dixon, but she didn't kill him."

"What history?"

"She didn't tell me the details."

"Oh, you've talked to her about this? Are you investigating her?"

"I'm not, but we *did* talk. I'm going to help her—"

"You're *what*?" Tyanne leaned into the table and stared at me. "There must be something wrong with my hearing."

"I'm not supposed to be talking about this," I said.

"Says who?" Tyanne said. "The enemy deputy who loves giving you the evil eye?"

"She's different now," I said. "She's concerned."

"About what?"

"You have to swear nobody else is going to hear any of this. Pinkie swear?" I placed my elbow on the table and offered my pinkie finger.

"We're not ten years old anymore," Ty said, but she linked her pinkie with mine anyway. "What's going on?"

"Since I last saw you, a lot."

"Apparently. You're in a video?"

"That happened before I was here yesterday, only I didn't find out about it until later. It's a video of the fight Tracey Powell had with Marty Dixon. Elise was there in the crowd, and so was I."

"I see," Tyanne said.

"Ethan heard Rosales arguing with Dixon, and he's concerned because she was, in his words, mad enough to kill."

Ty backed up. "Whoa, that sounds bad."

"I don't think it meant anything except that she was angry and spouting off. She was fine with Dixon living in Nashville, only she didn't want to see him here—or anywhere near her—ever again. That's my take."

"For anyone who cares to listen."

"The sheriff cares what I have to say, but I don't want to talk about Rosales to him. He called me in to see if I had any leads on the murder that would help him, so he places some value on my opinion."

"That's nice to know," Ty said.

"He talked to Nick and Matt and told them that the president of the fan club is using the money she makes to buy—or sell—drugs. We're not sure which, and she's missing at the moment. She was telling kids their money was to pay for some VIP fan club membership and/or a ticket to win a personal meeting with Colt Jamison. I'm pretty sure that's a total scam."

I paused, and Tyanne waited without comment.

"Tracey Powell is drinking too much and worried about her brother Chester—who always drank too much—because she's afraid he doesn't remember where he was at the time of the murder. He might have wandered into the woods and killed Dixon with no memory of the event."

"That's very worrisome," Ty agreed.

"Rosales was out at the Wild Pony last night, pretending to be just another woman in a bar and talking with Jamison's road crew. I'm not sure if she turned up anything useful. I, on the other hand, heard last night that Marty Dixon had a girlfriend here in Lavender, but I don't know who she is or if she had a reason to kill him."

"Is that all?" Ty said.

I shook my head. "There's a rumor that Marty Dixon wrote 'Broken Mirror.' Crazy people are throwing pieces of broken mirrors around on the street. Oh yeah, on a personal note, Luke took Nick and the boys out this morning for a day-in-the-life-of-a-game-warden day. And wait a second. I forgot the most relevant part. Rosales isn't working right now because she has a history with Marty Dixon—and I gather it's a bad history that she doesn't really want anyone to know, including me. So she's actually working, but on her own time. And she's looking to me—in a very roundabout way—to help her solve the case so that she doesn't get in trouble or have to tell anyone about this trouble she had with Dixon in the past."

"Oh. My. Lord." Tyanne slumped in the chair.

"Yeah," I said.

"What was the trouble about?"

"I don't know."

"You're a very good fiction writer," Ty said. "Is that what all of this was right now?"

I shook my head. "Nope. All true."

"That's what I was afraid of. I especially don't like the talk of drugs being sold here in town."

Ty had three young kids, and I was also concerned for them.

"Assuming you're going to continue looking into this, which I know you are," Ty said, "where on earth will you start?"

I let out a big sigh. "At the beginning. With the victim's life. I think I should pay a visit to Marty Dixon's mother."

Chapter 22

I wanted more than to quiz Wanda Dixon about the details of her son's life. I wanted to visit the grieving mother to pay my respects. She'd suffered a huge loss, maybe even more so because she'd been out of touch with Marty. My heart ached for the woman even though we had not yet met.

Tyanne knew where Wanda lived and offered to go with me. She could deliver a crafting book Wanda had ordered from her and hadn't picked up yet. She pulled the book from the "hold" shelf and placed it in a sack to take with us. I knew the real reason Tyanne offered to go along. She liked the investigation process of finding puzzle pieces and putting them together. She also thought of herself as a protector of sorts. I'd been known to get myself into some tight spots. A few times she'd been there with me, and her husband Bryan was no fan of mine for that reason. I wondered if she planned to accompany me all day long.

Hitchcock came with us—no way was I leaving him behind to skulk around town without supervision. I made a quick stop at the vet's office to buy a backup harness for my cat. Tyanne asked me to stop at the bakery, where she picked up a box of their scrumptious assorted muffins.

Wanda Dixon's home was situated on Pike Creek Road about five miles out of town. Tyanne pointed out the mailbox that marked the turn tucked into pink flowering oleander bushes, and I took the curvy driveway. We reached the house about half a mile in—white brick with a second-floor balcony and a covered front porch that held a couple of rockers. There were no cars in sight and no obvious tracks leading to a barn set back quite a distance from the house.

I pulled my car into a spot near the front sidewalk. "The place looks deserted."

"She's not the type of person to hang up a welcome sign and have pots of petunias on the porch," Ty said, "but we probably should have called ahead."

"We're here now," I said. "If she's home, she'll have heard us pull up."

"Mrreow," Hitchcock said.

Tyanne laughed. "Curiosity and the cat. He definitely wants to go in."

"Then let's go."

I carried Hitchcock as we approached the front door, though a dog on the premises would have made itself known by now. The porch rockers were covered with thick dust. Half a dozen pots held dried-up remains of dead plants. Someone who lived here had planted flowers in the distant past.

I didn't see a bell and knocked on the front door with my free hand. After a ten-second wait, I heard movement inside.

"Who's there?" came a scratchy voice.

Tyanne looked at me. "Wanda? It's Tyanne Clark from Knead to Read. I brought the book you ordered from us."

The door opened with more force than I expected, and a thin woman with spiky blonde hair and readers perched on her nose stared at us. She wore tan capris with a short-sleeved orange top made of crocheted squares that looked too warm for the weather.

"Which book?" she said.

"May we come in, Wanda?" Tyanne said. "This is my friend Sabrina."

Wanda leaned forward and focused on Hitchcock. "Is this the bad luck cat? I heard all kinds of stories about him."

"Mrreow," Hitchcock said.

I hadn't come out here to be turned away because of the dumb legend. "His name is Hitchcock," I said. "He's *not* bad luck at all."

The woman's laugh sounded like a cackle that for some reason made me think of the story about Hansel and Gretel. "Of course he's not bad luck," Wanda said, "but that's what they call him. I heard how he saved you out at the rodeo a while back."

I nodded, relieved. "That's right. He sure did."

Wanda moved aside and motioned for us to come in. The foyer held an antique hall tree and an ornate grandfather clock. A formal dining room table and chairs sat behind closed French doors to our left. The colorful rug we stood on felt plush under my feet.

Wanda motioned to us. "This way. Watch your step."

Once we moved away from the foyer, I saw the reason for her warning. I followed Tyanne on a narrow path into the living room. Except for the path, the entire floor was covered with boxes, stacked plastic bins, and large baskets filled with skeins of yarn of every color imaginable. Hundreds of them. Maybe thousands if we counted what I guessed was inside the cardboard boxes that were still sealed.

Tyanne turned to look at me, and I raised my eyebrows.

The yarn was divided by color groups. We passed shades of yellow, then orange, red, rust, cranberry, and so forth. We trekked on into the living room, where Wanda walked to the sofa and with a whoosh of her arm swept aside a heap of what looked like little baby caps in a multitude of colors. Wanda turned to us. "Have a seat."

Tyanne thrust out the box she'd carried in. "We brought you some muffins. There's an assortment. I, we, were so sorry to hear about the loss of your son."

I nodded my agreement, but Wanda didn't notice. She practically grabbed the muffins out of Tyanne's hand and dropped the box on the coffee table, where it scattered the variety of knitting and crocheting magazines. I lurched forward to stop them from avalanching into a basket of lime green yarn.

"Too late to be sorry," Wanda said. "Lost him years ago when he took off to Nashville. Didn't have the common decency to keep up with me. Hardly ever called, only if he wanted something. Usually money."

My heart went out to her. Maybe she'd held out hope that her son would turn over a new leaf—only now it was too late for Marty ever to change.

"I'm sorry to hear he wasn't a better son," I said, "and that he moved away to Nashville. Was he a musician?"

"Tried to be," Wanda said, "though he didn't have a speck of the talent his father had. My late husband was the musical one."

Tyanne sat down on the sofa, and I sat beside her with Hitchcock in my lap. I wondered about the alleged rumor that Wanda claimed Marty wrote "Broken Mirror." She didn't seem inclined to repeat the story to us. Maybe the rumor was only that—a rumor.

Wanda dropped into a chair to our left and picked up the crocheting that sat beside her. She straightened the pumpkin orange yarn, and her nimble fingers began working the crochet hook. She was making something round, and the circle quickly grew larger.

"Do you live here alone?" I said.

"Seems like it," she said. "My second husband likes to stay out back. Calls it his man cave."

Ty said, "My Bryan has one of those, too. Used to be our garage."

As we talked, Hitchcock eyed the containers filled with yarn like a small child might view the assortment of rides at an amusement park.

"Go ahead and let the cat down," Wanda said. "He wants to nose around."

"I'm not sure that's the best idea."

She waved a hand. "Oh, go on. It'll be nice to see somebody happy around here for a change."

I wasn't sure how to respond to that, so I did what she suggested and unhooked the leash from Hitchcock's harness. He didn't waste any time. After sniffing at the contents of the two closest containers, he bounded into the small spaces between containers like a deer bounding through a field.

The moves brought a laugh from Wanda. "See? He's having a ball."

I wasn't worried about Hitchcock hurting the piles of yarn, but the mantel and built-ins on either side of the fireplace were crowded with delicate knickknacks and framed photos. I hoped Hitchcock steered clear of them.

Wanda turned her attention from the cat and focused on us. "Why are you really here?"

"Your book." Tyanne pulled the bookstore sack from her handbag and handed it to Wanda. "The one you ordered. *Weird and Wacky Crocheted Animals.*"

Wanda took the book from Tyanne and pulled off the sack. The book cover showed a frog, a monkey, and a cat.

"Those look cute," I said. "The little baby caps are cute, too. You must have a plan for so many of them."

"I donate them to the hospital," Wanda said, before placing her new book on top of the coffee table magazines. "For the newborns."

From the sheer quantity of caps, I wondered if she were making donations to all the hospitals in Texas.

"Need to keep my fingers busy," she said. "Makes me feel useful. Speaking of which, can I bring you ladies something to drink? Coffee? Tea? Lemonade?"

"I'm fine." Tyanne shook her head.

I gave her a slight nod and said, "I'd love some coffee."

"On second thought," Tyanne said, "maybe I'll have a cup as well."

"I have some made," Wanda said and left the room.

Tyanne whispered, "What do you have up your sleeve?"

"I want to see those pictures. Then I'm gonna ask the tough questions."

I sidestepped the yarn containers and went to check the pictures on the fireplace mantel. Hitchcock sniffed around cardboard boxes at my feet as if he suspected a mouse hid inside. Next to a crystal vase that held blue silk hydrangeas sat a picture of a wedding party back in the day when bridesmaids wore floppy hats. The bride was a small woman — Wanda, I assumed.

In the center of the mantel an ornate crystal-framed mirror leaned against the fireplace brick. Next to it, the flame of a battery-operated pillar candle flickered, then came another picture with a wedding cake in the background. This one of an older Wanda with a different groom. If I ever married again, I didn't plan to keep a wedding picture from my first wedding on display.

I turned to the pictures lining the shelves. They told a story of a lone little blond boy growing older through the years with no apparent siblings. I gathered that Marty was most likely Wanda's only child. In this supposed timeline of Marty Dixon's life, yet another wedding picture appeared. This one of a groom who was undoubtedly Marty next to a lovely bride with flowing reddish hair.

"Psst," Tyanne said. "She's coming."

I picked my way back to the sofa and sat as Wanda returned with our coffees. Tyanne stacked magazines so there was room for Wanda to place the tray she carried on the coffee table.

After the three of us doctored our coffees the way we wanted them, I sat back against the sofa cushions, inhaled the warm, rich aroma and took a sip of coffee. Hitchcock was lying on his side on the fireplace hearth and batting at a skein of gray yarn.

"Wanda," I said, "I'm going to tell you why I've come here to see you."

"Spit it out," she said, "so I can get back to my work."

"I'm sure you've already spoken with the sheriff."

"I have."

"I hope you don't mind my asking you some questions about what happened and who might have done this to Marty."

"Why do you care?" she said.

"I didn't know your son, but I care that the right person is punished for what happened."

"Is that your job?"

"No, ma'am, it isn't. However, my nephew was one of the people who found your son. He, along with many other people, were nearby when the crime was discovered. All people who might be falsely accused if the killer goes free. I'm after the truth."

I stopped speaking to take another sip of coffee.

"Sabrina is very good at unraveling mysteries," Tyanne said. "She's helped the sheriff before with other mysteries."

"As you may already know, since you heard what happened out at the rodeo," I added.

Wanda didn't acknowledge my words. She fingered a partially made baby cap that sat on the chair next to her with a crochet hook looped through the yarn. After a minute, she said, "Go on."

I smiled and continued. "I know you've told us that Marty didn't stay in touch with you very well. When's the last time you saw him?"

She thought for a moment. "I'd say that was Mother's Day, not this year, but last."

Confirming what the sheriff had told me. "He came here to Lavender?"

"Yes, he did."

"Did he say anything about having trouble with anyone? Someone in Lavender? In Nashville? From his work? Anything at all?"

"That boy caused trouble wherever he went," she said.

"What do you mean?"

"He was disrespectful. Acted like he knew better than anyone else. He was an ungrateful, ungiving person."

"I'm sorry to hear that."

"I always wanted him to have a family," she said, "so that I could have the grandbabies I always wanted. But I know Marty wouldn't have been a good father any more than he could be a good husband or a good son."

"Marty was married?" I said.

"Was, then he got divorced." Wanda's voice caught on a sob. "Susan was a good woman, she would have been the perfect mother for my grandbabies, but he left her."

"I remember Susan," Tyanne said.

"You know she's remarried and has three children?" Wanda said. "Two girls and a boy."

Tyanne shook her head. "No, I didn't hear about them. She moved away, didn't she?"

Wanda nodded. "She lives in Georgetown, near Austin."

"Would there be any reason to believe Susan had an ax to grind with Marty?" I said. "Or maybe her new husband?"

"No," Wanda nearly shouted. "Don't you bring those good people into this mess."

"Okay, okay," I said. "I won't mention them again. How about any other people? Did Marty have old friends here in Lavender that he kept up with?"

"I doubt it."

"How about enemies? Did anyone pose a threat to your son?"

"You should ask the people in Nashville. They're the ones who saw my Marty from day to day. They would know."

"Now that you mention them," I said. "One of those people told me that Marty has a girlfriend here in Lavender."

"Girlfriend?" Wanda was on her feet and shouting. "A girlfriend? Here? Who is she?"

I tapped the air with my hand. "Calm down, please. I'm sorry, I didn't mean to excite you."

"Tell me who she is," Wanda said. "A mother should know these things."

"I don't know who she is," I said. "That's why I'm asking you."

From the corner of my eye I saw Hitchcock leap from the hearth to the fireplace mantel.

"I can't believe Marty had a woman," Wanda cried, "and he never told me."

"That's what I heard," I explained. "I don't know if it's true. I'm only asking you in case you knew of someone."

Hitchcock picked his way carefully around the framed pictures standing on the mantel.

"I need to meet this woman who held my Marty," Wanda said, "who comforted him when he needed comforting, who can comfort me now. Maybe we can bring comfort to each other."

The hopeful and forlorn tone of her voice tugged my heart strings. I moved toward her. "I'm so sorry I've upset you."

I decided not to mention the fact that I was asking about a girlfriend because she might have had a reason to murder Wanda's son.

"Hitchcock," Tyanne said, "don't—"

Too late.

When I looked up, Hitchcock stood on the mantel gnawing on the silk flowers while the crystal-framed mirror tumbled toward the floor. I took a wild leap and dove, barely missing the mirror as it fell.

You'd think the mountain of yarn would break the fall, but no such luck. The mirror struck the corner of a plastic container and cracked before sliding off a stack of yarn and landing on the floor.

Chapter 23

"I feel drained," I said, driving away from Wanda Dixon's house.

"Mrreow," Hitchcock said.

"You're the one who caused the trouble, you little scamp," I told him. "Now we have to see if we can find a beveled mirror to perfectly fit into that lady's antique frame. How're we gonna do that?"

"Mrr."

Tyanne stroked Hitchcock's head. "Sabrina's the one who decided to go over there. I had my doubts from the beginning."

I frowned. "Should have said so."

Ty looked at me. "Do you listen when I make recommendations? Ever?"

"I've probably listened to you a time or two." I drummed the steering wheel with my fingers. "I shouldn't have listened when Wanda told me to unleash Hitchcock."

"Who do you think will have the seven years of bad luck?" Ty said. "You, Hitchcock, me, Wanda, or all four of us?"

I glanced at her. "I'm not superstitious."

"Okay then. Let's put this event behind us and try to forget all about it. You're lucky the crystal frame around the mirror didn't break. That's irreplaceable."

I wasn't sure the frame had escaped unscathed. I'd have to inspect it for hairline fissures.

"What's your next move?" Ty said.

"Why? Are you going with me?"

Ty shook her head. "I believe I'm needed back at the store."

"Good excuse."

Ten minutes later, I dropped her outside Knead to Read. Tyanne opened her door to climb out.

I reached over and put a hand on her shoulder. "Seriously, Ty, thank you for going with me. I'm not sure I could have handled that visit on my own."

"You're welcome. I guess you didn't get much from Wanda. Maybe her husband could give you a different point of view on the situation."

"Do you know her husband?"

"I know who he is," she said. "His name's Ezekiel Farley. Wanda is still Dixon, by the way, she never took his name. The only thing I know about Zeke is he plays in a band, sometimes over at the Wild Pony.

Zeke, Mr. Scruffy. The singer.

I would never have placed a guy like that with Wanda Dixon.

"Thanks, Ty. I may talk to him at some point. Think I'll head over to Wagon Wheel Antiques. See if they can help me with the broken mirror."

"Good luck. Say hello to Twila for me."

• • •

The front porch theme at Wagon Wheel Antiques was obviously things with wheels. Everything from old and rusty Red Rider wagons to antique bicycles, a kids' John Deere tractor with pedals, and even a unicycle occupied the wide front porch.

I sat in my parked car and looked over at Hitchcock. "You are *not* coming off this leash while we're inside," I said. "Got it?"

"Mrreow," he said.

Based on the last time I'd seen Twila with her new hair color and clothes, I expected the interior of the antiques store to be updated as well. Of course, there's only so much updating a customer could reasonably expect in a place that specialized in all things old and collectible. I had hoped the ancient bowl of candy corn, the ghosts, and the fake spiderwebs would be gone. They weren't.

I walked in and didn't see anyone in the store.

"Hello," I called out.

"Why, hello, my dear," came the quavery reply, and Twila walked around an antique six-drawer chest that dwarfed her.

Today she wore a light pink top with gray slacks and a pair of stylish black sandals.

Twila said, "Welcome to you, Sabrina, and your special friend, Hitchcock. I'm so glad you've come to help me with my dear Connie."

I had also hoped she was past the issue of expecting her late husband Constantine to return from the grave. I took a step backward. "Hey, Twila. You look nice."

"Thank you, dear. Now, about Connie."

"Um, I thought you were working with the Chart Your Course lady, and I guess I assumed that was about finding your way for your own life, not looking back to your late husband."

"That's right," Twila said, "but he won't leave me alone."

I knew I should keep my mouth shut on the subject, but I couldn't help myself. "What's he doing this time? Did you tell him about your life changes?"

"He already knows. You see, he's watching me every day."

"Oh. I didn't know that."

"Don't you know he can see everything, being in that in-between state he's in?"

"No. Guess I didn't know the, um, rules, or whatever they're called." I looked at Hitchcock.

"Mrreow," he said.

Twila looked down at the cat. "That's a very good idea."

Say what?

"Mrreow."

"Okay," Twila said. "Thank you so much."

I didn't comment, and Twila moved on.

"So, Sabrina, is there something I can help you with?" She looked down at the package I held.

I was too stunned to remember what I'd come in for. Finally, I lifted my arm and remembered the mirror. I told Twila I was looking for a replacement mirror to fit a certain frame.

"Ernie is the one who could help you with that, but he's not here right now. You may leave your piece, and I'll bring it to his attention when he comes in."

I heard the noise of a loud motor approaching.

"Believe that's a truck I hear," Twila said. "Maybe it's Ernie."

It wasn't. Ernie's twin brother, Eddie, came in the back door from the warehouse followed by Chester Mosley. Eddie's expression, in my opinion, could only be described as smarmy. A slim man with unkempt hair, he was dressed in jeans with a shirt that had rolled-up short sleeves, James Dean style. Chester outweighed Eddie by at least a hundred pounds. I took it as a good sign that his eyes looked clear and his gait was steady.

Eddie grinned when he spotted me, but I didn't share his glad-to-see-you attitude. In my opinion, Eddie was the bad twin—he was the man Luke had saved me from at the Wild Pony when Eddie made a too-aggressive advance toward me.

"Are you here for the love seat?" Twila said.

"Yes'm," Chester said.

He came farther into the warehouse and spotted me. I could tell by the confused expression on his face that he wasn't placing me in this scenario.

"Hi, Chester. Sabrina. Remember me?"

He nodded. "Kind of," he said. "You came to see Tracey last night."

"Yes, I saw your sister," I said. "I didn't see you. Are you feeling better today?"

"I feel okay," he said, his expression unsure.

"You getting some furniture?" I said.

"Yup, for my office. Tracey's making me fix up the place. She's tryin' to get me to change my sloppy ways."

"Nice of her to help you," I said. "Sounds like she's giving you some good advice."

"Guess so."

Twila walked to her son. "Eddie, could you please come with me for a moment. I need a bit of help reaching something high up."

"Sure thing, Mom," Eddie said, and they walked out of sight.

Hitchcock leapt up on the arm of a chair next to where Chester stood, and the man jumped a foot. "Jeez, Louise—"

"That's only Hitchcock, my cat." I held the leash tighter to make sure Hitchcock didn't scare Chester off altogether. "I understand you were at the Wild Pony on the night Marty Dixon was killed."

"Ah, poor Marty," Chester whined. "I can't believe somebody killed him right after he apologized for everything."

"Everything being what?" I said.

"Huh?"

"What did he apologize for?"

"The thing with the concert, you know. What Tracey's so all-fired ticked about."

"You mean moving the concert out to Beckman Vineyards instead of having it at your place?"

"Yeah, that," Chester said. "He came purpose-like, to see me. To apologize."

"Very nice of him," I said.

Chester nodded and stuffed his hands in his pants pockets.

"Was that on Wednesday night?"

He looked at the ceiling for a moment. "Wednesday. Sure was."

"Are you certain of the day?"

"Yup. We were right there, in the woods, when he said 'Man, I'm sorry,' and I walked away 'cause I wasn't ready to say 'Nah, don't worry about it.' I might have said that later, but not right away."

"You were in the woods at the spot where his body was found?" I said.

"Yup," Chester said, "at least I think he was found there. I didn't find him, but they had the yellow tape strung up there."

"Sounds like the place he was found," I said.

Chester nodded again. "I thought it was a dream at first when he called. I didn't think there would be any apologizing."

"You mean he called, then he came over?"

"No. He was already there when he called and said to come out and meet him in the woods, so I did. Figured he didn't wanna come in and risk runnin' into my sister."

The back door thwacked into something, and Eddie Baxter strode into the room. He stared daggers at Chester.

"Dude! I told you not to talk about this to anyone, now I hear you tellin' this woman everything? What's wrong with you? They'll think you're a stone-cold killer."

Chapter 24

After Eddie Baxter chewed out Chester for telling me about his meeting with Marty Dixon on the night of Dixon's death, they loaded Chester's love seat into the bed of a pickup truck and drove away. A minute later, Eddie's twin brother, Ernie, the clean-cut twin, walked in through the back door. Ernie had a fresh haircut and wore his short-sleeved shirt tucked into starched khakis. He swiped his forehead with a handkerchief and greeted me with a smile.

"Mom tells me you need help with a broken mirror."

"That's right. It's this one here." I pointed to where I'd placed the mirror on the counter. "We had a little accident."

Ernie checked his watch and grimaced. "Please excuse me for one second. Be right back." Ernie returned to the warehouse and came back carrying an antique cane-backed chair that bore a tag marked *Sold* in black marker. He placed the chair at the end of the counter, reached underneath for a roll of Bubble Wrap, and placed the wrap on top of the chair.

"Sorry about that." He turned to me. "Have a customer on his way to pick up this chair and he's short on time."

"Not a problem," I said.

He looked at Wanda's mirror. "I'm happy to help someone fix a mirror for a change."

"What makes you say that?"

"A young man has been coming in here to buy mirrors. Any kind of mirror, he doesn't care. Heck, we might be sold out of mirrors now, and I'll be darned if I'm going to sell him a mirror from an antique dresser so he can smash it in the street. Ought to be a law against such craziness."

"I wish there was such a law," I said. "I've seen the road crews cleaning up all that mess. Who is this mirror-smashing trouble-maker?"

Ernie shrugged as he unclipped a tape measure from his waistband and measured Wanda's mirror. "Don't know him. I think he's an out-of-towner. Pays cash and doesn't give a name. To be honest, we don't ask for one when there's a cash purchase."

"You're saying he's buying mirrors simply to break them?"

"That's what I'm saying." Ernie nodded. "Crazy, huh?"

"Quite," I said. "Sheriff Crawford might want you to get a name if the guy comes back."

"I plan to. My bad that I didn't ask before now." Ernie looked down at the mirror I wanted repaired. "This isn't a standard size, but I have a great glass guy who'll be able to help you out."

"Oh, good. This belongs to Wanda Dixon, and I sure hate that we've added to her troubles."

Ernie glanced at a nearby settee, where Hitchcock lay sprawled as though he lived here. "Might I assume that this guy had something to do with the accident?"

Ernie knew Hitchcock, and I wasn't worried about him bringing up bad luck, but still. I sighed. "Unfortunately, yes. We went to pay our respects, and then this happened. I need to keep a closer eye on my cat. Like now, he shouldn't be leaving his hair all over your furniture. I meant to keep that leash in hand." I wasn't even sure when I'd relaxed my hold on the cat and hurried over to the settee to snatch Hitchcock up.

"I'm sure that piece has seen a lot worse," Ernie said. "If you want to leave Wanda's mirror, I can contact the glass man. Or I can give you his information."

"I have visitors in town this week. I'd be happy to pay you for handling the job, beginning to end."

"I'll take care of it." While Ernie filled out a form with my information, I tried to place him age-wise in relation to Marty Dixon.

"Are you familiar with the Dixon family?" I said.

Ernie nodded. "Know them well. Knew Marty, Sr., best. He passed at least ten years ago."

"Senior? So, the Marty who died this week was—"

"Marty, Jr.," Eddie said. "That boy was Senior's pride and joy. Good-lookin' young man, like his daddy was back in the day. Ladies' man."

"Senior or Junior?"

Ernie shrugged. "I'd say both of 'em. I can tell you I never attracted the ladies like either of those men. Now my brother Eddie, he's a different story. He has a knack."

A bad one, in my opinion. Eddie had a definite bad-boy vibe that Ernie didn't possess.

"The mirror job may be a week or more," he said. "Okay?"

"Whatever it takes," I said. "I want it back to good as new, if that's possible."

"Did Miss Wanda throw a fit when it happened?" Ernie asked.

I made a seesaw motion with my hand. "She wasn't happy, but she was focused on whether or not Marty had a girlfriend here in town. I'd heard he did, but Wanda didn't know anything about a woman. While she was going on about this alleged girlfriend, Hitchcock did his damage."

"Unless I'm mistaken, Marty hasn't been around much the past few years. If he has women, I'd look for them in Nashville."

"Women, plural?" I said.

Ernie nodded. "If he carries on the way he did when he lived here."

The door opened and a dark-haired man wearing a New York Mets baseball cap came in.

"You have the chair?" he said to Ernie, who was still filling out information related to fixing Wanda's mirror.

"Right there." Ernie nodded toward the antique chair. "After you inspect the chair, we'll wrap it up good for transporting."

"I'll just take it," the man said.

"You'll have to sign that you picked the chair up," Ernie said. "Make sure you have the right one and all."

"How do I know what she wants? I'm only the one with the truck."

"I thought you wanted to get on her good side," Ernie said. "Maybe send her a picture of the chair. You don't want to get home and find out it's the wrong one."

"*You* should know which freakin' one she wanted," the man said.

Ernie gave me an apologetic glance, then said, "I'll confirm that for you. Hang on a sec."

The man grunted his displeasure. "I don't have time to wait around."

"I'm finished here," I told Ernie, and took my claim check. "Thanks for the help."

I left him to deal with the disagreeable man.

After Hitchcock and I were out the door and back in the car, I noticed the Tower of Pizza logo on the pickup out front. The chair customer must have been Fritz, Bruno's son-in-law. I would have said hello to the man if I'd realized, or maybe not, given his bad mood. Thinking about him and pizza made me hungry. I looked at my watch.

"Time to eat," I said to Hitchcock. "How about we try the new taco stand."

"Mrreow," he said.

• • •

Take-a-Taco occupied a tiny building where the previous owner had sold sausage on a stick. The location for a take-out stand was perfect—near offices in the town square and the park. I'd heard the prior owner moved away to Amarillo, where he had family. I ordered three shredded chicken tacos—one with no sauce—and a lemonade and carried my lunch to a picnic table. A few teens occupied other tables, but most customers walked away with their Take-a-Taco sacks.

At our table, Hitchcock sat on the bench near me and licked his lips as I pulled chicken from the sauceless taco for him. Given the heat, I had carried water with me for Hitchcock. I took the bottle from my tote, along with a tiny bowl, and poured some for the cat.

As we ate, I thought over the morning's events. I wondered how Nick and the boys were faring on the game warden tour. Whether one or both of them would come back with grand ideas of becoming a game warden. They had each changed their career choices several times that I knew about. I wondered if Matt had more than a "pretend" interest in working as a profiler.

I thought about Deputy Rosales and what kind of deep dark secret she had that she didn't want the sheriff to find out. In my opinion, some personal information was better left to oneself. Sheriff Crawford might not agree when the secret keeper was one of his employees.

My thoughts drifted to Tracey and how serious she'd sounded when she asked me about the best way to kill someone without getting caught. What had we told her?

Make sure the body will never be found.

Whoever killed Dixon had not taken that advice. Possibly, the killer didn't have time to think about hiding the body. Or didn't have the strength to move the body, if the killer was a woman. No way to know that. Anyone might have taken Dixon by surprise and caused the neck wound that led to his death.

I took another bite of taco and chewed thoughtfully. Back to the girlfriend question. Ernie Baxter thought Dixon had been a ladies' man. He probably loved the bikini-clad girls in the group I'd seen following him to the pizza shop.

Aside from the teens and Tracey, who wasn't exhibiting any girlfriend tendencies, Elise and I had been the only other women outside on the lawn. Was Elise Marty Dixon's type? I didn't think so. I reminded myself that I hadn't seen anything that might pass for a personal connection between them. Not one little flick of a glance or a slight grin. Nada.

I had zero chance of figuring this out on my own. Maybe Jamison's work crew knew the identity of the mystery woman. I finished my last taco and looked down at Hitchcock, who was busy cleaning his face. "You up for a drive?"

"Mrreow," he said.

• • •

The trip to Beckman Vineyards took us down curvy country roads and over surrounding hills. I remembered listening to a speech about Beckman's history when Tyanne and I once visited the winery. I couldn't recall how many acres they had—hundreds, as far as the eye could see. Many of the acres were covered with grapevines. Some of the land was hilly, some flat. When I passed the landmark I remembered from my trip out here with Tyanne—a red metal building with flowering oleander bushes lining the drive—I knew we were very near our destination.

Shortly before two o'clock, I parked in the lot that faced the immense white stone building that housed the winemaking facilities, offices, a store, and a spacious wine-tasting hall. I supposed that most of the cars in the lot were visitors interested in the tours and wine-tasting. I checked Hitchcock's harness and leash to make sure I could keep him under control no matter what might catch his fancy while we walked around outdoors.

When we climbed from the car, I smelled barbequed meat rather than the scent of grapes or wine that I might have expected. Behind the main building sat the largest covered patio area I'd ever seen. People clustered at tables, and folks scurried to and from an outdoor kitchen. Feeding Jamison's work crew here made more sense than having them take off to find food during a lunch break.

Next to the patio, a windmill turned in the lazy summer breeze. Beyond that, a variety of trucks, trailers, and three buses were parked in the field. Workers, most of them wearing hard hats, scuttled around the vehicles and the structure that had to be the stage they were readying for the show. The sound of hammers, music playing, and shouted instructions filled the air.

They only had one more day to get everything set up. It seemed to me they had more than a day's work left, but this wasn't their first rodeo, so to speak, and they knew their deadline. In this scenario, I felt sure they'd work through the night if they had to.

The hottest point of the day was yet to come. Already the workers were stripped down to undershirts and wore sweat bands or rags tied around their heads. I stood on the periphery and scanned the people, thinking of Tandee and the fact that the girls at Hot Stuff had told me Tandee could be found out here.

I wondered when the girl who planned to get in line way in advance—Ms. Pink Glasses—planned to arrive. I didn't see any waiting line as of yet. Nor did I see Tandee or anyone who resembled her. I didn't think Tandee would be allowed inside the winery unless she lied about her age.

I walked along the outskirts of the work area, looking for the man Rosales had befriended the night before. Curious about what kind of story she'd told him. Hard to pick out a certain guy in this distracting sea of muscles and snug jeans.

"Hey," a man shouted. "You can't be out here." He approached me at a fast clip. "What are you doing? You need to step back."

"I'm not hurting anything," I said. "I'm a friend of Colt's."

The man, a rugged type in a gray T-shirt with the sleeves rolled up, shook his head and chuckled. "Right, and if I had a dollar for every time I've heard that I wouldn't be workin' anymore."

I took note of an ID card pinned to his shirt—*Bobby Hall*. "No, really, Bobby. I'm also a writer, and—"

"All due respect, I don't care what you are," he said. "I'm head of the production crew. You don't have an ID badge, you don't get in."

"I'm not technically *in*," I said. "If you could spare me just a minute, I need to know if you've seen a teenager out here today. Her name's Tandee."

He shook his head so fast he couldn't have given the question any thought.

"She's eighteen, long dark hair, about this tall?" I held my hand up to my chin.

"Haven't seen her," he said.

She's the president of the Colt Jamison fan club." According to the story she was using, which may or may not have a bit of truth to it.

"Heard something about a fan club," he said. "Don't know more than that. You and your cat need to skedaddle. Off the premises. Now."

"The winery is open for tourists," I said.

"Not out here." He pointed at the building. "Inside only."

"Have you worked with the Jamison crew for long?" I said.

"What are you, a reporter?" His attitude was making his already sunburned face even redder.

"No, only an interested resident of Lavender. Did you know Marty Dixon?"

My change of tack seemed to startle him. "Yeah."

"Did you know he was fired?"

"I heard about that, yeah. Why do you care?"

"I visited with his mother yesterday. Did Marty ever tell you about her?"

"We weren't exactly pals."

"What was Marty's relationship with Colt like? I'm sure you saw them together regularly seein' as how you and Marty both worked for Colt."

"This isn't your business," he said.

"Marty was fired, and he came to Lavender anyway," I continued, "but he didn't contact his mother, and now she'll never see him again. Somebody killed him. Do you know anyone who wanted Marty out of the way bad enough to commit murder? The killer might be someone right here working with y'all, and you might help—"

"What? Whoa. I'm not talkin' to you." He pulled out a phone. "I'm callin' security."

He walked a few yards from me, and I moved in the opposite direction. I couldn't identify anyone out here as the man Rosales had talked to, so I might need to find her and get her to share whether she'd learned anything useful from him. By Hall's reaction to my comment about the killer, I assumed the crew had been instructed to not speak about Dixon's death to anyone. I made a circle and headed back in the direction of the outdoor kitchen.

That's when I saw Sheriff Crawford climb out of his cruiser and adjust the bill of his cap. He'd parked next to a row of trailers, in the area that Bobby Hall would consider off-limits—for me, probably not for the sheriff.

I looked over my shoulder. Hall was slipping the phone into his pocket as he came my way.

"I have security coming," he called out, "so you can still walk away as I've asked you to. It'd be better if you were gone before—" He stopped talking when he noticed the sheriff's approach.

"I think Sheriff Crawford trumps whatever your security person would have to say," I told Bobby.

"What are you talkin' about?" he said.

I picked Hitchcock up and held him close. "The sheriff is a close personal friend of mine."

"Yeah, right," Hall said. "I've heard enough of your stories."

He waited beside me until the sheriff was within hearing distance. "Sheriff, this woman is trespassing and impeding progress on our job. I've asked—" He stopped talking when he realized the sheriff wasn't paying attention to him.

Sheriff Crawford nodded to me and Hitchcock. "Sabrina, is this man bothering you?"

Chapter 25

"I enjoyed that," Sheriff Crawford said after Bobby Hall walked away and was out of hearing distance. "This is my second run-in with Mr. Hall."

"When was the first?" I said.

"Yesterday, when I clocked him driving eighty-seven in a thirty-five, and he tried his darnedest to talk his way out of a speeding ticket."

"I guess that didn't work in his favor."

"No, it did not." He grinned at the memory, then turned his head to look at me. "Do you want to tell me why you're over here? I was pleased when you sent me the tip about Ms. Cushing. I assumed that you'd turned the information over and would let me do my job."

"I *was* turning it over. I mean, I did."

The sheriff gave me the stern expression that reminded me of my dad on the few childhood occasions when I'd crossed him. "I repeat," the sheriff said, "why are you here?"

I tried to reel in my unfocused thoughts. "A lot has happened since we last spoke."

"You say that as if we haven't seen each other in weeks," he said. "We talked yesterday. What new information have you learned?"

I thought for a moment and remembered several points.

Aunt Rowe wants to date you.

Deputy Rosales has skeletons in her closet.

Tracey thinks her brother killed Dixon while in a drunken stupor.

I settled on, "My brother told me about Tandee's possible drug issue. That's why I let you know of her suspected whereabouts."

"We've covered that."

"The young ladies who told me about seeing Tandee here at the winery said Tandee's selling hundred-dollar tickets for a contest to win a personal meeting with Colt Jamison."

"Is that so?" The sheriff nodded thoughtfully.

"If that's true, and I have no reason to believe those women would invent the story for my benefit, I'd guess the contest is bogus. I mean, he's charging for concert tickets. Why would a singer like Jamison be involved with such a contest?"

"I'll look into this," the sheriff said.

"Unless it were something to benefit a charity," I went on, "but I didn't hear anything about any donations being made on his behalf."

The sheriff blew out a breath. "Do you have more you'd like to get off your chest?"

"I heard Marty Dixon had a girlfriend he was eager to see here in Lavender, and that interested me because a significant other is always a suspect in a murder."

"Maybe not quite always," he said, "but you do have a point. Who is this woman?"

"No one has a name — at least nobody I've talked to."

"You mean no one who would share information with you," he said.

"Well, right, though I'm not sure why anyone would keep the name from me if they knew a name." I paused to think about that. "Wanda Dixon would surely not have kept the name a secret. She was stunned to hear there was a girlfriend, and she'd love to know who that person is."

"You visited with Wanda?" he said.

"I did. Tyanne and I went to pay our respects this morning."

"Uh-huh." His gaze traveled along the leash in my hand and down to the harness. "Hitchcock, did you go along?"

The cat paused in his jumping at bugs in the grass and looked up. "Mrreow."

"I thought as much," the sheriff said.

I started giggling and couldn't stop. "Now you're talking to him, too."

"I wasn't serious," he said.

"Hitchcock is like that. He brings it out in us."

"What's that? Craziness?"

"Something like that," I said.

"Have we covered everything?" the sheriff said.

I put a finger on my chin and looked up at the sky for a moment. Remembered a new and important fact and focused on the sheriff.

"Did you have a lightbulb moment?" he said.

"Kind of. I saw Chester Mosley at the antiques store today. He said Marty approached him on Wednesday night. Maybe you already knew this."

"No, I didn't." He shook his head. "Wednesday. The night of the murder?"

"Yes. He said Marty came to the Wild Pony because he wanted to apologize to Chester."

"For?"

"He was sorry the concert got moved over here, to Beckman Vineyards. Away from the Wild Pony, where it would have benefitted Chester's business."

"Did Chester's sister know about the apology?" the sheriff said.

"I didn't ask him that question."

The sheriff stroked his chin. "If Dixon died shortly after this alleged apology, Chester may have been the last person to see Dixon alive."

Aside from the killer.

Neither of us voiced the thought that had to be going through both of our minds right now.

"I need to get back to my office," the sheriff said. "To be clear, I'm only overlooking your taking such an active part in the case because of this week's big event. The Jamison show is bringing a good deal of publicity to Lavender, which should be a good thing. Unfortunately, the murder is bringing bad publicity. The sooner we can close the case, the better. I will not be as lenient in the future, Sabrina. Do you understand me?"

I nodded. "Yes, sheriff, I understand."

"If, God forbid, we're ever in this situation again, you are to stand clear and let me and my people handle everything."

"I understand," I repeated, though I wasn't sure I did. "What's next?"

"I need to figure out how to get in touch with Colt Jamison. I have a list of questions for that boy."

Guilt for keeping information from him raged against my loyalty to Aunt Rowe. She might make allowances under the circumstances and let out the secret of Jamison's whereabouts, but I couldn't make myself do it.

"That manager of Jamison's, Gary Weber, could probably arrange something for you," I said.

"Good idea." He turned and started toward his car.

"Wait," I said. "Aren't you gonna stay here and look for Tandee to ask her about the drugs?"

The sheriff gave me a smug grin. "I already have Tandee. Found her camped out at the old Stoddard place down the road."

"Have you already talked to her?"

"That's what I'm going to do now. Deputy Ainsley is transporting her to my office as we speak. I'll see *you* later." He tipped his hat to me and walked away.

• • •

I followed the sheriff as he drove away from the Beckman Vineyards and back toward town. I wondered why he'd come out to the winery at all if he already had Tandee. Looking for me, most likely.

"At least he didn't make a total fool of me," I told Hitchcock.

"Mrreow," he said.

"And you may keep your opinion to yourself."

In hindsight, I wished I'd asked Sheriff Crawford what new information *he* might have acquired since we last talked. His information plus my information might equal a breakthrough in the case. He wouldn't have been as forthcoming, though, as I was with him. I'd have ended up annoyed with him for not sharing, and that wouldn't help anything.

"I should let him run the case and mind my own business," I said to Hitchcock.

"Mrreow," he said.

We were almost back to town when my phone rang. The caller ID said Glenda, and I pushed the button on my steering wheel to answer hands-free.

"What's up, Glenda?"

"I hope you're in town and free to help, because I need some help."

"Why? What's wrong?"

"Nothin' wrong per se," she said, "but your aunt had this brain-storm. Out of the blue, she's invited a group for dinner tonight."

I could imagine why this threw Glenda for a loop. "How big a group?"

"Eight to ten," Glenda said. "Thomas is off to the meat market for steaks to grill. If you could stop by the grocery store for the other things I'm missing, that would be a great help."

"Sure, I can go to the store for you. Should I assume I'm invited to this shindig?"

"Of course you are," Glenda said. "You, Luke, Nick and the boys. A few others, including Violet, who's bringing a guest. It'll be a gang, and now I'm cookin' my heart out over here."

"Send me your list, I'll run by the store, and then I'll come home and help you get everything ready. I wonder why she didn't plan ahead for this."

"Lord knows. I sure can't explain it. Oh, and she's invited Sheriff Crawford, too. That was a surprise."

"Huh." He hadn't mentioned a word of that to me. Maybe when he said he'd see me later, he assumed I already knew about the dinner.

"I'll text you the list. It's not terribly long. I had enough of what I need to get a head start on the cooking."

"What time does she expect people to arrive?"

"Seven."

"Okay. I'm on it."

I disconnected the call and shook my head. "Aunt Rowe's having a party. I wonder what brought that on." I liked the idea of getting everyone together and wondered whether everyone she invited was going to be able to attend given the spur-of-the-moment invitation.

My phone buzzed with an incoming text. Glenda's list. I headed for the grocery store. Shopping might be a good way to clear my head of all my other concerns.

A few minutes later, I hit the outskirts of Lavender and headed through town toward the market. The streets were more heavily traveled than usual, and I drove slowly to watch out for jaywalking pedestrians. I spotted one man up ahead walking briskly down the sidewalk. He looked familiar, and I slowed even more.

The man had dark hair and wore jeans and tennies with a khaki short-sleeved shirt. I'd seen that shirt before. I recognized the man's gait. It was Nick.

What the heck was my brother doing here in town? I scanned the sidewalk for the boys but didn't see them. Had the day out with

Luke ended early? If so, where were the kids?

On impulse, I swerved into an empty parking spot along the street. Nick was moving fast. I pulled out my phone, saw the text from Glenda, and sent a quick message to Luke.

How's your day going?

I started to climb out of the car, then remembered Hitchcock and took the end of his leash.

"C'mon, boy. Quick walk?"

"Mrrreeeoooowww."

He wanted to continue his nap, but I picked him up and hurried to follow Nick. He walked with purpose, with a mission in mind. Was he running an errand for Glenda, too?

My phone buzzed, and I held it up. Luke had responded.

Good. On the lake. Kids are having a blast. Nick's off on an errand.

That raised my curiosity, but no point in asking a lot of questions of Luke. I asked only one.

Do you know about Rowe's dinner?

Yup. We'll be there.

Okay then. I slid the phone into my pocket. Hitchcock shifted in my arms. I knew he'd rather walk, but I didn't want to yank him along by the leash to keep up with Nick.

Should I shout out to my brother?

My furtive side wanted to know where he was going without calling attention to myself. I kept walking. He turned right at the next corner.

I was familiar with this stretch. We would pass the dry cleaners, then the new candle shop, then —

I took the corner, stopped, and waited. Nick went to the third entrance, opened a door, and walked inside.

He was going to Rita Colletti's office. The question was, why the heck did my brother need to visit a family law attorney?

Chapter 26

I carried the last of the groceries into the kitchen at Aunt Rowe's house and deposited them on the counter. I hoped I'd gotten everything Glenda needed because I was more focused on Nick than on her list as I shopped.

Why on earth would my brother go to see family law attorney Rita Colletti, my former Houston boss? They'd never worked together. Would he consider her a colleague because they were both attorneys? Still, that didn't mean he'd go to visit her while he was here. I remembered Luke telling me he'd seen Nick in town two days ago, his first day in Lavender. What if he'd gone to her office on that day, too?

Did my brother have some sort of deep dark secret that required legal advice? A secret no one was allowed to know? Not me? Or Aunt Rowe? The boys? Maybe not even his wife? I might be able to believe one visit to Rita's office simply to say hello. If there were two visits in such a short time I would find that very curious—and worrisome.

Stop jumping to conclusions, Sabrina.

I could attempt to put this out of my mind, but chances were this mystery would eat at me until I found out what was going on. I couldn't go up to Nick and blurt out "Why are you seeing Rita?" He wouldn't like my spying on him, and I had no viable defense because I *was* spying. If someone brought up Nick's afternoon errand, I could take advantage of the opening. A private conversation would be better, though. Tonight's dinner should be about enjoying each other's company and relaxing. For now, I'd keep this information to myself.

The back door opened as I made my decision, and Glenda came in. She saw the groceries and grinned. "Good job, girl. I sure do thank you."

"You're welcome," I said. "Something smells good."

"Calico beans," she said. "I just put them in the oven. Let's get those bakers scrubbed, and we can put them in there, too." She eyed Hitchcock, who was under the breakfast table and sniffing the floor. "Did you take *him* shopping with you?"

I nodded. "Guilty. I couldn't very well leave him in the hot car, so I slipped him into my tote and made a record-breaking dash down the grocery aisles with no one the wiser."

Hitchcock looked up at us. "Mrreow."

"Well, except for Libby the cashier. She has supersonic cat radar, and she adores him."

Glenda probably didn't approve of me taking a cat into the grocery store, but I honestly hadn't seen any other quick way around the issue.

"Hitchcock was very well behaved. The store employees probably think I'm a nut since I was talking to him the whole time."

"No doubt they've heard plenty about you and Hitchcock," Glenda said.

"I'm sure you mean that in a lighthearted who-doesn't-love-Hitchcock way."

"Of course I do." She winked at me. "Time to get this show on the road."

"I'll get the potatoes ready." I pulled a vegetable brush from a drawer and took the new sack of large russet potatoes over to the sink.

Glenda stowed sour cream and shredded cheese for the baked potatoes in the refrigerator. "Did you get some writing done today?"

"A bit," I said, "and Luke's going to ask about my word count. I may need to fudge a bit on that number."

Aunt Rowe walked into the kitchen and wagged her index finger at me. "Lying is never appropriate."

I grimaced. "How about if I stretch the truth a teensy bit?"

"If you must," she said, "but you could avoid the problem if you wrote huge quantities of words every day."

"I try, but there are so many interruptions. Speaking of which, what brought on the impromptu dinner party?"

Aunt Rowe shrugged. "I felt the need for a bash. The Jamison show is tomorrow, and we need to start the buzz. Feel the excitement."

"Are you going to the concert?" I said.

"Hadn't planned on it," she said.

"Then won't the excitement you're building tonight fall flat?"

"Not if I can get Jeb on board to spend the evening here with me while y'all are away at the show." Aunt Rowe smiled a devilish smile and wiggled her eyebrows.

"Aunt Rowe!" My cheeks felt flushed, and my aunt laughed.

"She's incorrigible," Glenda said.

"Sounds like you've invited an unexpected group to this dinner," I said to change the embarrassing topic. "Should be interesting."

"That's the plan," Aunt Rowe said and sashayed out of the kitchen.

I worked side by side with Glenda, and an hour later I finished two key lime pies for dessert after garnishing them with swirls of lime rind. I slid them into the refrigerator and looked at my cat.

"Hitchcock," I said, and he perked up from a kitchen chair where he'd been napping. "It's time for us to go and get cleaned up for dinner."

"Mrreow," he said.

• • •

We gathered for dinner on Aunt Rowe's deck, where the feast was laid out on a banquet table. The mouthwatering smell of grilled steaks, corn on the cob, and Glenda's calico beans filled the air. A mound of foil-wrapped baked potatoes sat in a wicker basket.

Aunt Rowe looked glamourous in a royal blue sundress as she addressed her guests. She'd swept her hair back and up into a casual twist fastened with a silver filigreed clip.

"Good to have y'all here," she said. "Thank you so much for coming."

Though she addressed the group as a whole, I noticed her frequent eye contact with the sheriff, who stood across the deck from her. Hitchcock had opted to stay inside. He sat on a windowsill with a direct view of the deck to assess the situation.

"This is definitely one of our long hot summer nights," Aunt Rowe continued, "so feel free to go inside if these fans we've set up don't do the trick. Otherwise, we have plenty of seating right here or at those tables under the trees. Y'all may be the most eclectic group I've ever entertained, and I hope you enjoy each other's company. Now, let's dig in."

Conversation buzzed as the group—a dozen of us in all—began to assemble into a buffet line.

Adam leaned toward his dad. "What's eclectic?"

"Diverse," Nick said.

I said, "People we wouldn't expect to see together in the same group."

"You can say that again." Matt eyed the sheriff and looked none too happy to see the lawman nearby.

Luke and I stood to the side with my brother, and I scanned the guests. I was surprised to see Tyanne and Abby, her oldest, and Gary Weber, whose name was on Around-the-World's guest register even though he wasn't staying in a cottage. No surprise that Colt Jamison wasn't in attendance.

I wanted to ask Sheriff Crawford about his meeting with Tandee, but Aunt Rowe had already taken me aside and made it clear that "business talk" was off-limits for the evening. I wouldn't ask Nick about his little trek over to Rita's office either, much as I wanted to.

Tyanne and Abby came over to join me and the guys. Abby, nine and mature for her age, smiled shyly at Adam. Tyanne said, "How did your day-in-the-life go?" She looked from Luke to the boys.

"I thought we had a great day," Luke said. "What did you think, guys?"

Adam's face lit up. "Luke caught speeders on the lake. We raced right up to them in his boat and pulled 'em over. I didn't know boats had sirens like cop cars. That was cool."

I watched Gary Weber as he got into the food line behind Bruno Krause, who'd accompanied Violet Howe to the dinner. Seemed there was more to Bruno's relationship with the woman than a little life coaching. The boys were eager to eat, and Nick gave them the nod to go and get in line.

"Being a game warden's a lot tougher than I would have guessed," my brother told Luke. "My office job's a piece of cake in comparison."

"The job can be a challenge," Luke said, "but I enjoy what I do."

Nick excused himself to join the boys, and Luke turned to me. "Before I forget, what was your word count for today?"

Tyanne burst out laughing at his question, and I gave her a stern look. "Honestly, I forgot to check the word count before shutting down my computer. I worked on a new book proposal, though, so asking about word count isn't a relevant question."

"I think it's very relevant," Tyanne said.

I laughed. "You would. Hey, and yes, I'm purposely changing the subject, where's the rest of your gang?"

"Bryan and the boys drove over to his dad's for the day. They won't be back until late, so your aunt's dinner invitation was very welcome."

"I'm glad you're here," I said. "You, too, Abby. I'm sorry, I should have introduced you to my nephews. You probably don't know many people here."

"I know some," she said. "Sheriff Crawford comes to the school every year to talk about safety." The girl looked around. "I know Noah's grandpa, too."

"Oh. You know Bruno?"

She nodded. "I babysit for Noah."

"At our house," Ty added, "so Abby's not alone with a four-year-old. Charlotte brings Noah over from time to time when the stress gets to her."

"I imagine chasing that little whirling dervish around could stress anyone," I said.

Luke looked at Abby. "I'm starting to drool, smelling this food."

Abby giggled, and they moved into the food line with Ty and me close behind. Ty leaned closer to my ear and lowered her voice. "Noah isn't the one stressing her. Hubby has some anger issues lately."

"Oh, dear." I recalled the tense conversation I'd partially overheard at the pizza shop and Fritz's attitude at the antiques store. The guy was wrapped tight.

We got our plates, and I filled mine quickly with a little of everything. Luke had chosen a seat at the table where the sheriff sat with Aunt Rowe and Gary Weber, so I went that way and sat beside him. Ty and Abby sat with Nick and the boys.

"So, Mr. Weber," the sheriff said.

Weber paused with a forkful of loaded baked potato in midair. "Gary, Sheriff. Call me Gary."

The sheriff smiled. "Gary it is. I heard that your client, I'm sure you can guess which one, will personally meet with the lucky winner of a contest. One of those back-stage-pass type things I hear about sometimes on the radio. Any truth to that happening here in Lavender?"

Weber put his fork down on his plate. "Where'd you get your information?"

"I'm the sheriff. You wouldn't believe half of what people tell me. They say proceeds from ticket sales are going to a charity. From your reaction, might I assume there's no truth to the rumor?"

"I haven't heard word one about any contest." Weber picked his fork back up and gave the sheriff what seemed like a forced smile. "Clients don't always tell me their plans, but I'd guess it's a scam."

The sheriff nodded as he cut his steak. "Do you run into a lot of them in your business? Scams?"

Weber shrugged. "Some days it seems like the whole world's full of scams and bad decisions."

I focused on stirring cheese into my baked potato and wondered why Weber had agreed to come here tonight. Had he known the sheriff would attend? Wanted to hear the latest about the murder investigation? Couldn't resist an invitation for a home-cooked meal? None of the options resonated with me.

"Scams, schwams," Aunt Rowe said. "This is the start of a party weekend, so let's act festive."

"I'm not sure what festive looks like," the sheriff said.

Aunt Rowe lifted an eyebrow. "I can help you with that, Jeb."

Violet and Bruno had taken seats at our table during the scam discussion. Violet said, "People, as a whole, need to work on finding their joy."

The men appeared at a loss for words, so I responded, "You're so right, Violet. The world would be a much better place if everyone took your advice."

Luke and I exchanged a glance, then he appeared to check out her hair with the feather and purple streak. I realized he hadn't met her and made introductions.

"Violet is a life coach," I said.

Luke addressed Violet. "Sounds like an interesting job. Are you here working or on vacation?"

"She's working," Aunt Rowe said, "and she's helped me see some things I need to tend to." She buttered an ear of corn on the cob.

The sheriff looked at Aunt Rowe. "Has she now?"

Aunt Rowe blushed as she regarded him. "She might say I'm a work in progress."

"You're making great strides, Rowe," Violet said. "As are you, Bruno." Attention shifted to Bruno.

Bruno swallowed a bite of beans. "Yes, I'm working with Violet, too. I admit it."

"Improving yourself is nothing to be ashamed of," Aunt Rowe said.

"I was kidding," Bruno said.

Violet beamed. "Bruno is getting his priorities in order, with that darling little grandson at the center of his world."

"As he should be," Aunt Rowe said.

"The apple of Bruno's eye," Violet said. "I wonder who came up with that saying."

"We could probably find out quickly." Luke made a move to pull out his phone then thought better of the idea. "Later. This is the time to enjoy the great food."

"And the pleasant company." Sheriff Crawford looked at Aunt Rowe. "Appreciate the invitation, Rowe. Too many times, I skip right past the dinner hour. A hazard of the job."

Aunt Rowe smiled. "You should break that bad habit, Jeb. You're doing good, so far. No work talk."

"And here I thought you might have engineered this dinner, Sheriff," Violet said, "to assemble a cast of suspects. Just like an Agatha Christie murder mystery."

"I assure you that's not what this is," the sheriff said.

"An intriguing idea, Violet," Aunt Rowe said. "I might host a mystery dinner one day. If you'll excuse me for a second, I'm going to start the coffee."

The sheriff watched as Aunt Rowe disappeared into the kitchen. I spotted Hitchcock slipping out as she went inside. When the door closed behind her, the sheriff turned to Weber.

"I do have a piece of business to mention to you, Gary, before I forget."

"What's that, Sheriff?" Weber said.

"I need to arrange a personal meeting with Colt Jamison."

Weber's fork accidentally knocked into his water with a noise so loud that everyone turned to stare. Weber caught the glass before it fell and said, "About what?"

"The case I'm investigating," the sheriff said. "You know the one."

"Yes, of course," Weber said, "but Colt has nothing to do with that. How could he when he's not even here?"

I wondered why Weber didn't give a simple answer, like, "I'll tell Colt you need to speak with him."

Why add the unnecessary lie?

Hitchcock jumped up on the patio chair nearest Weber and watched the man as if he, too, wanted to figure out Weber's angle.

"I'm sure Colt knew Marty Dixon," the sheriff said. "I have a few questions about his personal knowledge of the man."

"Any idea who's behind the pieces of broken mirror in the streets?" Bruno said, changing the subject. "Now that we're talking police business."

"We're in the process of putting up street cameras," the sheriff said, "and that's going to take some time."

"Ernie over at the antiques store has seen the man," I said. "Whoever it is bought some mirrors from their store. Did you know that?"

The sheriff shook his head. "That's new information. Thank you, Sabrina."

"I'll give you a hand with this problem, Sheriff," Luke said, "if you'd like my help."

"I may take you up on that. I have a feeling I'm going to need some extra hands over the coming weekend."

We ate in companionable silence for a few minutes before Gary Weber put his fork down and addressed the sheriff again.

"I have a wild stab of an idea," Weber said, "about the broken mirrors."

"What about them?" the sheriff said.

"Well, Dixon came up with some of the weirdest damn publicity stunts I ever heard of. Which is one of the reasons he got fired before we, before I, ever came here to Lavender."

"What are you saying?" Luke said.

"Throwing around pieces of mirrors sounds like the dumb kind of stunt Dixon might have concocted," Weber said. "You know, because of Colt's song. When you find the guy behind it, ask him if he was hired by Marty Dixon."

The sheriff sat back in his chair. "Okay. Good suggestion, and thank you for that, Gary." He glanced at the house as if to make sure Aunt Rowe was still inside, then turned to Bruno.

"Please tell your son-in-law I still need to speak with him, too."

"Why do you need to speak with Fritz?" Bruno said.

"Still working my way through interviews of everyone who was present when Mr. Dixon arrived at the pizza shop on Wednesday." The sheriff's brows drew together. "Do you know if Fritz knew Marty?"

Bruno shook his head. "You'd have to ask him, Sheriff."

"You may have a hard time solving the murder," Violet said. "With so many visitors in town, who's to say what happened? This could be a random act of violence."

"You're right." The sheriff nodded. "But I don't think that's what we're dealing with here."

I chewed a piece of steak and thought about the concept of a murder mystery dinner. Did we have any suspects here tonight? Did I think the murder could have been a random act of violence? Not after hearing negative comments about Marty Dixon from multiple people. Even from Marty's mother—but there were probably two sides to that story, and Marty's side would never be told.

Hitchcock jumped down from his perch and wove between table, chairs, and human legs as he nosed the floor. I saw Abby's arm fall to her side as she slipped a sliver of steak to the cat.

"Okay, no more murder talk," the sheriff said, picking up his cob of corn. "Let's get back to polite chitchat, all right? Or should I say festive chitchat?"

The door opened, and Aunt Rowe stuck her head out.

"Excuse me, Sheriff?" she called.

Sheriff Crawford looked at her, his expression questioning. "What is it, Rowe? You need a hand with something?"

"I suggest you put your corn down," she said. "You have a visitor."

With a frown, the sheriff placed the cob on his plate and pushed his chair back. "Who is it?"

"The gal from KTSU," Aunt Rowe said, but by the time the words left her mouth Kendra Steele had barreled around the side of the house with her photographer in tow.

The sheriff nearly stumbled as he disentangled himself from his chair and muttered, "What the —?"

The reporter practically bounced up the deck steps as she spoke into her microphone. "We're here live in Lavender, Texas, at Around-the-World Cottages, where Sheriff Jebediah Crawford is dining with friends. Sheriff Crawford, what can you tell us about your progress in the investigation of Marty Dixon's murder?"

She shoved the microphone into the sheriff's face.

"No comment," he said.

"I understand you have taken a person of interest into custody. What can you tell us about Tandee Cushing?"

"Still no comment."

"Is there a drug connection here, Sheriff?"

He glared at her. "I will not discuss an ongoing investigation with you."

"Then how about this, Sheriff Crawford? Perhaps the most pressing question. The public wants to know, and they have a right to know, more about the sighting of Colt Jamison on the streets of downtown Lavender on the very night of Marty Dixon's murder."

Chapter 27

Luke herded us into the house like a shepherd protecting his sheep from a wolf. "No need giving her a chance to ask each of us for our name, rank, and serial number," he said when he'd closed the door behind us.

"Good move," Aunt Rowe said. "Who wants dessert?"

Adam, who stood on tiptoes to peer out the window over the sink, glanced at the sweets Aunt Rowe had lined up on the counter, then turned back to the window.

No one took Aunt Rowe up on her offer.

"Is Colt Jamison already here in Lavender?" Matt said.

"You can't believe reporters," Gary Weber said. "They invent stories to stir people up."

My dinner sat like a lump of bricks in my stomach. Was Kendra Steele's question for real? *Had* someone seen Jamison in town on Wednesday night? I wouldn't put it past the reporter to say so for the sake of a sensational story, but I knew for a fact he was in Lavender. I clearly remembered seeing his truck pull in at the Athens cottage that night, and I needed to tell the sheriff what I saw.

Didn't I?

"Boys," Nick said. "In the living room."

"Aww, Dad," Adam moaned, but he followed Nick.

Matt trailed behind and looked at me. "Did the sheriff arrest Tandee? Is she, like, in jail?"

I patted him on the shoulder. "I don't know, Matt."

I thought about asking Gary Weber when Colt Jamison was expected to arrive in Lavender to see how he'd handle the question. When I poked my head into the living room, Weber was making a beeline for the front door.

"Thank y'all for dinner," he called over his shoulder. "I need to go before I get trapped by that reporter."

"I think we'll leave, too," Tyanne said. "Enjoyed dinner, Rowe. Everything was delicious. Bye, Sabrina." Ty put a hand on Abby's back to guide her out. The girl turned and gave Adam a shy wave.

"We'll talk tomorrow, Ty," I said. "Thanks for coming."

Aunt Rowe saw them out. Nick and the boys sat on the sofa.

Violet and Bruno perused Aunt Rowe's framed family photos on the mantel, apparently in no hurry to leave.

Maybe they had dessert on their minds.

I went to the back door, where Luke stood sentry. He pulled the door curtain aside every few seconds to look out.

"The sheriff could come inside with us," I said. "You look like you're ready to attempt a rescue."

Luke shook his head. "He won't walk away and give her an excuse to say he refused to cooperate. He'll stay out there until she leaves."

"But he won't comment," I said. "She'll put a negative spin on anything he says."

"He can handle her." Luke turned the doorknob and pulled. For a second, I thought he was going out, but he opened the door only enough for Hitchcock to slip inside.

The cat rubbed against my legs.

"Mrreow."

I bent to pat his head and heard his nervous purr. "You want to give us a report on what you heard out there?"

Hitchcock ignored my question and trotted into the kitchen. Luke put an arm across my shoulders, and we followed the cat. At the kitchen counter, Luke surveyed the selection of desserts. Unless we all had a major snack attack, we had enough sweets on hand to last until after Nick and the boys went home and then some.

Luke tipped his head to inspect my face. "What's wrong? You look pale."

I gave him a weak smile. "This whole thing has me feeling a little jumpy."

He watched me for a few seconds, then said, "What are you holding back?"

How did he do that?

I motioned for Luke to follow me down a hall opposite the living room into Aunt Rowe's office. I closed the door and faced him.

"I haven't told this to anyone before now."

"I'm listening."

"It's a two-part story," I said. "The first part is Aunt Rowe's secret." I explained that although Gary Weber's name was on the guest register for the Athens cottage, Weber was not the person staying there and who was.

"She swore us to secrecy," I said. "Me, Glenda, and Thomas."

Luke shook his head and chuckled. "I can't believe y'all have kept this quiet for days. Matt and Adam don't know, right?"

"Of course they don't. We've been trying to respect Jamison's privacy."

Luke sobered and said, "I guess part two is what's bothering you."

I nodded and told him how I'd seen Jamison's truck pull in on the night of the murder. He'd been out—somewhere—Lord knew where.

"Maybe he went stir crazy that night," Luke said. "Took a drive. Could be that simple."

"You're right. I don't know when he left, how long he'd been gone, or if he went to town, where somebody allegedly saw him."

"I don't think Steele made up the story. You know he went somewhere. She says somebody saw him. Odds are somebody really did see him."

"Which doesn't mean she should connect a simple trip into town to a murder," I said.

Luke came over to me and rested his hands on my hips. "It shouldn't mean that, but he needs to tell the sheriff his whereabouts that night same as everybody else."

I frowned. "I have to tell the sheriff what I saw, don't I?"

"You already know the answer," Luke said.

"Even though I don't believe Jamison did anything wrong."

"Sheriff needs all the facts."

I nodded. "Aunt Rowe won't like me giving up her secret."

"How about we make her give it up herself?"

"That's a very good idea."

We sealed the plan with a kiss before going back to the living room, where Nick and the boys sat by themselves watching a baseball game on TV.

"Where's everybody?" I said.

Nick looked up. "Violet and Bruno went home, or wherever. Aunt Rowe's outside talking to the sheriff. The reporter's gone."

"I'm bored," Adam said.

I thought of the concert tickets Gary Weber had given me. Showing them to the boys now would rev up their excitement level for tomorrow's concert. I should have done it while Gary Weber was here, and they could have personally thanked him.

Too late for that.

"I have a fun surprise for you guys," I said, "so stay right here. I need to talk to Aunt Rowe first, then I'll be back."

"What is it?" Adam said.

"You'll find out soon enough."

I walked to the door with Luke on my heels. "What's the surprise?" he said.

"You'll find out when they do," I said. "Be right back."

I took a tentative step out to the deck and listened. Night was falling fast, and the tree frogs had already begun their nightly chorus. The table had been cleared as if by magic. Glenda and/or Thomas must have taken everything to the storeroom given that Aunt Rowe had guests in the house.

The voices of Aunt Rowe and the sheriff came to me from a spot beyond the deck. I went in that direction and saw them seated at one of the tables under a shade tree. Now that I'd made up my mind to talk to the sheriff, I didn't want to delay. I walked toward them and hoped I wasn't interrupting a personal conversation.

Aunt Rowe saw me coming. "Jeb got rid of the pesky reporter," she said. "He no-commented that woman right out of here."

"Good job, Sheriff." I looked at Aunt Rowe. "Now there's something I need you to do."

"Well, sit right down here and tell me all about it," Aunt Rowe said.

She wouldn't be so cordial after I told her what I had on my mind. I sat in a chair across the table from them.

"About that secret in the Athens cottage," I said.

Aunt Rowe fidgeted in her seat and wouldn't meet my gaze. She didn't respond.

"What kind of secret, Sabrina?" the sheriff said.

"Aunt Rowe needs to tell you. After she does, I have something of my own to add."

"This is Gary Weber's secret to tell if anybody's gonna tell it," Aunt Rowe said.

I met her gaze head-on. "Obviously, he's not in the mood to say a word. He hightailed it out of here the second he got a chance."

"Is Weber at the Athens cottage now?" she said.

I lifted my arms to my sides, hands palms-up. "That's anybody's guess. I didn't follow him."

"My guests have a right to privacy," Aunt Rowe said.

"Under ordinary circumstances, I agree," I said.

The sheriff made a T with his hands. "Time out, ladies. Rowe, what's going on?"

She blew out a breath, then told him that Gary Weber had booked the Athens cottage through the following day. "He's staying elsewhere, I don't know where."

"And—" The sheriff made a rolling hand motion, trying to drag out more information.

"Colt Jamison is staying in the Athens cottage, has been since Wednesday," Aunt Rowe said in a rush. "He needs peace and quiet to write songs, so that's why he's here. To my knowledge, the only ones who know are Weber, me, Sabrina, Glenda, and Thomas."

The sheriff sat back in his chair and nodded. "Your coconspirators."

"If that's what you want to call them." Aunt Rowe huffed and crossed her arms over her chest.

The sheriff looked at me. "And what might you have to add to this revelation?"

"Let me begin by saying I have absolutely no idea where Colt Jamison went in his truck on Wednesday night. I only saw him when he pulled back into the spot beside the Athens cottage."

All traces of levity disappeared from the sheriff's expression. "And what time did this happen?"

"Actually, it was early Thursday by then. Around three in the morning," I said. "Maybe a little later."

The sheriff's brows drew together.

I tried to block out the irritation in Aunt Rowe's expression as I answered the sheriff. "I couldn't sleep, so I was going to bake. In Aunt Rowe's kitchen."

"She does that all the time, Jeb," Aunt Rowe said.

"This is probably not a big deal," I said and repeated the possible innocent reasons that Luke and I had discussed for Jamison being away from the cottage. "None of these things necessarily connect him to what happened to Dixon."

"I'll take up the investigation from here," the sheriff said. "So, let me get this straight. Neither of you ladies have spoken with Colt Jamison about the murder."

"Never talked to the man," Aunt Rowe said, "though I wouldn't mind. He sure is sexy."

The sheriff ignored her comment and I rolled my eyes.

"Sabrina?" the sheriff said.

I chewed my bottom lip for a few seconds. "I've only talked to him twice."

Aunt Rowe's head jerked in my direction.

"What did y'all talk about?" The sheriff nodded for me to go ahead with my story.

"That night I asked him if he'd seen Hitchcock. The cat and I left the Monte Carlo cottage together, then Hitchcock disappeared like he often does, and I went looking."

"Like he wanted you to meet Colt Jamison," Aunt Rowe said. "That's a smart cat."

The sheriff ignored her. "What did y'all talk about?"

"The cat going missing. That's about it 'cause then we found Hitchcock, and I came on up here to bake."

I skipped right over the part about my stalker-like behavior when I followed Jamison to the river. That was unrelated to him going somewhere in his truck, wasn't it?

The sheriff leaned forward and propped an elbow on the table. "Don't keep me in suspense. When was your second conversation with Jamison?"

"Early this morning. I couldn't sleep and went outside."

The sheriff waited.

"She's a bake-a-holic," Aunt Rowe said. "You should see all the desserts we have in my kitchen."

The sheriff kept his gaze on me, waiting.

"I heard music, so I headed toward the sound. You know how curious I am. Jamison was outside, singing, with Hitchcock in his lap. See, Sheriff, these are completely innocent stories. I can't imagine this man, who's very modest, by the way, would hurt a fly."

"What did y'all talk about this morning?" the sheriff said.

"Writing. He writes songs, I write fiction. We have writing in common."

"And you haven't told anyone that this singer is here."

"I told Luke ten minutes ago. He's the only one."

The sheriff pushed his chair back and stood. "I'm disappointed in you, Sabrina."

I swallowed hard and didn't respond.

"Yesterday, in my office, I specifically asked you to share anything you might learn. We're past the first forty-eight hours now, the best time frame in which to solve a murder."

"I understand."

"And yet you didn't tell me about Colt Jamison, the dead man's former employer, being here in Lavender and quite possibly away from his cottage when the murder took place. I'm pretty sure you were putting that timeline together in your head. Am I right?"

I gulped and nodded. "Yes, you are."

"If there's anything else you'd like to share, this would be the time."

He towered over me, all six-foot-three, and I felt like a kid in school being yelled at by the principal.

I looked up at him. "Yesterday, in your office, you told me that Dixon has a stepfather."

"That's right," the sheriff said.

"He was out here," I said, "early Thursday morning, when I went looking for Hitchcock and saw Colt Jamison for the first time. I think his name's Zeke Farley."

The sheriff nodded. "Right, that's his name. Where did you see him?"

"He and Jamison met up, down by the river."

"In the dark," the sheriff said, deadpan. "At three in the morning."

"Thereabouts." I paused, swallowed. "They talked for a few minutes. Farley had some papers in an envelope, gave them to Jamison."

"And you saw all of this. Did they see you?"

"No. I'm sorry, Sheriff. I saw Jamison walking down to the river, and I wanted to see where he was going, so I watched. From a distance."

Sheriff Crawford put his hands on his hips. "Thanks for coming clean, but don't think I'm finished with you because I'm not. Now,

I'm going to the Athens cottage to see if I can have a word with Mr. Colt Jamison."

I wanted to ask the sheriff about Tandee Cushing, but this probably wasn't the time. Aunt Rowe and I watched him walk away. He rounded the house and headed toward his car. The car started and crunched on the gravel. A minute later, we watched the sheriff drive in the direction of the Athens cottage.

"Well," Aunt Rowe said, "way to ruin my plan to cozy up to that man. Guess it's time for me to launch Plan B."

Chapter 28

The day of the concert dawned bright and hot, a steamy ninety-five degrees in the shade. I took my morning coffee out to my cottage's tiny porch and sat where I could let the caffeine seep in while I listened to the rushing river. Hitchcock jumped up on the porch rail and sat as still as a statue to watch the birds and squirrels. It was a peaceful scene—until I thought back to the events of the night before.

The sheriff wasn't happy with me for keeping information from him. Aunt Rowe was aggravated because I'd shared her secret information with the sheriff. Chances were that Colt Jamison was none too pleased that the sheriff came calling at the cottage where he was supposed to be hidden away from the public at all costs.

"The boys are excited, though, aren't they?" I said aloud.

"Mrreow," Hitchcock said.

After the sheriff took off, I'd shared my surprise with Matt and Adam, who whooped and hollered when I showed them the front-row concert tickets. Adam leapt up so high I thought he'd hit his head on the living room ceiling. Matt abandoned all inhibitions and gave me a giant bear hug. Adam held his ticket almost lovingly against his cheek. I grinned as I recalled him asking if he could sleep with the ticket under his pillow.

I took a sip of coffee and stared into the distance. My grin dimmed as I thought about the murder. Who the heck had killed Marty Dixon and why? It seemed the sheriff was no closer to solving the case, and I wished I could do something to help. Sheriff Crawford would disagree with that sentiment, I knew. That didn't keep me from feeling the need to take action.

Maybe Rosales had made some headway in her private investigation. I pulled out my phone and punched her number to place a call. After five rings, the call went to her voicemail.

"You've reached Deputy Patricia Rosales. Leave your message at the tone."

Short and to the point. No promise of a return call. After the beep I felt tongue-tied for a moment, unsure of what to say.

When I feared the ending beep might sound before I said a word, I spit out, "Hi, Deputy, it's Sabrina. Sabrina Tate. Maybe we could touch base. Compare notes. You know. Call me." I punched the End button.

That sounded dumb.

"Do you think Rosales will call me?" I said.

Hitchcock turned his head toward me. "Mrreow."

I made a face. "I won't hold my breath."

The whole concept of Rosales taking personal time off to solve a case, which is what she'd ordinarily do on the job, struck me as weird. What was she hiding?

I mulled that over for a while and my plotting brain kicked into gear. What if the very secret Rosales was keeping held the answer to solving the murder? She wasn't willing to share the information. Who else would know what she knew?

Her family.

I didn't know who they were. Were her parents still around? Where did they live? Did she have siblings? Where did Rosales live herself? I had no idea. Until a couple of days ago the woman would barely acknowledge me, much less share details of her personal life.

The sheriff's office would have contact information, but I didn't want to go there. How many times had Laurel told me she wasn't supposed to give out any information?

Maybe I could log on to one of the public data sites and find out where she lived. Assuming the passwords I used when I worked in Houston at the law office hadn't changed, I might find her that way. I drummed my fingers on the bench, thinking, and looked across the lawn, when I heard the overhead door of the storage building sliding up.

Looked like Thomas was preparing to mow, so the peaceful morning was about to be interrupted.

I stood to go inside and opened the door, then paused and turned around to look at Thomas. He'd lived here his whole life. I was certain his Hispanic family had a wide circle of friends. Maybe they knew Deputy Rosales's family.

I put my coffee cup down on the bench and hurried across the lawn to catch Thomas before he started the mower.

He saw me coming and seemed wary as I approached. I looked behind me and saw the reason for his expression. Hitchcock followed in my footsteps. Thomas had adjusted well to the fact that the cat he used to refer to as "El Gato Diablo" lived here on the premises, but he wasn't quite over the superstition borne of the old legend.

When we reached the building, Thomas held a Weed eater upside down to refill the spool. Hitchcock made a wide circle to come around Thomas and jumped up on the seat of the riding mower, one of his favorite places to sit.

"Miss Sabrina." Thomas tipped his straw hat, then glanced at Hitchcock. "And Mr. Hitchcock. Good morning."

"Morning, Thomas."

"What will you and your nephews do today?" he said.

"They announced last night they were going to sleep in. Then Nick's taking them to the Snake House, without me." I had driven by the building decorated with colorful painted snakes on the highway between Lavender and Emerald Springs and knew I would never willingly set foot inside.

"You no like snakes?" Thomas grinned. "I enjoyed the Snake House when I was a boy. Visited many times."

"I don't understand the attraction," I said. "I'd feel slithery for a month if I went in there and looked at those things."

"The boys will have a good time." He adjusted the line, then paused to look to me. "Something I can help you with?"

"Perhaps," I said. "You know Deputy Rosales, right?"

He pursed his lips and answered in a cautious tone. "Sí."

"How long have you known her?"

"No sé. Ten years maybe."

"Is that when she came to live in Lavender?" I said. "Ten years ago?"

"I don't know if she lived here then or now. She works here, but where she lives?" He shrugged.

I frowned. "She hasn't worked for the sheriff's department ten years. How did you know her before?"

"From my church," he said. "Her family attends. The deputy, not so much these days."

"Where does her family live?"

"Closer to Riverview." Thomas rested the Weed eater against the mower and turned to face me. "Why do you want to know?"

How to answer that one?

"Let's say I'm interested in gathering a little family history," I said.

"You should not show up askin' questions at her folks' house," Thomas said. "Her daddy doesn't take to strangers."

I lifted my brows. "That doesn't sound like a good Christian man."

Thomas pulled his gloves off and slapped them against his palm. "You want to know about the Rosales family, Reggie Burt's the one to ask. He lives down the road from them. Has for a long time. Sees everything, knows a lot."

"You mean he's a gossip?"

"Not exactly," Thomas said. "He doesn't go around running his mouth. If you want to talk, though, he'll talk. You should go see him. So long as you like birds."

"Birds? What's up with that?"

"They call him Burt the bird man. He collects them. Has an aviary right there at his house."

"I'd take birds over snakes any day," I said.

• • •

Reggie Burt and Deputy Rosales's family lived on the outskirts of Riverview town proper, in an area where everyone had an acre or two of land. Twenty minutes after we passed Thomas's church, I found the county road that would take me to the bird man's house. I'd brought Hitchcock with me. Maybe not the greatest idea for visiting a man who loved birds, but I'd watch the cat closely. Hitchcock loved road trips and acted more like a dog than a cat while in the car. I loved watching the way he sat up in the passenger seat with his paws on the door sill so he could look out as we drove. I counted it a point in his favor that he didn't slobber on the window the way a dog would.

Thomas had told me that Reggie Burt almost never left his house and loved visitors. I could see he was right the second I pulled into the driveway in front of the modest one-story clapboard house. A thin white-haired man in denim overalls worn over a T-shirt had retrieved the newspaper from his box by the street. He waited to greet me with a big smile when I opened my car door.

"Howdy there, miss," he said. "How can I help you on this fine day?"

I climbed out and returned his infectious smile, then introduced myself. "I came from Lavender to visit you. My cat and I enjoyed the drive over."

He stooped to look into the car at Hitchcock, and I noticed a small set of binoculars stuffed into the front pocket of his overalls.

"Mighty fine-lookin' cat he is, too," Reggie said.

"I heard you're a bird lover, so I hope you won't mind that I brought Hitchcock with me." I paused to gauge his reaction, and there was no change in his expression. "He wears a harness, and I'll be sure to keep a hold of his leash so he doesn't make any inappropriate moves around your birds."

"Come on and make yourselves at home. Would you like to come around back and see the birds?"

"I'd love that," I said.

"Mrreow," Hitchcock added.

Reggie chuckled. "I'll bet he would."

"Are you sure it's okay?" I said. "For the cat to be here, I mean?"

Reggie waved a hand. "He's fine. My little feathered friends are locked up tight."

We took a sidewalk that wound around to the back of the house, and I could hear the birds chirping and twittering before I saw the elaborate domed structure that contained them. A huge assortment of colorful birds flew around or rested on perches inside the aviary. A vestibule with a door on either end would allow Reggie to go in and out without birds escaping while he did so.

"This is my largest one yet," he said. "I seem to keep building 'em bigger and bigger."

"I'm impressed," I said. "The birds are lovely. How many do you have in there?"

"Upwards of seventy last count," he said. "I could sit and watch them all day. Some days that's what I do."

"I would, too," I said, "if I were you."

I felt a tug at the leash as Hitchcock darted closer to the birdcage. He made what sounded like chirping deep in his throat.

"No, Hitchcock," I said. "You can look, but don't rile them up."

"Have a seat and don't worry yourself," Burt said, indicating a glider under a nearby tree. He sat and placed the newspaper on the seat beside him. "Here's my favorite watchin' place."

I joined him on the glider and held Hitchcock in my lap.

"Who told you about me and my birds?" Burt said.

"Thomas Cortez." I explained my relationship to Thomas and how he'd explained that Burt knew the Rosales family well.

"Sure, I know them," he said. "They have a large bunch, lots of kiddos. Not sure I recall Thomas, though."

Thomas hadn't explained how he knew about Burt, so I let that statement go.

"I didn't come specifically to see your birds," I said, "though they're very nice. I was wondering about something else entirely."

"What would that be?" Reggie said.

"I assume you know Patricia Rosales?"

Burt put his head back and scratched at the whiskers under his chin. "Patricia. Hmm, let me see. There's Elena, the oldest, Sofia, Alita, then Patricia. Yes, I know Patricia." He paused and counted on his fingers. "After Patricia, Anna, and Lucita."

"All girls?" I said.

"Six girls, one boy." He wet his lips. "Sadly, Lorenzo is gone."

"At seventeen," I said. "Patricia told me."

Burt looked at me, surprise in his eyes. "You are a friend of Patricia's?"

"I'm not sure you'd call us friends. I know her. She works in Lavender where I live. I didn't know she has five sisters. She only mentioned her brother to me this week."

"Patricia doesn't come around," he said, "not like the others."

The deputy had always seemed so aloof—not to mention alone—not like someone who'd come from a whole houseful of sisters. But I didn't have a sister, so who was I to judge?

"Alita is nearby." Burt pointed. "See the house across the way? The one with the red shutters, barely visible from here?"

Through the trees, I spotted red shutters. "Yes, I see them."

"That one is Alita's house. She has four little ones of her own. The closer house with the wrought iron balcony on the second story? That's Patricia's parents' home."

Reggie Burt had a straight shot to watching what went on at the Rosales home. I thought of his binoculars and decided I wouldn't want to live within watching distance of this guy, no matter how nice he seemed.

"Where does Patricia live now?" I said.

He shook his head. "Can't help you there. She moved out of these parts before she went to work for the sheriff. Keeps to herself, that one does."

I rested against the back of the glider. "Did you live here when Lorenzo died?"

He nodded. "Moved here when I was thirty, long time before the tragic event."

"What happened to him?"

Burt made a tsk-tsk noise that took Hitchcock's attention away from the birds for a second. "I'm not sayin' anything you couldn't find out from looking in the papers from back in the day," he said.

"I understand."

He paused a beat before going on. "That boy got hooked up with a bad crowd."

"That's a shame." I waited. Hitchcock curled up on my lap, sensing my tension.

"The story went this way. Lorenzo and the gang he was with broke into a house. Thought the owner was out of town." Reggie looked at me and made the tsk-tsk noise again. "He wasn't. Kids tried to get out. You know about the rights of a homeowner in Texas?" Another pause.

I nodded.

"Lorenzo didn't make it," he said.

"The owner shot him?" I guessed.

Reggie nodded. "He was dead inside the house."

"What about the other kids?"

"Never knew who they were." Reggie pushed his feet against the ground and set the glider in motion. "Don't think anybody looked very hard. They didn't have time enough to steal anything. Owner wasn't charged."

I could only imagine the anger that Patricia Rosales felt over the situation and the death of her brother.

"Did it happen near here?" I said.

"No." Reggie shook his head. "They went over to Emerald Springs. Homeowner owned a car dealership. Had a good bit of money. Big house."

My earlier feeling that something in Rosales's past might figure into this week's crime fizzled. On a whim I asked the next question.

"Reggie," I said, "did you know Marty Dixon?"

"Kid who was killed in Lavender?"

"Yes."

"I been thinkin' about him a lot the past couple of days." He patted the newspaper by his side. "I read the paper every day and saw a piece about that murder. At first I thought nah, couldn't be the same Marty Dixon, but damn if I didn't recognize him by that picture they ran."

"You knew him pretty well then."

"Not as good as Lorenzo Rosales did. Marty was one of his friends."

"Was Marty in the gang of kids who broke into that man's house?" I said.

"Nope, Marty was a good egg. Was about to go off to college in the fall that year."

"How could anyone be sure he wasn't with Lorenzo that night?"

"At first, Lorenzo's parents believed Marty was in on it, since he and Lorenzo were buddies." Reggie folded his arms. "They were wrong, but they didn't like the truth any better."

"Why do you say it that way?"

"Because they found out Patricia was with Marty that night. All night."

"You mean they spent the night together?"

"Looked that way," Reggie said. "Patricia turned up at home the next morning after being gone all night. Said she and Marty Dixon were together the whole time."

Chapter 29

"I thought you were helping Deputy Rosales," Tyanne said after I'd told her about my meeting with Reggie Burt. "How does learning this story—possibly the very reason Rosales carries that huge chip on her shoulder—help the woman?"

I'd driven straight to Hilltop City Park on the outskirts of Lavender when I learned Ty had brought Abby here for a friend's birthday party. Ty planned to wait for the hour or so that the party would last, then go back to work at the bookstore with Abby in tow. This was my perfect opportunity to get my friend's take on what I'd learned from Reggie Burt.

We stood a distance from the party bus emblazoned with *Let's Dance* on the sides and blasting hip-hop music. The birthday group of a dozen girls had piled inside, and their giggling rocked the vehicle.

I paused a moment for Ty's statement to soak in. "This is why I come to you. You zero in on the crux of the matter."

"Moms have to," she said. "That's our job."

"I don't get it."

"If we didn't, then our kids might—"

"I mean I don't get how you connect that chip on the deputy's shoulder to what Reggie Burt told me."

Ty put a hand on one hip. "Think of the Rosales family, all those girls and their baby brother. Finally, a boy."

"Okay. So?"

"He was a very important part of that family."

"Did you know him?"

She blew out a breath. "No, I didn't know him, and maybe those parents were going to keep having babies until they had seven no matter what. But I'm sure they treasured that boy when he came. They all did, and older sisters would feel protective over their baby brother."

"Okay, I'm with you."

Hitchcock sidled around Ty's legs and she picked him up. "So on the night he's murdered, Patricia was out with a boyfriend, stayed out all night no matter what anyone thought, and then she got the shock of her lifetime. Her brother is gone. I think she'd blame herself from the time she found out what happened and never stop. If only she hadn't left with Dixon, if only she had spent the night with her brother, et cetera. Hence, the chip."

"Mrreow," Hitchcock said.

"And maybe that's the reason she went into law enforcement," I said. "To keep people safe, to solve crimes, because she didn't solve the one that mattered most."

"Or prevent the one that mattered the most," Ty said.

I nodded thoughtfully. "You think that's why she was still ticked at Marty Dixon when he showed up here in Lavender all these years later?"

Ty shrugged and let Hitchcock down when he squirmed in her arms. "Not to the extent she'd want to murder him, if that's what you're getting at. My question stands. How will learning this history about Rosales help her?"

"I don't know yet," I said. "For someone who used to be a friend, Dixon sure acted like a jerk when he saw her outside the pizza shop."

"She did, too, according to what Ethan witnessed."

"True." I walked a few steps closer to Hitchcock, who'd stretched out the leash to claw on the trunk of the tree we stood under. "Do you think there's any chance Rosales was the girlfriend Dixon planned to see? The one his mother would love to find so they can be BFFs?"

"Zero percent chance," Ty said. "Have you talked to Dixon's stepfather yet?"

"No, but I will today. Timing may be tricky. I have reason to believe the sheriff will talk to Zeke Farley soon, if he hasn't already. I don't want to run into him."

"You and Sheriff Crawford are on the outs?"

"Kind of," I said. "He's upset with me for keeping information to myself."

"That's nothing new," she said.

"He wants me to share everything in this case with him, more than ever."

"So you'll tell him about your meeting with this birdman guy?"

"And let him know I was checking up on Deputy Rosales?" I shook my head. "Not on your life."

• • •

As we left Tyanne and walked through the park to return to the car, I spotted several other birthday party themes. A woman dressed as Ariel from *The Little Mermaid*—red wig and all—held the attention of a group of young girls. Darth Vader entertained some boys. An adult-sized Scooby-Doo scampered across the lawn ahead of us toward some picnic tables.

"Hitchcock." The child's voice called out from behind me, and I turned to see Noah Hansen zoom toward us. His eyes glittered with excitement. "Hitchcock's coming to the party, too?" he said.

I laughed. "No, cats don't usually get invited to parties. I came to the park to see my friend, and Hitchcock happened to be with me."

Noah dropped to his knees and put his chubby little hands on either side of the cat's face to look him in the eye. "Scooby-Doo the dog is coming here," the boy told Hitchcock, "so you have to be super careful." The cat accepted the boy's attention, but he gave me a look that I read as "help me."

"Noah, come back here." Charlotte Hansen jogged across the grass toward us with a wrapped birthday gift tucked under her arm.

"He's okay," I said. "He and Hitchcock are buddies."

"He's supposed to be at his friend's party," she said.

"If it's the Scooby-Doo party, I don't think it's started yet," I said.

"Yes, that's the one." She cast a frantic glance toward Noah, who was busy acting like his mom was invisible, then over to what I assumed was the party site.

"Has the sheriff talked to Fritz yet?" I said, recalling Sheriff Crawford's comment of the previous night.

"What?" The expression in her eyes went from annoyance to concern. "Why would he?"

"I'm sure it's not a big deal. I happened to see the sheriff at dinner last night. Your father was there, too. At my Aunt Rowe's."

"Dad mentioned the dinner," she said.

"The sheriff asked him to pass a message to Fritz," I said. "That he wants to interview him about what happened outside your pizza shop. You already know he talked to many other people, but he hasn't caught up with Fritz yet."

Her expression lightened. "I'm sure Dad told Fritz. Men. They don't tell me what's happening."

"Men are from Mars, women from Venus," I said. "A lot of truth in that saying."

Charlotte laughed and seemed to relax a tad. "Nice to see you again. We need to go."

She bent to put a hand around Noah's forearm, but the boy struggled, and she let go.

"It is *so* hard," she said, "to raise a boy this age."

"He probably listens better to his father," I said. "That's usually how it goes."

"Not in our case," she said. "Thank the Lord for *my* father. Dad and Noah are like this." She crossed an index and middle finger. "Fritz has *no* patience with Noah. Or with me. With nothing, actually."

"I noticed that about Fritz," I said. "Yesterday, when I saw him in town, he was in an impatient mood."

"Sounds like Fritz," she said. "I hope this rough patch will pass. With the business to worry about and the bills, there's a lot." She tapped the toe of her sneaker against her son's leg. "Noah, please. Now."

I knew I should help her corral the boy, but this was a chance for me to ask a question I'd wondered about.

"I saw you the other day in the sheriff's office," I said.

She turned to me. "Yes, I remember."

"I'm sorry about what happened to your friend," I said.

"Friend?" Her expression seemed blank.

"Marty Dixon," I said. "The man who, the victim of —"

"I know the name," she said, "but not the man."

"Oh, I assumed." I gave a small laugh. "That's never a good idea. I assumed you knew him well because you appeared to be crying when you left, after talking to the sheriff."

"I cry too easy," she said, "And I think speaking of murder is always an upsetting thing."

"So true." I nodded and looked down at Noah, who now lay sprawled in the grass with my cat.

"Noah," I said, "Hitchcock and I are leaving now, and you need to go to your party." When I bent to pick up the cat, my phone slipped out of my shirt pocket and hit the ground, bouncing once before coming to rest.

"Noah," Charlotte said, "remember Papa said he would come. I think he's already here."

Noah popped up and spoke excitedly. "Papa is here?"

My phone rang, and the caller ID on the screen read "Deputy Rosales."

"Oh, I need that call." I juggled Hitchcock and took a step toward the phone. Charlotte was closer. She grabbed my phone and handed it to me.

She took Noah's arm again and pointed toward the party area. "See Papa? There he is."

I answered the call. "Hello."

"Sabrina, I have something," Rosales said. "Can we meet? About thirty minutes?"

"Sure. I think so. Where?"

I looked in the direction Charlotte pointed and saw Bruno standing with the Scooby-Doo group. Noah ran full throttle toward his grandfather. Such a cute kid.

Bruno noticed me and lifted an arm in greeting. I waved back, then headed for my car. Three days ago I'd have never guessed I would listen to instructions from Patricia Rosales. Yet here I was. Curiosity had me hanging on the deputy's every word.

Chapter 30

I met Rosales in the parking lot behind the city's water district office. The building was closed for the weekend, and the only thing in sight besides us and our vehicles was a weathered bench sitting outside the back door. A place for employees to take a break from their desks, I figured. I parked next to the deputy's SUV and watched her pace on the sidewalk.

Four paces to the right, about-face, four to the left. Repeat.

After watching two rounds of the pacing, I got out and left the engine running for Hitchcock to have AC while Rosales and I talked.

"What's up with the car?" she said when I approached her.

"Hitchcock's with me," I said. "Not much shade here, so he's better off left inside."

Rosales surprised me by not making a snide remark about the cat. She was out of uniform again, in beige shorts with a coral shirt that gave her a more feminine appearance than usual. She looked exhausted, though, with dark circles under her eyes and the pallid complexion of someone who hadn't slept well lately. I wanted to know if she'd kept up with Dixon all these years since her brother's death, but I knew better than to come right out and ask her.

The bench was situated in the building's shadow, out of the glaring sun, so I went to it and sat. "What do you have to tell me?"

She continued pacing as she talked. "The solution lies with the girl," she said, "and the drug connection."

I frowned. "Tandee Cushing?"

"Right," Rosales said.

"Does the sheriff have her in custody?"

She shook her head. "He didn't have evidence. Had to let her go, but we can find some. Help him button up the case."

"I'm not sure I understand. Does Sheriff Crawford think she's selling drugs?"

I wondered where Rosales was getting her information since she wasn't working this week. Maybe she'd talked to the sheriff or logged in to read the file. She stopped pacing to look at me.

"I'm not in the sheriff's head, so I don't know what he thinks at this moment. Plus, it's not the drugs I'm thinking about right now. In my opinion, the girl killed Marty Dixon."

I felt a jolt of surprise. "But you said there was a drug connection."

Rosales gave me a withering look. "The connection being that when Dixon found out about the drugs, he threatened to tell the authorities and have her arrested."

"Why would he care what this girl was up to? I doubt that they ran in the same circles. She's eighteen, and he was what? In his thirties?"

"Thirty-two," she said.

"Tandee lived here. Dixon lived in Nashville. They each had a connection to Colt Jamison, but so what?"

"Here's my take," she said. "As Colt Jamison's P.R. guy, Dixon needed to maintain the singer's good reputation, which might take a hit if the president of his fan club had a drug problem."

"Yeah, but do you have any evidence that they kept up with each other's activities? Why would you think Marty knew anything about Tandee?"

Rosales glared at me. "I called you for help to find the evidence to nail her, not for you to argue with me."

"Give me a minute." I sat back and propped my elbow on the bench arm, rested my chin on my fist. Dixon had allegedly been fired from his job, but he came to Lavender anyway to continue promoting Jamison. If he believed Tandee could hurt the singer or the upcoming show in any way, he might have threatened to turn her in. I had wondered myself about the possibility that Tandee purposely led Matthew into those woods to find a body that she already knew was there.

I turned to look at Rosales. "Okay, if you want help, I need more information."

"Like what?" she said.

"You must have done some research about Tandee's background. What can you tell me about the girl?"

"All right." Rosales came and sat beside me on the bench. "She was born and raised here in Lavender. Parents took off to live in California. They're some kind of transients, sorry excuses for parents if you ask me. Left the girl with Mom's brother when she was six, and he raised her ever since."

"What do you know about the brother?"

"Decent guy," she said. "Works in a car repair shop for the past twenty-something years. Did the best he could with the girl, but through no fault of his that I can tell she has a record. Two arrests for drug possession."

"Anything violent in her past?"

Rosales shrugged. "She had a friend a couple years back who died of a drug overdose. There was speculation that she got the drugs for the friend. No proof. Tandee went to the girlfriend's bedroom and found her dead. Took it hard."

Thinking back to Tandee's horrified reaction as she looked at Dixon's body in the woods, I wondered if she might have flashed back to the discovery of her friend's body. At the time, I had no idea what her chanting "not my fault" might have meant. Now, I wondered if she believed she'd been at fault in that death.

"I don't think she killed Dixon," I said.

"And where is this conclusion coming from?" Rosales said.

"For one thing, Tandee told me she didn't know Dixon well."

"Maybe she lied. The girl had means, motive, and opportunity."

"I don't accept your slim possibility of a motive," I said.

"She was right there in the vicinity," Rosales said. "She didn't even run, just boldly took your nephew into those woods to show him what she'd done." She paused, her dark gaze boring into mine. "Unless she talked him into doing the killing for her. That's another possibility."

I stood up and looked down at the deputy. My heart thudded so hard it seemed like it might explode out of my chest.

"Do *not* go there," I said. "Matthew had nothing to do with this except he was with Tandee when they discovered the body. That's it—do you hear me?"

"I hear you," Rosales said, her tone icy.

"I don't see this girl as a killer. You're trying to make some square facts fit into a round hole." I couldn't keep my voice from rising as my words rushed out. "You have no evidence. Why are you doing this? Is it because you and Dixon still had a relationship? Had you and he kept up with each other all these years?"

Rosales popped up like a jumping bean. "A relationship? What in God's name are you talking about?"

Her dark eyes were wide, and her usually sleek hair stood out at odd angles. Maybe grief was causing Rosales to lose her grip on reality. Grief over Marty's death on top of leftover grief about her brother. Movement inside my car caught my attention. Hitchcock stood on the dash and watched us. His mouth worked, and I read the silent meow as a warning.

Don't push Rosales too far.

"I heard Dixon had a girlfriend in Lavender," I said. "So far, I haven't confirmed the identity of the woman, but you and he knew each other back in the day. Naturally I wondered if there was still a relationship between you two."

"There was *not*," she said, "any romantic relationship between me and Marty Dixon. Not now — not ever."

"Okay. I didn't think so, because you appeared to hate the sight of him the other day outside the pizza shop. I'm probably not the only person to wonder."

"Wonder *what*?" she said.

"Why you were so nasty to him, for one thing, and whether you had a motive to want him dead. Which obviously you must, or you wouldn't be concerned that someone would accuse you of killing him."

I stood stock-still, hoping I hadn't pushed her too far.

She began to pace again — six steps in each direction this time.

Sweat trickled down my back as I waited. After a bit more pacing, Rosales stopped and faced me. "Obviously, you've learned more than I thought you could about my background. Do you believe I'm guilty?"

"Maybe of holding on to something from the past that you should let go," I said. "Not of killing Marty Dixon. I never thought you killed him."

"And you don't think Tandee did it either. So after all the nosing around you've done thus far, who do you peg as the killer?"

"There's no one person I'm ready to name," I said, "but I'll let you know when that changes."

Chapter 31

"Mrreow," Hitchcock said as we drove away from Rosales and the public works building.

"I know I should have kept quiet, but why'd she have to bring Matthew's name into the discussion? She knows Matt didn't do anything wrong. She was purposely goading me, like that would change my opinion about Tandee. She shouldn't have asked for my help if she didn't want to know what I thought."

I stopped at an intersection and checked both ways. Then I looked at Hitchcock. "I still don't know why she held such a grudge against Dixon."

Hitchcock, sprawled on the passenger seat, slitted his eyes in response. I was glad someone felt relaxed.

I wasn't ready to tell anyone the names on my suspect list, especially not Rosales, who seemed hell-bent on closing the case and locking up a killer, with or without evidence. She was obviously operating on emotions and not on her training or common sense. Probably better that she was spouting off her conclusions to me and not to the sheriff.

The problem with my suspect list was it seemed no one had a huge enough motive to kill. The people with the most at stake—financially and reputation-wise—were Gary Weber and Colt Jamison. Had Dixon put a kink in their plans somehow? There could be other suspects in the entertainment industry that I didn't even know.

Maybe if I gathered more information some important fact would come to light and turn everything I thought I knew on its head.

Worth a try.

"Let's go visit Zeke Farley," I said, "and see what he can tell us about his stepson. Then I'll take you home so you can get in your afternoon nap."

"Mrreow," Hitchcock said with a little zip at the end.

• • •

This time when I took the driveway toward Wanda Dixon's house I saw a pickup parked at the barn. I took that as a sign that Zeke was home and drove on by the house to park beside the shiny black Ford with a King Ranch insignia on the back. Of course, Zeke might be in the house with his wife, but I had a hard time picturing the musician hanging out in there with her and all that yarn.

"How about you slip into the tote for now?" I said to Hitchcock, remembering the broken mirror incident during our last visit. Hitchcock went willingly and sat with his head poked out, curious to see where we were going.

Near the tall sliding barn doors, a smaller door stood slightly ajar. I heard what sounded like someone might be tuning a guitar.

I knocked and called at the same time. "Hello?"

"Yeah," came the reply. "Who is it?"

Before I could answer, Zeke Farley came to the door and pushed it open. Up close, I could see he was a good decade younger than Willie Nelson, though the long braid still reminded me of the legendary singer.

I said hello and introduced myself. "I came to visit your wife yesterday, but you weren't here."

"And?" he said. "What can I do for you that she couldn't? Besides appreciate a visit from a pretty lady? That I can surely do." He gave me a once-over, then added, "Come on in."

I hesitated and Hitchcock made a rumbling noise deep in his throat.

"Settle down, boy," I whispered. "He's only joking around."

I stepped into the barn and my breath caught. There was nothing barn-like about the interior. I stood in the doorway of what reminded me of the homes or studios of famous musicians I'd seen on television interviews from time to time. On a smaller scale, maybe. A collection of guitars lined one long wall. Plaques, some of them holding vinyl records under glass, and framed photographs hung on another. A third wall held a large flat-screen TV between two shuttered windows.

"Wow," I said. "This place is awesome."

Zeke sat on a stool next to a bar, where it appeared he'd recently had lunch, judging from the empty take-out container and crumpled napkin nearby. He grabbed a guitar and went back to the tuning. "Have a seat if you like," he said. "Look around. Whatever. There something special you came here for?"

I considered the L-shaped brown velour sofa and plush

armchairs and chose to inspect the wall hangings. The first photograph I studied portrayed a trio of singers. I recognized one of them as Vince Gill.

"I wanted to say how sorry I am about what happened to your stepson. I hope you and Wanda are doing okay."

"You the one told her there was a woman in the kid's life?" he said. "Shouldn't have done that. Now I'm gonna listen to her wailing about some nonexistent relationship over and over forever."

"But—"

"Like that song," he continued. "Forever and ever, amen. That's what it'll be like around here."

"Sorry," I said. "She kind of jumped to a conclusion."

"Yeah," he said. "She does that."

"I only mentioned I heard a rumor about a girlfriend."

"Doesn't take much to get Wanda going." He continued twisting the things that tuned the guitar strings. They must have a name, but I had no idea what that might be or how someone could tell when a guitar was tuned properly.

"Did *you* know anything about Marty's personal life, like whether he had a girlfriend or not?"

"I met his ex once, that's it. Kid didn't even talk to his mama, sure didn't talk to me."

"So you wouldn't know if he had trouble with someone."

"Somebody who'd knock him off, you mean? Nope."

This guy's attitude bugged me. I sure hoped he showed a little compassion around his wife.

"How long have you and Wanda been married?"

"Seems like forever." He chuckled. "Does that count?"

I forced a smile. "I guess so."

"Kid was about sixteen at the time," he said. "Already had a car. Nicer than the one I drove."

He couldn't complain now, judging by the pricey truck sitting outside the barn.

"Were you and Marty ever close?" I said.

"Not hardly. Didn't come to me unless his mama wasn't home and he wanted money. Kid always had his hand out."

I cringed inwardly, not liking the fact that Zeke would talk to a stranger this way about Marty only a few days after his death. I wondered if he'd ever had a kind word for his stepson. I continued to study the things hanging on the wall. Some were awards given to Marty Dixon, Sr. Some were family photos, including one I guessed was a family portrait of Marty, Sr., Wanda, and little Marty, Jr. Nothing on the wall, as far as I could tell, related personally to Zeke.

"I heard you play at the Wild Pony a couple nights ago. Always thought it would be fun to be a musician."

"Has its moments," he said.

I went to the sofa and sat down, resting the weight of my tote on the cushion. Hitchcock kept his head low and didn't attempt to jump out. If Zeke realized I had a cat with me, he didn't comment.

I scanned the wall of instruments. "Are all of these guitars yours?"

Zeke followed my gaze. "A couple of 'em are. Rest belonged to my wife's first husband. This was his place. Guess you could say I'm a pale imitation of the man who first played his guitar in this room."

"Don't sell yourself short," I said. "You have a heckuva lot more musical talent than I'll ever have."

"Nice of you to say so." He smiled and fiddled some more with the guitar strings.

"Did you find it useful to have a stepson in the Nashville music business?"

"Useful?" he said in a tone filled with scorn. "I'm not sure what all he was doin' over there in Nashville, but it wasn't earnin' a good livin', that's for sure."

"I meant useful because he might be able to get your music heard by somebody in the business. In case you had a song you wanted to sell."

"Nope. I'm no country music star and have no designs on becoming one."

I thought about Zeke's meeting with Jamison at the river and wondered how he'd made a connection with the famous singer if it wasn't through Marty.

"Small towns need country music, too," I said. "Not everyone's going to be a big star like that guy who's putting on the concert tonight, right?"

"Colt Jamison," Zeke said.

I nodded. "Yeah, Colt. You going to the show?"

Zeke shook his head. "Nah. I'm playing at the Pony tonight."

"I know Tracey appreciates having you there."

His attention turned away from the guitar and toward me. "You know Tracey?"

"We're acquainted."

"She's a pistol, that one is." He chuckled, shaking his head. "She sure was ticked off with Marty."

I didn't want to get into discussing Tracey and her fight with Dixon. I had a burning question for this man, and I needed to ask it before he ended our meeting and sent me on my way.

"Have you ever met Colt Jamison?" I zeroed in on Zeke, staring at him until he looked up and met my gaze.

"Never had the pleasure," he said.

Chapter 32

Even though I'd told Hitchcock we'd head home after seeing Zeke Farley, I had one more quick stop to make. I had some questions Tracey Powell might be able to help me with. I wanted so badly to solve the mystery of who killed Marty Dixon. Finding the solution would put Nick and Matt at ease so they could enjoy the rest of their stay, and would help the sheriff, and yes, solving the case would help Patricia Rosales with her problem that I didn't fully understand. If only I could line everything up properly for the pieces to start making sense.

Parking at the Wild Pony in the middle of the day was a cinch. I snagged a front-row spot, bundled Hitchcock into the tote again, and jogged up the steps and inside. The area around the bar was deserted. With no one to stop me, I headed toward the back where I'd seen Tracey come out of a door the other night. I knocked and then walked through the door when no one answered.

"Mrreow." Hitchcock squirmed in the tote.

"I know, and I'm sorry. I'll make it up to you, buddy."

"Who are you talking to?"

The voice came from behind me and I turned to see Elise Lister in a room to my right. She held a handful of rolls of red, white, and blue ribbon.

"Hi, Elise," I said. "Didn't expect to see you here. I'm talking to my cat, and I'm here looking for Tracey."

"Where's the cat?" she said.

"In my tote."

"Good Lord, don't make him suffocate in there. Let him out."

"I don't know if I should," I said, but Hitchcock was rumbling and squirmy. I poured him out of the tote onto the floor and picked up the end of his leash.

"There, that's much better," Elise said. "Hello, you handsome boy. Come right this way with your mom. Tracey and I are making goodie bags to hand out tonight."

Elise sounded so relaxed and more pleasant than the other times I'd spoken with her. I couldn't help but wonder what she'd had to drink. I followed her down a hallway to a larger room. Tracey stood behind a long folding table that held a lineup of shallow baskets holding what looked like giveaways. Bottle openers, refrigerator magnets, and pens with the Wild Pony logo. Free drink coupons. Pocket-sized maps of Lavender's shops. A few other things I couldn't identify from a distance.

Tracey held a cellophane packet and went down the row, picking up an item from each basket to assemble the goodie bag. I guessed they would tie the finished product with the ribbon Elise had brought in.

"Sabrina," Tracey said when she noticed me. "What a surprise. Did you come to help?"

"I didn't know you needed help, so that's not why I came. I don't mind helping you, though, if you need me to." I noticed a couple of nearly-empty cocktail glasses sitting on the table behind Tracey.

She'd seen me looking. "Get you anything?"

I smiled. "Some water for my cat might be nice."

"Sure." Tracey looked at Hitchcock. "Long as he doesn't get any ideas about playing with my goodie bags. I have a couple hundred more to make before five."

Elise moved the rolls of ribbon out of Hitchcock's view. "Let's not tempt fate. I'll get the water."

"Thanks." I watched Tracey beginning to fill another packet.

"What can I do for you?" she said.

"I'd like to know more about Zeke Farley," I said.

She smirked. "You have that hunky boyfriend. Why'd you be asking about Zeke?"

I ignored her reference to Luke. "I just came from talking with Zeke over at his place. Sounds like you and he saw eye to eye on your opinion of Marty Dixon."

She looked up. "Why d'you say that?"

"Well, he was Marty's stepfather, but he sure isn't sad that Marty's gone. Sounded like he's rid of a major thorn in his side if you ask me. I wondered if he ever talked to you about Marty."

She shook her head. "Never thought to bring Marty up with him. Zeke comes here and plays, and that's about it between him and me."

"Do you know where Zeke's from?" I said.

Her forehead wrinkled as she considered the question. "Odessa, maybe. Someplace where there's not much except dust. I heard him say that once."

"Any idea how long he's been here in Lavender?"

"Since he married Wanda. Don't remember how long ago that was."

"Now that I've met both of them, I wonder how they got together. They're kind of opposite types. Do you know her?"

Tracey shook her head, but Elise had come back into the room with a bowl of water for Hitchcock. She set the bowl on the floor. "I think Wanda got a flat tire out on the highway, and Zeke stopped and changed it for her. I heard somebody say that's how they met."

"An interesting way to meet a husband," I said.

"Zeke says that was his lucky day," Elise said. "I always thought it sounded sweet, though I did wonder what was in it for Wanda. He's not exactly a catch."

"Maybe he has money," I said.

Tracey burst out laughing. "Then why's he always begging me to pay him in advance?"

The statement made me pause, but I didn't expand on the issue. "Does he have any other family," I said, "besides Wanda? Kids from a prior marriage?"

"Don't think so," Elise said.

"And Marty was Wanda's only child?" I said.

"Far as I know." Elise picked up a cellophane packet and went down the other side of the table, helping Tracey with her project.

Hitchcock finished having a drink and walked under the table to where a pen had fallen. Before I could pick the pen up, he'd batted it across the room. I retrieved the pen and returned it to the basket with the others.

"Has the sheriff been here to see you again, Tracey?" I said. "Or Chester?"

"No, thank goodness, I think he's finally convinced that neither of us killed Marty."

"That's good," I said.

I checked my watch and reminded myself that any mention of the concert might set Tracey off. "I've had Hitchcock out all morning, so we really need to get back home. Poor cat puts up with a lot."

"He looks happy, though," Elise said. "He's not bored."

"No, that he's not. One more question for you ladies." They paused and looked at me.

"What is it?" Tracey said.

"There's a rumor that Marty Dixon was eager to see his girlfriend here in Lavender, but nobody knows who she was. So I was wondering—"

I paused and looked at each of them.

Tracey burst into laughter again. "You think it was one of us?" She looked at Elise, and they both laughed hysterically and so loudly I wasn't sure I'd be able to hear what I said next.

"Well, it *could* be one of you. How am I to know?"

"The knock-down, drag-out fight didn't convince you?" Tracey said, laughing so hard she could hardly speak.

I shrugged.

Elise doubled over with laughter and held her side when she tried to straighten, gasping to catch her breath. "I'm in enough trouble with the man I have," she said. "He thought I was in New Orleans for my job on Wednesday, but I didn't want to go out of town with him to visit his sister."

Their gales of laughter continued. I giggled along, but I didn't really know what was so funny.

"Then somebody makes a danged video," Elise said, still gasping, "and it's on YouTube of all things. I still don't know what I'll say if he sees the video."

"You weren't doing anything suspicious on the video," I said, not getting the point.

"But he *thought* I'd gone out of town, and I never did. I was only making an excuse. I wanted a break."

"Oh." I looked at Tracey, who nodded in confirmation.

I didn't really care to ask Elise why she had to lie about wanting a break or why she said she'd gone to New Orleans.

"Bottom line is that neither of you were Marty Dixon's girl-friend."

"Absolutely not," Elise said.

"Never," Tracey added.

I thought of one more question and nodded toward the cocktail glasses. "What the heck is in those drinks that's making y'all so giggly?"

"That's my anti–Colt Jamison special," Tracey said, "and the ingredients are top secret. Get 'em here. Two ninety-nine. Tonight only."

Chapter 33

I took Hitchcock home to the Monte Carlo cottage, where he quickly assumed his napping position in the center of my bed. I'd missed lunch, and my refrigerator was bare except for one lone yogurt container. After the emotion-packed day I'd had so far, I needed something a lot more hearty than yogurt. I needed comfort food.

I headed for Aunt Rowe's, where I was always welcome to the leftovers. Maybe with a full tummy I'd be able to examine what I'd learned in my discussions with Rosales, Zeke, Tracey and Elise and pull out something to help solve the case. Stranger things had happened.

I was eager to hear the boys' report on their visit to the Snake House, but Nick's vehicle wasn't back yet. Matt and Adam would be excited, for sure, and I didn't mind listening to stories about snakes so long as I didn't have to see them.

Partway to the house, I noticed Violet sitting in an Adirondack chair under a large oak tree. She wore a pink gingham dress that matched her hair feather and slip-on sandals. A yellow tablet sat on the wide chair arm, and she wrote steadily until she noticed me and stopped to wave.

I walked over to her. "Hope I'm not interrupting your work."

"No, dear," she said. "I'm only making some notes for a seminar I'm holding in Lubbock next month."

"I guess you stay pretty busy with the life-coaching business."

"I do, but simply because I'm leaving on Monday doesn't mean you've missed your chance. I'd be happy to make arrangements to work with you."

"Maybe someday when there's not so much else on my plate. Today's the big day my nephews have been waiting for. Are you going to the concert tonight?"

"No," she said. "Bruno says the pizza shop will be extra busy this evening. That the end-of-summer crowd is always heavy."

I grinned. "Is there something going on between you and Bruno? Seems like you two hit it off quickly."

Violet cocked her head. "I thought there might have been a spark there, but now I'm not sure. If it's meant to be, it will be." She

209

looked at me. "Rowe tells me you have a knack for investigating. Is that what you've been doing today?"

"A little bit," I hedged. "My big question of the day remains a mystery."

"What's the question?" she said.

"Who was the victim's girlfriend? He allegedly had one here in Lavender, but no one seems to know her name."

"I can't help you there," Violet said.

"I'm giving up on that for now," I said. "I want to catch the guys when they come back from their visit to the Snake House."

"They've already come and gone," Violet said. "They left with Rowe about thirty minutes ago."

I felt a pang of disappointment that I'd missed them, but maybe this worked out for the best. I'd have a chance to sort through the thoughts racing through my brain while the new information I'd gathered was still fresh.

"Not a problem," I told Violet. "I'll be seeing the guys soon enough at the concert."

I left Violet to get back to her project and continued on to the house. When I reached the empty kitchen, I fixed myself a bowl of calico beans and put them in the microwave to heat. I checked my phone and realized I'd put it on silent before my meeting with Rosales. I'd missed several texts from Nick and read through them.

Aunt Rowe had offered to introduce them to a friend of hers who owned an ostrich farm. The farm was in the vicinity of the concert site, and he and the boys could head straight to the show from the farm. Matt and Adam wanted to arrive early to enjoy the full Colt Jamison experience, and they would meet me at the front-row seats.

I wondered what they'd think about the concert experience after they'd spent hour upon hour in the ninety-degree heat. The thought made me grin. The heat probably wouldn't faze them. I felt guilty for being out of pocket today, but we'd have the next two days together before they headed back to Houston.

I sliced some of the leftover steak, cut a piece of corn bread to complete my meal, and sat at the breakfast table to enjoy my late lunch. As I ate, I thought about the case. I needed to drop the whole idea of a girlfriend who might not even exist. Dixon's death was more likely about something bigger. He'd been involved with the music business in Nashville, for crying out loud. A place where people dealt with fame and fortune.

Thinking about the case as money-driven rather than an emotional crime put a different spin on everything. Who would benefit monetarily from Marty Dixon's death, if anyone? He didn't seem like the kind of guy who'd buy a life insurance policy, but his mother might have bought one for him. Wanda and Zeke seemed to live very nicely, though, judging by their home and possessions. If there was a policy, it probably wouldn't amount to a change in their lifestyle.

Zeke was the shifty person in that family. He'd outright lied to me about not knowing Colt Jamison. I had witnessed him accepting what appeared to be a wad of cash from Jamison in exchange for something. Wanda said her first husband was the talented one. What if Zeke was selling off things that belonged to Marty, Sr., and what if Marty, Jr., found out what he was doing and threatened to tell his mother?

But Dixon hadn't been in touch with his mother for more than a year and had made no move to contact her before his death.

I got up to check out the desserts and cut an extra-large piece of key lime pie. I stood at the kitchen counter and ate the dessert way too fast, then cleaned up and put my dirty dishes in the dishwasher. I checked the time—not too early to shower and get ready for tonight. I hadn't decided what to wear—slacks with a shirt or a casual maxi-dress.

I mulled over the decision on my way back to my place, but my attention was drawn to the Athens cottage when I realized that both Colt Jamison's pickup and Gary Weber's black SUV were parked there. I would have thought the star of the show would have to arrive way ahead of time, but it appeared both he and his manager were still here. Maybe Jamison would be driven in at the last moment when the fans were all in place and excitement had built to a fever pitch.

I felt a jolt of adrenaline thinking about it, but what I heard now was not the joy of someone eager for the show to begin. Was it shouting? No, not quite that loud, but not happy conversation either. The voices definitely came from the Athens cottage.

I jogged in that direction, listening carefully. When I arrived at the cottage door I realized the sound came from around back.

"Do you have any idea what's at stake here?" a man said.

Weber.

"Of course I do. I'm not stupid, which is apparently what you're trying to say."

Jamison's softer voice.

"What about the songs? Have you come up with anything yet?"

"Maybe," Jamison said.

"You've been sitting here for three straight days and all you have is a maybe?" Weber said.

"I'm kind of collaborating with someone," Jamison said.

"Who?" Weber said.

"You don't know him."

"Ever think you should run this by your manager first, so I could check the guy out?"

"No need," Jamison said. "He's dead, and I might not use the stuff anyway."

Weber's voice rose. "What the hell are you talking about?"

"I bought his notes. They're rough. Nothing's finished."

I remembered the exchange at the river. Zeke Farley had likely sold Jamison the papers left behind by Marty Dixon, Sr. I wondered if he'd run this idea by his wife before doing so.

"Of all the damn fool ideas," Weber said. "Did you talk to a lawyer about this first? No, of course you didn't."

"Look." Jamison's tone grew testy. "If I use anything at all, I'll give credit to the guy, to his estate, whatever. Then I might consult a lawyer. I'm not going to claim something I didn't write as my own. If you don't know that, you don't know me very well."

"Do you have any idea how much money people have sunk into you?"

"How about you try composing a song," Jamison said. "See how far you get. And, by the way, your attitude doesn't help one bit."

"Well, it sure doesn't help that you left this place on the night of the murder. What the hell were you thinking?"

"I was *thinking* I wanted a bag of peanuts. No law against that. The old man behind the counter didn't let the cat out of the bag. He had no idea who I was."

Good Lord, I was the one who'd done that when I told the sheriff

Jamison was staying here. But what the heck was Weber thinking by dressing Jamison down today, the day of the show? He was acting like a bully.

Without weighing the pros and cons, I marched around the cottage to the back deck. The men stood there face-to-face. Weber's complexion was beet red. Jamison, with a Coke in hand, appeared relaxed.

"Excuse me," I said to draw their attention, and they both turned to me.

"Did you lose your cat again?" Jamison said.

"No, he's at home asleep, thank you. But you two are way out of line here."

"And what makes our private discussion any of your business?" Weber said.

"You men have a beef with each other you'd better get over it right quick," I said. "There's a concert tonight."

"We know that," Weber said.

"How do you expect Colt to put on a good show after you finish raking him over the coals? You're acting ridiculous."

"Where do you get off telling me anything?" Weber said.

"She makes a lot of sense, you ask me," Jamison said.

"Thank you, Colt," I said. "Mr. Weber, you might not understand what it's like to be creative. Coming up with a great finished product takes talent and solitude and plenty of time. A creative spirit has to get into the right frame of mind to do well, and your behavior will not improve the situation. You can't badger him this way and hope to get what you want."

Jamison nodded in agreement.

Weber crossed his arms over his chest. "I've spent many a year in Nashville. You can't tell me how to do my job."

"You're right," I said, "but if you have a problem with Colt today, you need to cool your britches. There's a concert to put on."

I caught Colt Jamison's grin as I turned around. He'd taken my interruption in a good-natured way. Weber didn't, and I sure hoped that man didn't have anything at hand to throw at my back as I walked away.

Chapter 34

"We're dealing with an all-time-high tourist attendance this weekend," Luke told me when we touched base by phone an hour later. "Seems like a thousand kids are out here on the river. I'm hoping things calm down when some of them take off for the concert." I heard the whine of his boat's motor and the rush of water in the background. "I won't know until then whether I can get away to join y'all there."

"The sheriff may need your help, too," I said.

"There's that," he agreed.

"So if you get to the concert, text me, and I'll meet you at the gate with your ticket."

"Sounds like a plan," he said. "I'll try my best. Hate to miss a chance to spend time with you, Sabrina."

I grinned. "Me, too."

We ended the call, and I tossed my phone on the bed near Hitchcock.

"That was Luke," I said. "He might get to the concert, might not. His work sure can put a kink in plans."

"Mrreow," Hitchcock said sleepily.

I bent to run my hand from his head to his tail, and he began to purr.

"You're gonna be a good boy and stay at home while I'm out, right?"

"Mrr."

"Now, to make the final decision on what to wear."

I turned to the closet and chose white capri pants with a blue-and-white print shirt. The pants were a tad snug after all the food I'd eaten, but I counted on the fact that they'd stretch out after a little while. I added strappy flat sandals, made sure my phone and the concert tickets were in my tote, and took off for town.

I figured I had enough time to check in with the sheriff and give him the new bits of information I'd gathered today. That way he couldn't accuse me of keeping a single solitary thing to myself.

The traffic downtown made me eager for the summer tourists to go back to wherever they all came from. The sidewalks were as jammed as the streets, and pedestrians didn't seem to care where they crossed the road or if they risked their lives by stepping out between moving cars. I drummed my fingers on the steering wheel as we inched down Main Street. This reminded me of the Houston traffic that I hadn't missed for one second since I'd moved to Lavender.

When I reached the next intersection, I turned right and wound my way toward the sheriff's office by taking back roads. I should have called ahead, because when I arrived I found the new deputy about to climb into the only car in the parking lot. I pulled up beside him and rolled down my window.

"Hey, Deputy Salazar." I reminded him who I was and explained that I had some information for the sheriff that I'd like to pass along in person. "Any idea where I might find him?"

Salazar nodded. "He got a call from Frank's Floats. Sounded like some kids got into it. One of 'em pulled a knife. Imagine he's still there."

"Okay. Thanks. I guess you're short-handed here, especially with Deputy Rosales out."

"She said she'd come in tonight to help work security, but I haven't seen her yet," he said.

"If she said she'd work, she'll show up," I said. "Thanks for the information."

Salazar got into his car and drove away. Rosales hadn't said anything about going back to work when I saw her this morning. If she was working security at the concert, maybe she'd gone straight there. I hesitated for a few seconds, then pulled out my phone and sent her a text message.

"Sorry about earlier. Think we're getting close. Have info about MD's stepfather. Off to concert. Talk later."

I stowed my phone, then made a U-turn in the street to head for Frank's Floats. I was familiar with the business along the Glidden River that rented tubes and the narrow winding road that would take me there. A traffic nightmare even on a good day.

I took a detour to approach from a more lightly traveled direction. I was making pretty good time until I neared a roadside rest and noticed a man standing on top of one of the picnic tables. I checked my rearview and, seeing nothing behind me, I slowed to watch the man. He spun in a circle and dumped pieces of something small and shiny from a pouch onto the ground around the table. He threw that pouch down and picked up another from the tabletop, then repeated the process.

Good Lord. Is that what I think it is?

I pulled off the road and took out my phone to call the sheriff's personal cell number. Five rings. No answer. I called the sheriff's office and got Laurel.

"I found the guy throwing pieces of broken mirror around. He's at the roadside rest." I explained to her where I was, but I didn't think she'd have anyone that could get here quickly. "Looks like he's driving an older model Hyundai. A Santa Fe." I read her the license plate number.

"Leave him alone, Sabrina," Laurel said. "I'll have someone come out there."

"Okay. I'm headed to the concert."

"Maybe I'll see you there," she said. "I'm off in fifteen."

She might have wanted me to stay on the line, but I ended the call and pulled into the parking area. The guy was on top of a different table now. I got out of my car and approached. He had a nerdy look about him, with shaggy hair and black-framed glasses.

"Hi," I said, glancing at the pieces of broken mirror scattered on the ground. "What're you doing?"

He stopped spinning and looked at me. "Working."

"Working at what? Littering?"

"I'm advertising."

"You need to stop that right now," I said. "The sheriff will be interested in talking to you."

His eyes went wide. "About what? I was hired to do this job."

"Seriously? Who hired you?"

"Marty Dixon."

Huh. Gary Weber had been right about Dixon's odd marketing ideas.

This guy obviously didn't see me as a threat and went on to explain, "Marty asked me if I wanted a trip to Texas, and I'd never been here before so I told him yeah, sure, I want to go to Texas and make some money."

"What's your name?"

"Logan," he said.

"Well, Logan, I think your job ended when Marty died."

"Died?" he shouted. "He's not dead."

I nodded. "Marty Dixon is dead. He was murdered on Wednesday."

Logan clasped the sides of his face with his palms. "Ohmigod, I didn't know he was dead. I thought he was with his kid."

I stared at him, and my thoughts raced. His kid? Marty Dixon's kid?

Logan watched me curiously as I worked through this new piece of information.

"Are you okay?" he said after half a minute had ticked by.

"Sure." I nodded. "Yes, I am. Logan, what do you know about this kid. Did Marty tell you he has a kid?"

"He did." Logan nodded vigorously. "He has a son."

"Did he happen to mention the boy's name?"

Logan's face scrunched up as he thought hard. "That guy with the animals. He had lots of animals."

I remembered the pictures at Wanda Dixon's house—there were no pictures of a baby, and she surely didn't know anything about a grandchild. Marty hadn't told her about any grandchild.

"I know it, I know it," Logan cried and jumped down from the tabletop to land in front of me.

"What is it?" I said.

"Noah."

• • •

Logan got back into his car and raced away before anyone arrived from the sheriff's office. I didn't much care. I had given them Logan's license plate number and that would have to do. I continued on my way to Frank's Floats, eager to talk to the sheriff and tell him about the boy. If Noah was Dixon's child and Fritz knew the truth, that could explain why he'd been in such a bad mood lately.

I could imagine news of a grandchild putting someone else in a bad mood—Zeke. He didn't tolerate Marty well, and I didn't picture him as a welcoming grandfather either—especially not if Wanda spent a lot of money on the boy, which she would. This new information—if it was true—could certainly have an impact on the investigation.

The route to Frank's Floats held a slow parade of traffic. I was finally getting close to the turnoff when my phone buzzed. I pulled it out, hoping for a call from the sheriff. It was a text from Deputy Rosales.

I know everything. Meet me ASAP. Red building near Beckman.

I wanted to respond that I was kind of busy at the moment. Instead, I sent her a thumbs-up emoji. I didn't believe she knew everything, but chances were good that when we combined what I'd just learned with what she knew, we could figure out who'd killed Marty Dixon. I passed the traffic that was headed for Frank's Floats and kept on going.

At least I knew the building Rosales referred to, and it was on my route to the concert. All good. As I drove, I turned the car radio to a country music station to get in the mood for tonight's concert. A fair number of vehicles were headed in the same direction I was driving, but I saw no sign of people camped out along the roadsides, as Tyanne thought they might. I wondered if the predictions about a huge attendance had been exaggerated.

I made good time reaching the meeting place and turned into the drive at the appointed red building. The structure was partly obscured from the road by trees and the flowering oleanders, and I saw no cars. I assumed this place was some part of the winery operation, but there was no sign to indicate a company name or the building's purpose. A concrete porch with an iron railing wrapped around the side of the building, so I followed the driveway that made a turn in the same direction.

Rosales's SUV was parked alongside the building, but she wasn't in the vehicle. I wondered what had made her choose to meet now when she was supposed to work concert security. Probably impatience. She wanted to tell me what she knew right now, not wait for several more hours. I could relate.

I parked next to her vehicle and got out of the car. When I turned back to grab my phone, I saw a flash of black. Hitchcock shot from my feet to the concrete apron, then rubbed against the iron railing and looked at me with a dare in his expression.

"Good Lord, what are *you* doing here?" The cat had not only faked me out with that nap on my bed, but he'd somehow managed to follow me and slip into the car. I couldn't believe he'd ridden with me this whole time with me none the wiser.

"What am I going to do with you now?" I said.

Hitchcock didn't respond to my words. Instead, he darted over to the building and ran up to the corner, then paused before disappearing around the edge. I wasn't sure why I was so shocked to see him. The darned cat hitched rides with people on a regular enough basis. I'd rather have him with me than with a stranger. At least I knew where he was. But I couldn't leave the cat in my car with the motor running all night during the concert. So how was I going to handle this problem?

Find Rosales first. Then corral the cat.

I walked in the direction Hitchcock had gone, took the corner, and came upon an enormous three-tier metal rack that held row upon row of wine barrels.

That stopped me for a moment. I'd never seen anything like it. I wondered if they were all filled with wine. Wouldn't they store full barrels standing upright? These were more likely empty at this point.

Makes no difference, Sabrina. You're not going to become a winemaker.

"Hello," I called out. "Rosales?"

No answer.

I walked to the other side of the barrels and saw a patio table and chairs, then stopped short. My breath caught. Patricia Rosales was here and dressed in her uniform, but she was duct-taped to the chair closest to the building. Her arms were secured behind her, her legs taped together, her mouth taped shut. She appeared to be alone, but she hadn't given herself the bruised knot on her forehead.

I ran to her. "Oh, my gosh, what's going on? What happened?" I dropped to my knees next to her and pulled at the tape around her ankles. She needed to be able to run. As I worked at the tape, Rosales groaned and grunted.

"I found that guy throwing pieces of broken mirrors around," I said. "Was he here? Is he the one who did this?"

Rosales rocked side to side as she shook her head.

"Hold still." I worked at the tape and finally got a good enough hold to make a rip and unwind the tape from her ankles. I crumpled the tape and threw it aside, then sat up to undo her hands.

Rosales moaned, and I looked at her face. She was focused on a spot between me and the wall of barrels.

"Oh, Sabrina." The man's voice caused chill bumps to run up my arms. "You're much more predictable than the characters you write."

I stood slowly and turned to face him.

"I knew you couldn't resist the mystery," Bruno Krause said.

He stood beside the wall of barrels, his right arm extended. He held a handgun in a gloved hand, possibly Rosales's own weapon. My first unreasonably calm thought was that Bruno wasn't wearing his usual Tower of Pizza apron. I'd never seen him without the white apron, yet here he was, dressed in all black—pants, shirt, gloves. An outfit chosen by a man who premeditated his moves.

My mind raced. The text message was sent by Bruno, not Rosales. He must have kept tabs on our actions, knew we were collaborating to solve the case. I would have never imagined Bruno could get the drop on Rosales, yet here he was—in control of the situation.

I only wished these pieces had fallen into place for me sooner. Fritz wasn't the culprit. Fritz might have known about Noah's biological father, but odds were he hadn't killed Marty Dixon. Bruno had. What the heck was he thinking now? How could I best handle this situation? Would he give me enough time to decide? I had to start talking. Invent a story.

"Bruno, thank goodness you got here," I said, trying for feigned relief. "I can't believe that Deputy Rosales committed murder, but she did have a good motive. A great motive, in fact, to kill Marty Dixon. If it weren't for him, her brother Lorenzo might still be with us today."

Despite the tape, I heard Rosales's gasp.

I glanced at her, then to Bruno, whose forehead creased in confusion. He said, "What are you—"

"Lorenzo's death occurred many years ago," I interrupted. "You'd think she'd have gotten over that by now, but I imagine it's hard to forgive something so horrific. From the moment Dixon arrived in Lavender, he was a marked man. She was out to get him."

I saw Hitchcock slinking behind the barrels and wondered if the cat was aware of the gravity of our situation. I reached toward the pocket that held my phone. "Anyway, you seem to have her under control, and boy am I relieved that you do, but I can give you a hand now and make a call to—"

"No, you won't." Bruno took a step closer to me. "Take out your phone, nice and slow. Throw it down on the ground, and kick it over to me."

I reluctantly obeyed him.

"I don't believe you think Deputy Rosales is guilty," Bruno said. "Nice try, but c'mon, give me more credit than that."

"Why should I? You're not thinking straight. Remember when you told Tracey that killing Dixon would be a dumb move? Then you went and did it yourself. Were you hoping to frame her?"

"Maybe." He paused as though the idea hadn't occurred to him. "But I'm the one making the decisions here. I'm the one with the gun."

I faced him. "And you're planning to do what?"

"I need to get rid of both of you. I'm sorry."

He was sorry. Oh, that was rich.

"Why, Bruno?" I said. "Because we're figuring out too much? Because we know Marty Dixon was Noah's biological father?"

Heat flooded Bruno's reddening face. "I am Noah's grandfather, and he belongs here with his family."

Rosales looked at me. I saw her working at the tape around her wrists.

"Of course he does," I said.

"No one is going to take that boy away."

"Did Marty Dixon threaten you? Charlotte?"

"He would have," Bruno said. "He'd know as soon as he got a good look at the boy. That man was a threat to my grandson. To my daughter. To her marriage. To the family. To everything I hold dear. He had to go. And now, unfortunately, so do the two of you."

"Bruno, you're not seriously going to harm a sheriff's deputy," I said, more alarmed about Rosales's safety than my own.

"But I am," he said. "I have no choice. You two are the threat now."

I wasn't sure why he hadn't already put a bullet in each of us, but if my blabbing was giving us more time, I could blab till kingdom come.

"What are you going to do with us?" I said. "You can't get away with a crime if you leave our bodies where they can be discovered. Remember? We talked about this."

"I remember," Bruno shouted.

"No bodies, no conviction," I went on. "You leave us here, they find us, they'll track you down. You know they will. What will happen to Noah then?"

"Sit down and shut up," he said. "Sit in that chair." He motioned with his gun hand and backed away from me as I moved forward and took the chair nearest Rosales. She and I exchanged a glance. I scanned my surroundings, looking for Hitchcock. Rosales's gaze flicked up for a moment, and I chanced a look, too.

Hitchcock stood on top of a barrel on the top row, gnawing on some kind of rubber strap. Below the cat, Bruno seemed to be analyzing his options.

"I will not leave any bodies to be found." He glanced at the rack. "I believe these barrels will work well for what I have in mind."

Good Lord, did he plan to shoot us and stuff our bodies into barrels? Then what? Bury us somewhere? This man was supposed to be serving pizzas tonight, for crying out loud. Doing his nice innocent job, not out here killing people. Killing us. Me and Rosales.

My heart thudded so hard it might give out before he did anything at all. Either that or I might drown in the sweat that drenched my body.

"Noah has a grandmother, you know," I said. "Marty Dixon's mother. She has rights, and Noah deserves to know her. All she'd have to do is take one look at the boy, like you said, and she'd recognize he's the spitting image of his daddy. What are you planning to do? Hide your grandson in the attic? Move him out of town before he starts school?"

"Stop it," Bruno cried and turned the gun on me. I saw his trigger finger move.

And that's when Hitchcock launched himself at the first barrel in the top row. The rubber strap that held the barrels in place, weakened by the cat's chewing, snapped. The barrels began to roll. Bruno heard the rumbling noise and looked up as a barrel toppled straight for him.

The falling barrel knocked Bruno to the ground. The gun flew from his hand and skittered across the concrete. I breathed a sigh of relief when the second barrel lodged against the rack, preventing an avalanche.

Bruno moaned, but Rosales was already on the move. She grabbed the weapon and, in two seconds, had the gun trained on Bruno. She struggled out of the remaining tape on her wrists, then ripped the piece of tape from her face and glared at me.

"What the hell, girl?" she yelled. "When were you going to get this danged tape off my mouth?"

Chapter 35

I never got to sit in my front-row seat at the Colt Jamison concert that night. After Rosales secured Bruno Krause and Sheriff Crawford took Bruno off to jail, I sent Nick and Luke a message saying I'd been detained, but no worries. I'd fill them in later. We didn't totally miss the concert. Rosales and I sat on the Beckman Vineyard's patio with Hitchcock. We were near enough to hear Colt Jamison sing, but in a quiet enough place to discuss the specifics of the evening's events. In spite of the fact that Hitchcock and I may have saved Rosales's life, the deputy was all business, taking notes to put into her official report. When she paused and seemed about to bring the interview to a close, I gathered my courage. "May I ask *you* a question now?"

Rosales looked up at me, her expression wary. "One question?"

I nodded and blurted out what was on my mind. "Why did you take time off from your job even though you continued to work on this case?"

Rosales thought about that for a moment and took a deep breath before responding. "For one thing, I didn't want to take orders from anyone. I wasn't going to waste time getting called out to some fender bender in the next county. I had to solve this murder before anyone began asking me questions I'd refuse to answer, because what happened in the past was not relevant to finding Dixon's killer."

"Oh." I pulled Hitchcock into my lap and stroked his head. I sure wanted to know more about the questions Rosales would refuse to answer, but I knew when to shut up. "Thank goodness the killer's in custody now."

"Mrreow," Hitchcock said.

"Yes." Rosales gathered her things and stood. "Mission accomplished."

• • •

The next morning dawned bright and hot—a typical August day. Aunt Rowe and Violet had gone somewhere together. Glenda had off Sunday mornings. I sat in the dining room having breakfast with Nick and the boys, feeling grateful to be alive—knowing full well that if Bruno Krause had been more decisive he could have shot me and Rosales and been out of there in seconds with no one the wiser. I had to believe there was some shred of goodness inside that man that kept him from doing exactly that.

Matt and Adam chattered about the concert, their favorite songs, and the awesome guitars that Colt Jamison had played. They'd heard the whole story about what happened the night before and knew the murderer was behind bars. They still had unanswered questions.

Adam took his last bite of bacon, then turned to me. "Aunt Sabrina, what's going to happen to that man now?"

"I don't know. He's hired a lawyer to help him with his case."

"He doesn't deserve help," Matt said. "What kind of grandfather thinks it's a good idea to kill a guy who might be his grandson's dad?"

Nick turned to his older son. "I understand your feelings, Matt, but everyone deserves a defense. Seems like somewhere along the line, a switch must have flipped. He wasn't thinking about what was best for the boy anymore."

"Will they tell Noah what happened?" Adam said.

I shrugged. "Maybe not right away. He's only four, and he's going to miss his grandfather. His parents will have some hard decisions to make." I hoped one of them was to introduce Noah to Wanda Dixon, assuming a DNA test proved what I already believed in my heart was true—that she was Noah's grandmother.

Through the front window, I noticed a sheriff's department car pulling up with Deputy Rosales at the wheel. I placed my napkin beside my plate of untouched food.

"I think I have a visitor." I stood. "Excuse me."

I walked out into the glaring sun and approached the deputy. Hitchcock raced out from under the hedge as if he'd expected this visitor and was excited about her arrival.

"How are you this morning?" I said.

Rosales nodded. "Okay. You?"

Hitchcock rubbed against my leg, and I picked him up. "Glad to be here. Do you have news?"

"No." Rosales cleared her throat. "I had to come, though, to say thanks."

For a moment, I couldn't speak around the lump in my throat. "Don't mention it," I said.

"No, I have things to say." She paused and looked up at the clear blue sky for a moment. "I keep too much to myself. *Way* too much."

"Do you want to sit down?" I said. "Come in for some breakfast? Coffee?"

"No." She shook her head. "Let me just tell you what I came to say."

"Mrreow," Hitchcock said.

Rosales laughed briefly and patted the cat's head. Then she sobered. "I'm sure you're wondering why I would hang on to my anger against Marty for all these years since my brother's death."

I nodded. "Yes, as a matter of fact."

"You're way too good at figuring out secrets," she said, "so I may as well tell you what's what. First of all, you were right when you said I needed to tell Sheriff Crawford everything. I've done that."

"Good." I waited.

"On the night that Lorenzo died," she said, "he and his pals set out to commit a burglary. He'd started running with a bad crowd, you see, one that Marty had nothing to do with. We, Marty and I, found out about their plan. We went after them." Her voice dropped to a near whisper. "We went to stop them, but we got there too late. I heard the gunshot that killed my brother. I saw Lorenzo, his sightless eyes. I knew there was nothing we could do."

I swallowed hard. "I'm so sorry."

"Marty grabbed me," she continued. "Said we had to run, that we would be arrested and probably charged with a crime if we didn't go. I knew he was right, so we ran and made a pact to never tell anyone that we were there. My brother died, and I ran away. Marty came up with the story that we'd spent the night together. We'd have an airtight alibi."

"Maybe that was for the best," I said. "You *didn't* commit a crime."

"Not exactly." Rosales's watery gaze met mine. "But in my heart, running out on my brother was the worst thing I could have done."

I felt the tears in my own eyes as I looked at her. "If there's anything I can do to help."

She shook her head and reached out to run a hand down Hitchcock's back. "I already owe a debt to the two of you. Again, thank you."

She got into her car and started the engine, then nodded to us before driving away.

I cuddled Hitchcock to my chest. "Now I know why she held that anger against Marty Dixon. She never forgave him. Or herself."

"Mrr," Hitchcock said.

I walked back into the house and found Nick doing dishes in the kitchen. I put Hitchcock down, and he went to his dish and crunched on his food.

"I left your plate if you want it," Nick said.

I shook my head. "I don't have any appetite."

"What'd the deputy want?" he said.

"To thank me and Hitchcock," I said.

He grinned. "Are you two going to be pals now?"

"Don't count on it." I wasn't going to tell him everything about Rosales and her brother. I understood her feeling that she'd let Lorenzo down.

"We talked about brothers for a bit," I said.

"Oh?" Nick looked at me. "What brought that on?"

I shrugged. "Sisters and brothers need to help each other, you know. Stick together. Rosales had a thing with her brother when he needed help, and she tried to help. Tracey, over at the Wild Pony, is doing a great job of helping her brother Chester with his business." I mulled over my next words before speaking. "You know I'd be happy to help you out with anything you might need, right?"

"Sure," Nick said. "Where are you going with this?"

"I have a small confession to make."

He dried his hands on a dish towel and turned to lean against the kitchen counter. "What might that be?"

"I saw you in town yesterday, going into Rita Colletti's office. You know I worked for her a long time, so I have experience, and I would help you if you need help—" I paused when I noticed Nick's amused expression.

He chuckled, then glanced toward the dining room and lowered his voice. "You think I need help with a divorce? No, that's not what's going on."

"Then what *is* going on?" I whispered back. "Why would you go to see Rita?"

He took my arm and led me into the living room, farther from the boys. "We're talking about her experiences in switching from being a big-city lawyer to a country lawyer. Does she have any regrets? Is it the best move she ever made? Like that. I'm asking her a lot of questions to get a feel for the reality of making such a change."

His words took me totally by surprise. "Because?"

"I'm questioning a lot of things now that I've turned forty," he said. "Can't see doing exactly what I'm doing now from here on out. The time for change might be now."

"I totally understand," I said, remembering my decision to move to Lavender.

"Melanie and I are considering moving the boys out of the city," Nick said. "Not to Lavender. Into the country, though, closer to her parents."

"Wow."

"Yeah, wow," he said. "Mom will throw a fit if we decide to make this move away from her, so keep it to yourself for now."

"I can only imagine what our mother will say." I shook my head, laughing. "Okay, my lips are sealed. Sorry I was snooping into your business."

He grinned. "I'd expect nothing less."

I heard the back door, and Aunt Rowe called out, "I'm back, y'all, and I have a great big surprise. C'mon out back and meet Colt Jamison."

The boys practically flew out the back door.

Nick looked at me. "Seriously?"

I shrugged, and we followed the boys. Hitchcock scurried out ahead of us.

On the deck, Matt and Adam appeared starstruck as Colt Jamison shook hands with them.

"I happen to have autographed pictures here for y'all," the singer said as he pulled something a bit larger than baseball cards from his pocket to hand to the boys.

"Did I do good?" Aunt Rowe stood beside Colt and beamed at her great-nephews.

"This is awesome," Adam said.

"Great to meet you," Matt said.

Nick approached Colt and shook his hand. "Appreciate you taking the time. My boys have been talking about your music pretty much nonstop for months. You put on a great show last night."

"Thanks." Colt looked at me. "Sorry you couldn't exactly make it, but I heard you helped the sheriff figure out what happened to Dixon. Thanks for that."

"I'm glad to help," I said.

Except for that part where I might have been shot.

"I wanted to let y'all know one other thing." Colt grinned as he looked at Hitchcock sitting on the deck railing. "I've had some special inspiration here in Lavender this week, and I'm working on a brand-new song. Would y'all like to hear what I have so far?"

The boys nodded eagerly.

"Sure," I said.

"Understand, this isn't going to sound polished, seeing as I don't have my guitar here with me," Colt said, "but the song's about a missing black cat, and it goes like this."

Recipes

Icebox Layer Cake

1 cup flour
½ cup butter
1 cup nuts
8 ounces cream cheese
½ cup powdered sugar
9 ounces Cool Whip
3 cups milk
2 small boxes instant pudding (chocolate OR vanilla)

First layer
Combine flour, butter and one-half cup of the nuts. Press in a 9x13 pan and bake at 350 degrees for 15 minutes. Cool.

Second layer
Mix cream cheese, powdered sugar, and 1 cup of the Cool Whip. Spread over crust.

Third layer
Add milk to the pudding and beat until thick. Pour over second layer.

Fourth layer
Spread the remaining Cool Whip on top and sprinkle with the remaining nuts.

Refrigerate for 4 hours before serving.

Blueberry Coffee Cake

½ cup butter
1 cup sugar
2 eggs
1 cup sour cream
2 cups flour
1½ teaspoons baking powder
½ teaspoon baking soda
½ teaspoon salt
1 teaspoon vanilla
1 can blueberry pie filling

For Topping

1/3 cup butter
½ cup sugar
½ teaspoon cinnamon
¾ cup flour

Cream butter with sugar. Add eggs and sour cream. Sift flour, baking powder, baking soda, and salt, add to creamed mixture. Add vanilla. Place ½ of batter in a greased and floured 9x13-inch pan. Spread 1 can blueberry pie filling over batter. Add remaining batter.

Combine all topping ingredients and sprinkle over cake.

Bake at 350 degrees for 45 to 50 minutes.

Key Lime Pie
(low-fat version)

1 box (3 ounces) sugar-free lime gelatin
¼ cup boiling water
2 containers (8 ounces each) of key lime pie–flavored light yogurt
1 container (8 ounces) of frozen fat-free whipped topping, thawed
1 prepared 9-inch reduced-fat graham cracker crust

Dissolve gelatin in boiling water; with wire whisk, stir in yogurt; with wooden spoon, fold in whipped topping. Transfer to crust; refrigerate overnight or at least 2 hours before serving.

About the Author

Kay Finch is the national bestselling author of the Bad Luck Cat Mysteries. Though her character, Sabrina Tate, is a mystery writer who's left the paralegal profession behind to move to the Texas Hill Country, Kay still works as a paralegal at a Houston law firm. A country girl at heart, Kay grew up on a farm in Pennsylvania, and she loves the huge cattle-filled fields near her Texas home. She resides in a Houston suburb with her husband and rescue pets. Visit her at www.kayfinch.com.

CPSIA information can be obtained
at www.ICGtesting.com
Printed in the USA
LVHW041327220721
693398LV00007B/714